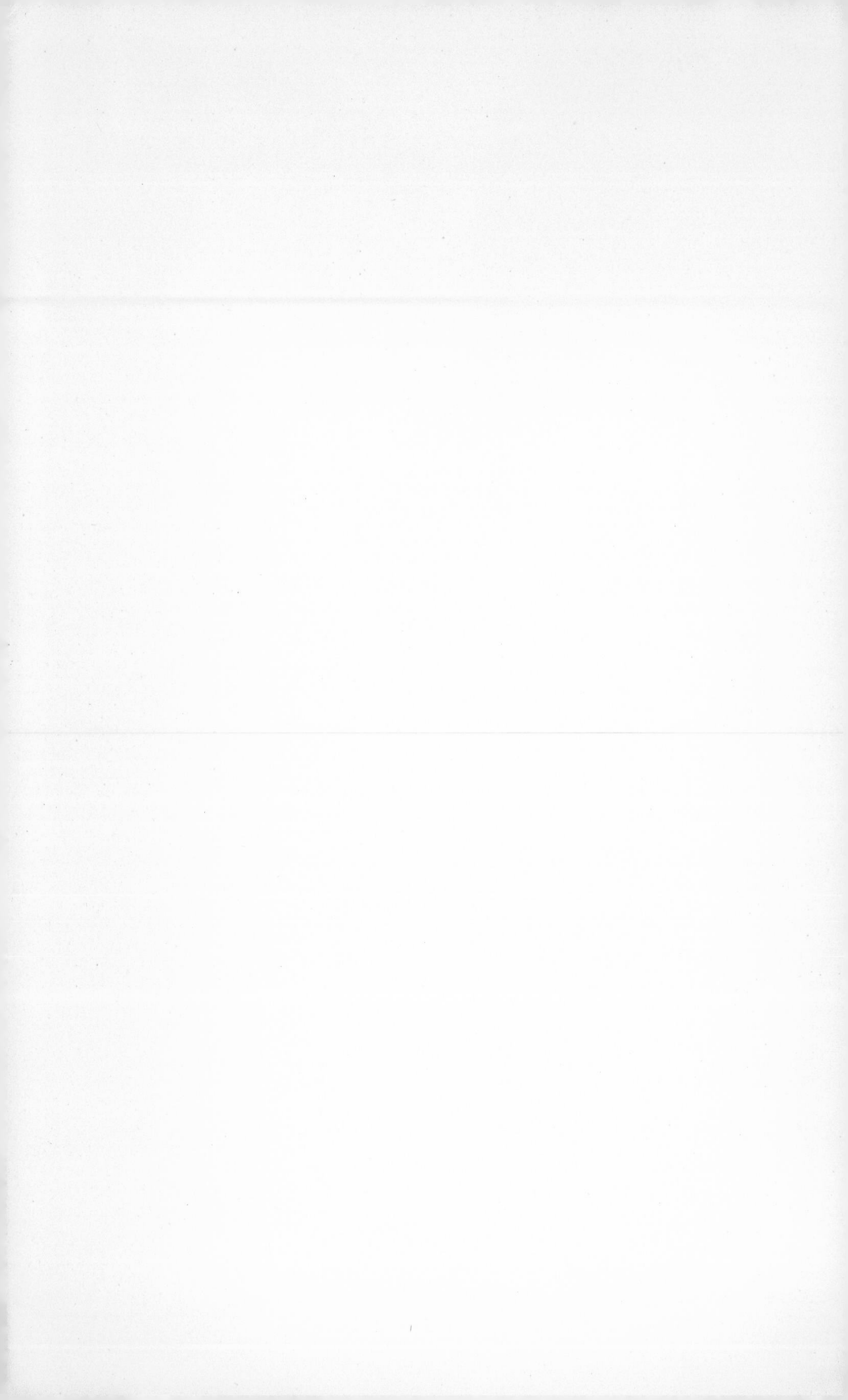

AN INTERPRETATION AND CRITIQUE OF WITTGENSTEIN'S TRACTATUS

SCANDINAVIAN UNIVERSITY BOOKS

DENMARK MUNKSGAARD *Copenhagen*

NORWAY UNIVERSITETSFORLAGET *Oslo, Bergen*

SWEDEN SVENSKA BOKFÖRLAGET Norstedts - Bonniers *Stockholm*

AKADEMIFÖRLAGET - GUMPERTS *Gothenburg*

UNISKOL Universitet och Skola *Lund*

AN INTERPRETATION AND CRITIQUE OF WITTGENSTEIN'S TRACTATUS

by

David Favrholdt

Third printing

HUMANITIES PRESS, INC.

NEW YORK

1. printing 1964
2. printing 1965
3. printing 1967

Published simultaneously in the United States by Humanity Press, Inc.

Printing composed by P. J. Schmidt A/S, Vojens, Denmark
Printed in Denmark by Villadsen og Christensen, Copenhagen

CONTENTS

PREFACE

This work was begun in the Spring of 1962 at the suggestion of Thomas Bredsdorff of the University of Copenhagen, who thought my views on Wittgenstein's *Tractatus Logico-Philosophicus* should be gathered into a volume. During my work on the book, I have profited from discussions with Professor Jørgen Jørgensen, Povl Dalsgård-Hansen, Helmuth Hansen, Arne Thing Mortensen, Dr. Peter Zinkernagel, and Mogens Asmussen, all of Copenhagen, and Bertel Fønss of Ribe; I have also benefited from letters from Professor Erik Stenius (University of Åbo, Finland), Professor Georg Henrik von Wright (University of Helsinki, Finland), and Professor Gustav Bergmann (The State University of Iowa, U. S.); in expressing my gratitude to them here, I must at the same time absolve them from any errors or misconceptions in the book, which are wholly mine.

My interest in the young Wittgenstein's ideas began with the reading of Justus Hartnack's *Wittgenstein og den moderne filosofi,* and was fortified by the work of G. E. M. Anscombe and Erik Stenius. The reader will notice that my viewpoint is divided. On the one hand, I consider the *Tractatus* over-estimated, for it contains many mistakes, and could be improved in all respects. On the other hand, I am convinced that some valuable points of the book have been overlooked by the commentators on Wittgenstein, and that his own fundamental viewpoint has never been understood. I am counsel for the prosecution and counsel for the defence in one. I hope this attitude is constructive, not confusing.

I pay a special debt to Lektor Bertel Fønss for his translation into Danish of much of the Italian work on the subject, and to my wife, Nina Favrholdt, for her great patience and assistance in typing, proof-reading, and the other arduous labours without which the book could not get into print. Furthermore I wish to thank Timothy Pearce, (at present lecturer in English at the University of Copenhagen,) for having undertaken the task of removing the worst mistakes in my English.

I am indebted to the Danish National Science Foundation for grants which have facilitated the work on this volume.

Finally I wish to thank my former teachers, Professors Jørgen Jørgensen, Bent Schultzer and Johannes Witt-Hansen for their sympathy towards my work which was completed October, 1963 and which they have accepted for defence as a doctoral dissertation at Copenhagen University.

Copenhagen, Spring, 1964.

David Favrholdt.

I
INTRODUCTORY REMARKS

a. On the cohesion of the theses in the Tractatus.

The viewpoints in this book on Wittgenstein's *Tractatus* (as his *Tractatus Logico-Philosophicus* will be called hereafter for the sake of brevity) are not intended to deliver an exhaustive account or even an outline of Wittgenstein's thoughts. Primarily they deal with what one may call the philosophical ideas of the book (as distinct from the mathematical and formal-logical ideas in it). The investigations which I present here are especially centred in the tacit assumptions in Wittgenstein's line of thought, i. e. in the philosophical, psychological and metaphysical theses which Wittgenstein has been bound, wittingly or unwittingly, to accept when writing the *Tractatus*. I believe that it may be of some interest for philosophy today to make a close examination of these theses, because many views of the *Tractatus* still prevail in philosophical discussions though most frequently without reference to their original connection with other problems, a connection which sometimes has to be re-established if they are to be treated satisfactorily. An example of this is Wittgenstein's theory of meaning, set out in the *Tractatus*, which has been revived and improved recently by Professor Erik Stenius (in his book *Wittgenstein's 'Tractatus')* but has not been viewed in connection with the 'theory of mind', i. e. the subtle account of the 'essence' and 'function' of the mind, which is indicated in the *Tractatus* as a necessary presupposition of the theory of meaning. To me the task of analysing the theory of mind in the *Tractatus* and unveiling its connection with the theory of meaning seems to be important not only for the history of philosophy but also for the current discussions of the concept of meaning.

None of these problems has been worked out by those philosophers who have been occupied with the *Tractatus* up to this time, and for this reason, and no other, they have not succeeded in pointing out the intimate connection that is to be found between the many 'theses' of the book. Rather they have been content either to deliver a successive exposition of Wittgenstein's viewpoints and to concatenate the expositions of each point with one another by means of some neutral remarks (as Weinberg has done in *An Examination of Logical Positivism,* Anscombe in *An Introduction to Wittgenstein's*

Tractatus and Maslow in *A Study in Wittgenstein's Tractatus)* or they have limited themselves to a few problems (as Stenius, for instance, in the book mentioned above). None of Wittgenstein's contemporaries has sought the unity in his early philosophy, not even Russell or Ramsey, though they should be the first to understand the thoughts of the young Wittgenstein. Instead they seem to have conceived of the *Tractatus* as an intelligent chat on epistemological and logical problems, and like the later 'Wiener-Kreis' they borrowed from the book the ideas that they could make use of and left the rest of it untouched.

In the thirties and forties, it was customary to place the *Tractatus* as a work which, in line with the philosophies of Ernst Mach and Bertrand Russell, was to be regarded as a predecessor of logical empiricism. This way of viewing the matter was in no way unjustified for in many respects the book actually shares viewpoints with logical empiricism though there always has been a remarkable difference between the metaphysical mood of Wittgenstein's book and the rigorous style of the 'Wiener-Kreis'. Some commentators (for instance Feibleman in *Inside the Great Mirror,* p. 51) regard the *Tractatus* as a sort of commentary on the *Principia Mathematica*. This, indeed, it is, but it is beyond doubt that both of these judgments only emphasize a few features of the *Tractatus*. In my opinion the book is primarily an account of a philosophical view, not only comprising some logical and semantic problems but, according to the intentions of its author, comprising all philosophy, every single problem belonging to the body of philosophy. Its main purpose is not to lay the foundations of a theory of truth-functions or of meaning. Above all it is to show what can be said and what cannot be said — what can be thought and what cannot be thought — (as Wittgenstein emphasizes at the end of his book as well as in the preface). About *what,* one may ask, and the answer is, about the 'eternal' problems in European philosophy, about the problem of substance, the problem of truth, the foundations of knowledge, about materialism, idealism, solipsism, the I, God, free will, life, and death. Wittgenstein's fundamental aim was to show what could be said and what could not be said on these topics. All the other themes of the book, the notes on the *Principia Mathematica,* the theory of meaning, the theory of inference etc. are steps only on the way to fulfilling this purpose.

This has been emphasized by Wittgenstein in a letter to Russell, as well as in the *Tractatus*. He writes: 'Now I'm afraid you haven't really got hold of my main contention, to which the whole business of logical propositions is only corollary. The main point is the theory of what can be expressed (*gesagt*) by propositions — i. e. by language (and what comes to the same, what can be *thought*); which I believe is the cardinal problem of philosophy.

(Anscombe: *An Introduction,* p. 161. Why this passage is left out in Wittgenstein: *Notebooks 1914 - 16* I do not know.)

*

In the following exposition, I shall try to demonstrate, while analysing the tacit assumptions in Wittgenstein's line of thought, the intimate connection between the different parts of the *Tractatus*. In my opinion this connection has hitherto been overlooked. In my exposition I will project a certain line of reasoning into Wittgenstein's thoughts to the following effect, in brief: The fundamental thesis of the *Tractatus* is the thesis of extensionality, i. e. the thesis that all sentences are truth-functions of elementary propositions and that these in turn are truth-functions of themselves. In the *Tractatus* this thesis is set forth as a postulate although it is supported by a particular doctrine explaining how truth-functions are to be developed by means of a special sort of negation-operation which will be described below. The theory of meaning introduced by Wittgenstein, which from now on will be named the picture theory, is a consequence of the thesis of extensionality. The doctrine that formal concepts and logical relations can never be described but only shown, which means that no meta-language can ever be established, is a consequence of the thesis of extensionality taken together with some aspects of the picture theory. Moreover, the picture theory has two further consequences: A theory of the structure of the world and a theory of the structure of mind. In continuation of these theories the Wittgensteinian solipsism is developed, and on the basis of the forementioned theses, the doctrine of the ineffable, i. e. the determination of what can be said and what cannot be said. My use of the word 'consequence' must be read with reservation. It is not a matter of course that the picture theory, for instance, *is* in fact a consequence of the thesis of extensionality but Wittgenstein must have conceived it so.

As to the forementioned steps in the train of ideas in the *Tractatus,* it should be noted that the most obscure are the theory of the structure of the world and the theory of the structure of mind. At these two stages in the development of his thought, Wittgenstein seems to have met with extreme difficulties, and, as I will show later in this book, these parts of his thought are presented in a postulating manner that goes to show that he has shut his eyes to the problems after realizing how difficult they were.

It may not be so that the line which I project into Wittgenstein's train of thoughts corresponds in every particular to the actual philosophical development which he underwent during the years from 1911 until the *Tractatus* was completed. It is not my aim to exclude other possibilities as to the line of argumentation in his book in advance. I only wish to present the one indicated above partly in order to stress the unity of the *Tractatus* in a simple manner, partly because it is in harmony with what we know about Wittgenstein's development from 1911 to 1918. Naturally it is for ever impossible to know exactly what Wittgenstein thought of first and what next, just as it is impossible to know how clear his thoughts were at the different stages of their development, but from the material presented in *Wittgenstein: Notebooks 1914 - 16* we can discover something of what occupied him most at various times.

In the *Notebooks* we find an extract of letters from Wittgenstein to Russell 1912 - 20, Wittgenstein's *Notes on Logic* completed September, 1913, his *Notes dictated to G. E. Moore in Norway* written in April, 1914, and finally his philosophical journal from 22nd August, 1914, to 10th January, 1917. In the letters from 22nd June, 1912, to 30th October, 1913 apparently only logical technicalities were dealt with.[1] The *Notes on Logic* open with some remarks on philosophy, which is defined as 'the doctrine of the logical form of scientific propositions (not primitive propositions only)' (*Notebooks*, p. 93). Later, it is pointed out that the propositions of logic must be unique and Wittgenstein meditates on the nature of the proposition ('Indefinables are of two sorts: names and forms. Propositions cannot consist of names alone, they cannot be classes of names.' *Notebooks*, p. 98). Here we are presented with the first speculations on the properties of propositions. Of interest in connection with the stages in Wittgenstein's development mentioned above, we find furthermore some remarks on propositions of the type '*A* says *p*', '*A* believes *p*', '*A* judges that *p*'. These propositions came into focus as a result of the idea that the logistics of the *Principia Mathematica* had no boundaries in respect of application. In the first edition of the *Principia Mathematica* we see these propositions mentioned as early as page 8 where they serve as instances of propositions which are not truth-functions, in spite of their being compound. Wittgenstein's attempt to show that propositions of the type '*A* says *p*' do not limit the applicability of logistics may be viewed as a sign that already at that time the thesis of extensionality was being regarded as a possibility, though no argumentation in favour of it had yet been given.

In November, 1913, Wittgenstein for the first time presents the viewpoint that one may, *a priori*, only by looking at the sentences of logic — and by this is obviously meant those truth-functions which are tautologies — decide

1. Unfortunately only part of the letters have been printed. I have not had the opportunity to read them in the original and must therefore take the chance that Anscombe, von Wright and Rhees, whose qualifications are undoubted, have not omitted any philosophical sections of the letters.

their truth-value, whereas the truth-values of non-logical sentences (these apparantly are the remaining truth-functions and elementary propositions) must be determined through experience ('It is the peculiar (and most important) characteristic of *non*-logical propositions, that their truth cannot be seen in the propositional sign itself. If I say, for example, 'Meier is stupid', you cannot tell whether this proposition is true or false by looking at it. But the propositions of logic — and they alone — have the property of expressing their truth or falsehood in the very sign itself.' *Notebooks*, p. 127). At this point the picture theory has not been mentioned, so therefore the excellent concordance between the picture theory and the doctrine that logical truth shows itself, as I will point out later, should, perhaps, be conceived of rather as a fusion of the two ideas than as an entailment-relation between them. In any case, it is hardly credible that the picture theory should be a consequence of the alleged fact that logical truths show themselves in the propositional signs alone. In *Notes dictated to G. E. Moore* this theory of the nature of logical truth is presented once more (*Notebooks*, p. 107) and later (*Notebooks*, p. 111), but independently of this theory, some viewpoints are set forth which may be the first germs of the picture theory. From 22nd September, 1914, forward, the speculations on the picture theory occupy a great part of the philosophical diary. At the same time as these speculations we find some preparatory remarks on the theory of the nature of reality. On 22nd August, 1914, Wittgenstein asks himself whether a point in the visual field can serve as an instance of an object and in the course of time, from 13th May, until 22nd June, 1915, he is intensely taken up by the attempt to find examples of objects that will satisfy the loose sketch of the picture theory which is before us at this point. On the 28th October, 1914, the viewpoint that there exist pseudo-propositions, the sense of which can only be shown and never expressed (see later, chap. IV, a) occurs for the first time. Wittgenstein writes: 'What the pseudo-proposition "There are *n* things" tries to express, shows in language by the presence of *n* proper names with different references.' (*Notebooks*, p. 20). On the 17th April, 1915, Wittgenstein, without further comment, writes 'The subjective universe' and from 23rd May, 1915, forward, he is working on the problem of solipsism, and thoughts about God, death and the freedom of the will. In connection with the problem of solipsism he touches upon the problem of the I, here conceiving of the 'I' as 'a comprehending subject'. Further comments on the concept of mind are not given. On 12th September, 1916, Wittgenstein suddenly discovers why thinking must be considered a sort of language ('Now it is becoming clear why I thought that thinking and language were the same. For thinking is a kind of language. For a thought too is, of course, a logical picture of the proposition, and therefore it just is a kind of proposition.' (*Notebooks*, p. 82)). But further thoughts on the relation between language and thought do not appear before January, 1917, at which time the diary ends. Likewise the first parts of the *Tractatus* (1-2.225) dealing with the world and the relation between picture and reality must be composed later than January, 1917. They are likely to be the parts of the book that are written last. Of course, the possibility exists that Wittgenstein worked on the *Tractatus* from 1913, besides writing in his philosophical notebooks, but as these do not contain one single hint on the theory of the nature of reality (in the form of remarks on the concepts of 'fact', 'state of affairs', or 'substance') nor more than one reflection on the relation between thought and language, this seems very improbable. It is most probable that these theories were developed in the time between January, 1917 and the time of the completion of his first opus.

In my interpretation of the connection between the theses of the *Tractatus* the following time-table (which must be read with reservation) has served as a guiding principle:

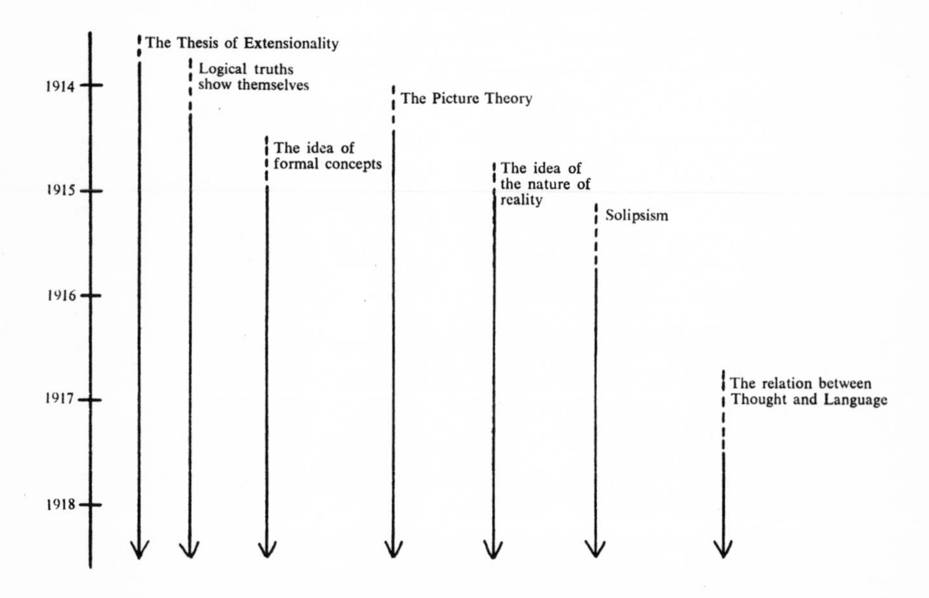

The space of time in which the lines of thought have developed are indicated by the arrows and dotted lines mark the approximate time of their conception. As a whole this table is in accordance with von Wright's observation (probably based on an examination of Wittgenstein's papers) that 'The oldest parts of the Tractatus are those dealing with logic.' (*Biographical Sketch*, p. 7). von Wright informs us that the book was accomplished when Wittgenstein visited Vienna during a leave in August, 1918 (op. cit., p. 8), so it seems clear that the items, which I have called 'Thoughts on the nature of reality' and 'The relation between language and thought', cannot be based on long-lasting reflections.

There can be no doubt that Wittgenstein, as far back as one can trace his thoughts in the notebooks, has held an extensional viewpoint of logic. When he hit upon the idea that all language should be conceived of as extensional, i. e. truth-functional, is unknown, but this idea seems to have directed his thoughts before he wrote the *Notes on Logic*.

I think it is suitable for the purpose of understanding the Tractatus to regard the thesis of extensionality as the fundamental thesis of the book, even if a later historical investigation should happen to disclose, for example, that Wittgenstein's solipsism is older still, and therefore in this chapter I will briefly describe this thesis and the consequences it has.

b. The thesis of extensionality.

The designation 'The thesis of extensionality' originates from Rudolf Carnap's book *The Logical Syntax of Language* (p. 245) where it represents Wittgenstein's thesis. However, Carnap develops the thesis in a special fashion suited to his theory of a universal language of science which is not relevant to this study. As mentioned before the thesis of extensionality is the assertion that all sentences, i. e. all that can be comprised under 'senseful language', are either elementary propositions or truth-functions of elementary propositions. As will be explained further on (chapter IV, *b.*), Wittgenstein regards an elementary proposition as a truth-function of itself and the thesis therefore can be shortened to: Any sentence is a truth-function.

In order to grasp this thesis it is useful to read Russell's *The Principles of Mathematics* and the *Principia Mathematica* by Whitehead and Russell. In the propositional logic of the *Principia* (and in fact it is only propositional logic Wittgenstein refers to when he speaks of extensionality) it is presupposed that the variables can only be interpreted as propositions and in the strict sense only as elementary propositions, i. e. propositions that in no way can be split into other propositions. It follows that elementary propositions cannot contain variables nor words such as 'all' or 'some', nor the definite article. In the *Principia* 'this is red', and 'this is earlier than that', are given as suitable examples (Introduction to the second edition, p. XV). Other examples used in the text are 'Newton was a man', 'the sun is hot' and 'Caesar died'. The concept of truth-function is defined as follows: 'We may call a function $f(p)$ a "truth-function" when its argument p is a proposition, and the truth-value of $f(p)$ depends only upon the truth-value of p.' (p. 8). The authors, however, point out that such functions are not the only possible compounds of sentences. For instance, '*A* believes *p*' is a compound proposition containing p, but its truth-value does not depend upon the truth-value of p. Whether p is true or false, this has no influence on the truth or falsity of 'A believes p'. The *Principia*, however, confines itself to dealing with truth-functions only, as its authors consider this sufficient for the solution of the main-problem of the book which is to show that all pure mathematics can be deduced from logical principles alone, and that all mathematical concepts in accordance with this can be defined solely by means of logical concepts. In the 2nd edition of the *Principia*, however, the authors have subscribed to Wittgenstein's remarks on sentences of the type 'A believes p'. I will return to this later (chap. III, *c*.).

Normally, a deductive system of propositions, the theorems of which are all truth-functions as these are defined above, is called truth-functional or extensional. The word 'extensional' is usually opposed to 'intensional' and both have had various connotations in the history of logic (*vide* Jørgensen: *A Treatise of Formal Logic*, vol. I, the footnote p. 46 and L. S. Stebbing: *A Modern Introduction to Logic*, pp. 27–30), but the discussion about the thesis of extensionality is, so to speak, always displayed on the arena of propositional and functional logic. Here the extensional viewpoint is that only external relations can subsist between elementary propositions. External relations do not in any way modify their relates (the propositions) and on the other hand are not modified by them either. According to the extensional viewpoint, propositions are, when dealt with in a divalent logical calculus, characterized exhaustively by their truth-values, whereas the intensional viewpoint consists in the contention that if the logic of propositions is to be applicable to all sorts of elementary propositions, it must necessarily consider the sense of the propositions and not only their truth-value, as internal relations between elementary propositions are possible.

The extensional viewpoint was set up in this form by Russell in his *Principles of Mathematics*. Russell opens his exposition with the following thesis: 'Pure Mathematics is the class of all propositions of the form "p implies q", where p and q are propositions, and neither p nor q contains any constants except logical constants.' In the explanation of the form 'p implies q' Russell introduces his famous distinction between formal and material implication (*Principles*, p. 14). By material implication is understood an implication between two constants whose values do not depend on the circumstance that a variable is ascribed a value, while a formal implication is an implication between two propositional functions, which have not been given any values. "Socrates is a human being' implies 'Socrates is mortal" is an example of a material implication, while $(x) : \varphi x . \supset . \psi x$ is a formal implication. As to the definition of 'implication' Russell urges that it is a fundamental concept and he writes: 'If p implies q, then both are false or both true, or p is false and q true; it is impossible to have q false and p true, and it is necessary to have q true or p false. In fact, the assertion that q is true or p false turns out to be strictly equivalent to "p implies q" .... It follows from the above equivalence that of any two propositions there must be one which implies the other, that false propositions imply all propositions, and true propositions are implied by all propositions.'

In the *Principles of Mathematics* and the *Principia* this definition is applied, since both material implication and formal implication are used in the construction of the propositional logic (*vide Principia Mathematica*, pp. 94–95). That this definition of implication expresses an extensional view of logic shows itself in that it, together with all the other logical constants of the propositional logic, only pays regard to the truth-values of the propositions, not to their sense. This view has been strongly criticized because, by this definition of implication, logistics are apparently cut off from treating of propositions expressing that one thing necessarily follows from another, or, as has also been pointed out, is in opposition to the use of the word, implication, in ordinary language and the language of natural science. This was pointed out as early as 1908 by Hugh McColl in his article *If and Imply* and was followed up later in C. I. Lewis' strong critique of the opinions of Russell.

Lewis, in his first plea against Russell (in *Implication and the Algebra of Logic*), contends that Russell has overlooked that a disjunction, as Russell applies it when defining $p \supset q. = . \sim p v q$ *Df* (*Principia Mathematica*, p. 94), can be conceived of in more than one way, and he illustrates this point by the following examples: 1. 'Either Caesar is dead or the moon is made of green cheese.' and 2. 'Either Mathilda does not love me or else somebody loves me.' In both disjunctions at least one of the entering propositions is true, but in 1. it is only maintained that one of them is at least true, while it is maintained in 2. that one of them is *necessarily* true. This implies that to find out whether 1. is true, we have to know that at least one of the entering propositions is true, while we do not have to know whether any of the entering propositions in 2. are true in order to know the truth of 2. Lewis writes: 'The second disjunction is such that its truth is independent of the truth of either member separately. Or, more accurately, its truth can be known, while it is still problematic which of its lemmas is the true one.' (p. 523). For this reason, Lewis distinguishes between molecular propositions of the first kind which he calls extensional disjunctions, and those of the second kind which he calls intensional disjunctions. By means of the intensional disjunction, he defines the relation which he calls strict implication and conceives of as a substitute for Russell's material implication, a substitute that avoids the paradoxes that spring from the material implication.

Although Lewis's argumentation in this article can scarcely be regarded as conclusive (it is my impression that the example Lewis gives of an intensional disjunction is a masked tautology, as its form is '$\sim\varphi y \vee (Ex).\varphi x$') the logicians in the following years divided themselves into two groups, one swearing allegiance to the extensional viewpoint, the other embracing the intensional, and the discussion turned upon the question whether an extensional logic presupposed an intensional logic or vice versa, a manner of viewing the problem which goes back to Russell's first treatment of the subject (*vide Principles of Mathematics*, pp. 66–81). Among the most essential contributions to the intensional viewpoint we find Paul Weiss' *Entailment and the Future of Logic* and Jørgen Jørgensen's *Über die Ziele und Probleme der Logistik*. Many logicians adhered to the extensional viewpoint which attains its most perfect formulation in Carnap's *Logical Syntax of Language*.

It is a characteristic of this discussion, the main theme of which was continuously the concept of implication, that it was not concerned with the question of what definitions of implication had to be introduced in different regions of human knowledge, but only concentrated on the question: what is the "right" definition of implication. The main aim of *Principia Mathematica* was to establish the connection between logic and pure mathematics, and whatever one may think about the concept of implication, the first task must be to examine whether Russell's definition of material implication really is the necessary requirement for solving this problem. It certainly cannot be automatically assumed that the 'if-then', which is applied in the reasonings of pure mathematics, is identical with the 'if-then' which is applied in everyday descriptive language, or in the investigations of natural science. However, the vigorous reaction against Russell's definition is understandable because Russell himself chose from the very outset subject-predicate-sentences and relational propositions of ordinary language as examples of the values of the variables of propositional logic (cfr. the examples above, p. 13). In his answers to the critics, Russell adhered to the view that his definition of implication was not only suited to mathematical matters but also suited perfectly well to any kind of inference. In so far as it had to be agreed that Russell's definition involved the statement that a true proposition is implied by any proposition and that sentences such as 'Socrates is a human being' and 'Caesar is dead' are instances of propositions for this purpose, the concept of implication was inevitably tinged with absurdity. However, Russell never put limits to the field of application of his definition. On the contrary he looked for empirical propositions that could fit in with the extensional logic of *Principia Mathematica*. In a number of books [*The Problems of Philosophy* (1912), *Our Knowledge of the External World* (1914), *The*

Relation of Sense-data to Physics (1914) and *The Ultimate Constituents of Matter* (1915)] Russell developed his logical atomism which later culminated in a neutral monism, of which the fundamental point was that all empirical propositions could be broken down into sense-data-propositions and that these could only be related to each other in ways that were in accordance with the extensional logic in the *Principia*. This involved an ontology: The world had to consist of a number of facts that were connected with each other by external relations only and as Urmson phrases it (in *Philosophical Analysis*, p. 6–7) the main thesis of logical atomism can be said to be simply that the world has a structure similar to the structure of Russell's mathematical logic.

*

Like Russell, Wittgenstein accepted the view that the logistics of the *Principia* had an unlimited range of applicability. But with regard to philosophical questions he displayed a greater precaution than Russell. It is a characteristic feature of the *Tractatus* that it adduces no examples of elementary propositions. Wittgenstein has never questioned the validity of the thesis of extensionality and the fact that ordinary language can show no examples of elementary propositions in the sense of the *Tractatus* never worried him. His work primarily consisted in deducing the philosophical consequences of the thesis of extensionality and in a way the *Tractatus* presents us with no more than this. As mentioned above, by 1915, he had already started looking for an instance of an object which could fit in with his picture theory, and in defiance of the fact that he did not succeed in finding any interpretation of his whole theory, he had the *Tractatus* published, nevertheless, probably being convinced that all the concepts in the book could be exemplified in principle.

It appears from the schedule in 5.101 that Wittgenstein adheres to Russell's definition of implication by ascribing the matrix (*TTFT*) (p,q) to $p \supset q$. It also appears that the concept of 'truth-function' is the same as in *Principia Mathematica*.

Carnap (in *Logical Syntax*, p. 245) mentions three places in the *Tractatus* where the thesis of extensionality is put forward but others can be found. The following sentences from the book all form parts of the thesis:

4.41 Truth-possibilities of elementary propositions are the conditions of the truth and falsity of propositions.

4.51 Suppose that I am given *all* elementary propositions: then I can simply ask what propositions I can construct out of them. And there I have *all* propositions, and *that* fixes their limits.

4.52 Propositions comprise all that follows from the totality of all elementary propositions (and, of course, from its being the *totality* of them *all*). (Thus, in a certain sense, it could be said that *all* propositions were generalizations of elementary propositions.)

5 A proposition is a truth-function of elementary propositions. (An elementary proposition is a truth-function of itself.)

5.01 Elementary propositions are the truth-arguments of propositions.

5.234 Truth-functions of elementary propositions are results of operations with elementary propositions as bases. (These operations I call truth-operations.)

5.3 All propositions are results of truth-operations on elementary propositions.

....

Every proposition is the result of truth-operations on elementary propositions.

5.54 In the general propositional form propositions occur in other propositions only as bases of truth-operations.

6.001 ....every proposition is a result of successive applications to elementary propositions of the operation N (ξ).

I will not deal with the concept of operation until chap. IV, b.; but from the statements quoted it will be seen that *all* sentences are conceived of as truth-functions of elementary propositions, i. e. as sentences the truth-values of which solely depend upon the truth-values of the elementary propositions that form their parts. This matter can be stated more clearly. In *An Inquiry into Meaning and Truth*, p. 211, Russell states the so-called principle of extensionality (which must not be confused with the thesis of extensionality) in this way:

'I. The truth-value of any function of a proposition depends only upon the truth-value of the argument, i. e. if p and q are both true or both false, then any sentence containing p remains true or false, as the case may be, if q is substituted for p.

II. The truth-value of any function of a function depends only on the extension of the function, i. e. if whenever φx is true, ψx is true, and vice versa, then any sentence about the function φ remains true or false, as the case may be, if ψ is substituted for φ.'

If we add to this that all sentences are truth-functions and that all elementary propositions are truth-functions of themselves (5), we arrive at Wittgenstein's thesis of extensionality. The circumstance that any elementary proposition is a truth-function of itself involves the idea that the truth-value of any elementary proposition is independent of the truth-values of other elementary propositions for as Russell has it: 'The truth-value of any function of a proposition depends only upon the truth-value of the argument.' The mutual independence of the elementary propositions therefore is an aspect of the thesis of extensionality and is stressed in the following sentences in the *Tractatus:*

4.211 It is a sign of a proposition's being elementary that there can be no elementary proposition contradicting it.
5.134 One elementary proposition cannot be deduced from another.
5.152 .... Two elementary propositions give one another the probability ½ ....
6.3751 .... (It is clear that the logical product of two elementary propositions can neither be a tautology nor a contradiction..)[1]

Wittgenstein, like Russell and Carnap, apparently implies that *a proposition cannot form part of a compound proposition without functioning as an argument, i. e. determining its truth-value.* This is an important feature of the thesis of extensionality, which is not included in the statement that every proposition is a truth-function. It therefore has to be maintained separately. It cannot be doubted, however, that Wittgenstein has implied this allegation in the *Tractatus,* which I hope the following discussion will show.

One passage in the *Tractatus* seems to indicate that Wittgenstein transcends the extensional viewpoint and opens the way to the possibility of an intensional. I am thinking of 5.2341 where he says: 'The sense of a truth-function of p is a function of the sense of p.' ... '(Negation reverses the sense of a proposition.)' As the extensional viewpoint is sometimes distinguished from the intensional by the indication that the former only considers the truth-values of propositions whereas the latter takes the sense of the propositions into consideration (*vide* e. g. Jørgensen: *Über die Ziele,* p. 93) it may seem that 5.2341 shows that Wittgenstein mixes the two viewpoints. But this is not necessarily so. That a truth-function such as pvq has a sense which is determined by the senses of p and q does not imply that it cannot be defined solely by the indication of its truth-values. According to the thesis of extensionality, its truth-value will remain constant when, for example, r is substituted for p, if $p \equiv r$. But the two expressions pvq and pvr obviously can differ in sense, because the fact that p is equivalent to r implies nothing about their sense. The circumstance that the sense of a truth-function may depend upon the sense of each of its arguments does not contradict the thesis of extensionality. Only if you maintain that it is possible to make an inference from the truth of one proposition about the truth of another by considering only their sense, are you holding an intensional view. But this Wittgenstein does not maintain. Probably it is quite a different thing he tries to stress in 5.2341, namely

1. The reader must not be misled by 5.5262: '.... If an elementary proposition is true, that means, at any rate, *one more* true elementary proposition....' When viewed in connection with the whole of 5.5262 the idea appears to be that if an elementary proposition p becomes true, the structure of the world is altered. For in this case, at any rate, *one more* elementary proposition, namely p, is true.

that the sense of a truth-function depends *solely* on the senses of the arguments, a view which is connected with his theory that logical constants are not representatives (*vide* 4.0312, 5.4).

Wittgenstein did not take part in the debate whether Russell's definitions of 'implication' and 'logical inference' were 'valid', i. e. in accordance with the unphilosophical use of these concepts in daily life and in the natural sciences. His assertion of the thesis of extensionality is dogmatic in character and he never explicitly considers what could serve as instances of elementary propositions. Certainly examples can be found in the *Tractatus* (e. g. 'it is raining' in 4.461) but we are not told whether examples of this sort are satisfying, and we have no reasons for supposing that Wittgenstein thought that they were. I believe that Wittgenstein would have objected to the criticism of the extensional view, which was set forth in the years between McColl's article from 1908 and the appearance of Carnap's book in 1934, by pointing out that the examples referred to in the debate simply were not examples of elementary propositions as these are to be conceived of according to the thesis of extensionality. Probably Wittgenstein would not have accepted the examples of 'atomic propositions' which McColl, Lewis — and Russell — advance. On the contrary, he would, in all probability, have maintained that the alleged absurdities in Russell's viewpoints arose because the participants of the discussion erroneously regarded sentences such as 'Socrates is a human being' as logically simple. When it was maintained that it was possible to make inferences solely by considering the senses of the propositions not knowing their truth-values, an adherent of the *Tractatus* view could object that sentences of this kind *per definition* could not be elementary propositions. It is, anyhow, evident (from the passage on the notion of 'object' in the *Notebooks, vide* chap. II) that Wittgenstein, when confronted with the schism between logic and ontology, in an eleatic way, took the side of logic, and he obviously expected that further research would reveal that there really was no schism but that reality, when further analysed, would give in to the logical system. As far as I know only one among the many *Tractatus*-specialists has clearly noticed that Wittgenstein's ontological conceptions are determined by his conceptions of logic and language and not the other way round, namely Campanale (*vide Studi,* p. 38).

c. Consequences of the thesis of extensionality.

The view of logic which follows from Wittgenstein's thesis of extensionality sets some definite limits to what sort of theory of meaning can be established.

First, it is definite that propositions have to have a sense in order that truth-values can be ascribed to them. Truth and falsity are qualities which cannot be ascribed to entities that can be described thoroughly by means of physical concepts only. They can only be attributed to something which, although it has physical appearances (e. g. as the written sentence has), states one thing about another thing. Wittgenstein does not elaborate this point but in 6.124 he writes: 'The propositions of logic describe the scaffolding of the world, or rather they represent it. They have no 'subject-matter'. *They presuppose that names have meaning and elementary propositions sense;* and that is their connexion with the world.' (My italics).

In 4.221 it is stated with similar confidence that elementary propositions exist: 'It is obvious that the analysis of propositions must bring us to elementary propositions which consist of names in immediate combination. . .' This assertion, however, is connected with a number of other ideas concerning the picture theory. In order that sentences can be dealt with in logic at all they have to have a 'definite sense' and when one is to explain where they get this from it is useless to answer: from other sentences, for this raises the question, where have they obtained *their* definite sense. At some point or other, we have to end up with sentences that refer to something beyond the province of language, sentences the sense of which is grasped *via* something that is non-linguistic. *So there must be something of a non-linguistic sort that enables us to ascribe sense to sentences.* This is expressed (though in quite another connection) in 2.0211: 'If the world had no substance, then whether a proposition had sense would depend on whether another proposition was true', and here Wittgenstein must imply that in case of this we would get entangled in an infinite regression (cfr. Waismann: *Was ist logische Analyse,* pp. 274 - 75 where one aspect of this thought is clearly emphasized.)

If a sentence is to have a definite sense this must imply that each of the symbols constituting the sentence must possess a definite meaning. This would not be possible if all of them were defined by means of other symbols. Here again it is necessary that some elements of language refer to something outside or beyond language. The symbols that refer to or represent something non-linguistic Wittgenstein calls names or simple signs (3.2-3.202). The necessity of these signs is stated in 3.23: 'The requirement that simple signs be possible is the requirement that sense be determinate.' The whole idea is summed up by Wittgenstein in *Logical Form:* 'If we try to analyze any given propositions we shall find in general that they are logical sums, products or other truth-functions of simpler propositions. But our analysis, if carried far enough, must come to the point where it reaches propositional forms which are not themselves composed of simpler propositional forms. We must eventually reach the ultimate connection of the terms, the immediate connection which cannot be broken without destroying the propositional form as such. The propositions which represent this ultimate connexion of terms ... then, are the kernels of every proposition, *they* contain the material, and all the rest is only a development of this material. It is to them we have to look for the subject-matter of propositions.' (pp. 162 - 63).

The extensional logic in a way helps us to give reality a structure. Wittgenstein starts from 'das Faktum der Logik' and this fact compels us to maintain that sentences have a definite sense, and that therefore elementary propositions as well as simple symbols must exist. Logic in itself does not 'contain' any assertion about the existence of elementary propositions and simple symbols. As a formal, deductive system, logic can only contain formally true sentences. Assertions about the existence of elementary propositions and simple symbols are materially true sentences. They are neither postulates nor theorems in any logical system, and therefore cannot be anticipated from logic. But as soon as logic is applied, logic itself determines part of the nature of the matter to which it is applied. Wittgenstein expresses this in 5.557: 'The *application* of logic decides what elementary propositions there are. / What belongs to its application, logic cannot anticipate. / It is clear that logic must not clash with its application. / But logic has to be in contact with its application. / Therefore logic and its application must not overlap.'

That elementary propositions exist is revealed whenever logic is applied to something. This insight belongs to the application of logic and, as it cannot belong to logic alone, logic, of course, cannot clash with its application. Logic helps us to endow reality with a structure without giving us any informations as to what is the case and what is not. It only tells us what may possibly be the case (by indicating that elementary propositions exist, but not telling us anything about their contents). And this is to say that the world does not come into existence until logic is applied to it, and that the limits of logic (i. e. what is logically possible) are therefore also the limits of the world. I will return to this affair in chap. V. For the time being I shall only quote 5.61: 'Logic pervades the world: the limits of the world are also its limits' as an illustration of what is stated here.

However, the consequence which is the most important for the understanding of the *Tractatus* as a whole is this: One sentence cannot deal with another. *One sentence cannot assert anything about the sense, truth, or falsity, of another sentence*. For the acknowledgment of this puts narrow bounds to the task of introducing a theory of meaning for language.

The allegation that one sentence cannot assert anything about another follows from the thesis that any sentence is a truth-function, and that *no propositions can form part of a compound sentence without functioning as an argument*. A sentence dealing with another such as 'What is meant by 'it is raining' is that drops of water are falling to the ground' violates this principle, because its truth-value is not dependent upon the truth-value of 'it is raining' (no more than its sense is dependent upon the sense of 'it is raining', cfr. 5.2341). Therefore it is not a truth-function and consequently neither a sentence nor an expression with sense. Propositions can only be connected with each other by means of logical constants and only form parts of truth-functions.

The result is that a theory of meaning must be constructed in a manner that gives an answer to the question how an elementary proposition obtains its sense independently of all other propositions. When no sentence can deal with any other the sense of any sentence has to be grasped from the sentence itself by some act of perceiving or thinking. From the outset, no attempt to explain the sense of it by means of other sentences is permitted as this would be against the thesis of extensionality. Therefore any possible theory of meaning must be of a sort that does not demand any meta-language. On the contrary it must show that a meta-language never can be established.

Furthermore a theory of meaning must be constructed in such a way that internal relations between elementary propositions are excluded. According to the thesis of extensionality the truth-values of elementary propositions are independent of each other, i. e. one cannot infer anything about the truth-value of an elementary proposition from the knowledge of truth-values of other elementary propositions. As mentioned above this must imply that it is impossible to make an inference from the sense of one elementary proposition to the sense of another. Hence, a theory of meaning is necessarily atomic in the sense that it 'explains' the sense of any elementary proposition independently of all other propositions. *But not only must it show how it is possible to understand an elementary proposition independently of all other propositions; in addition, it must exclude the possibility that one should discover, having perceived the senses of two arbitrary elementary propositions, that the senses in question have any relation to each other,* which would be the case if f. i. part or the whole of the sense of one was 'contained' in the sense of the other.

The demands on an eventual theory of meaning enumerated here are not formulated like this in the *Tractatus*. The following statements, however, show that they form part of Wittgenstein's thoughts:

4.021 A proposition is a picture of reality: for if I understand a proposition, I know the situation that it represents. *And I understand the proposition without having its sense explained to me.*

4.022 A proposition *shows* its sense ....

4.461 Propositions show what they say ....

6.4 All propositions are of equal value.

5.556 There cannot be any hierarchy of the forms of elementary propositions....

(The italics in 4.021 are mine). 4.021 states that the sense of a proposition can be perceived without any explanations, i. e. independently of other elementary propositions. (The same matter is emphasized in 4.016 which I will comment on further on and in 4.02). If the sense was to be explained by means of other propositions this would presuppose that sentences can deal with each other. But as this is not possible, propositions must necessarily show their sense as mentioned in 4.022 and 4.461. This does not imply that the sense of one elementary proposition has no relation to the sense of any other. This circumstance is, however, emphasized in the *Tractatus* in connection with the development of the picture theory, where it is said that the sense of an elementary proposition is the state of affairs it describes (vide 2.201, 2.202 and 2.221) and that these states of affairs are independent of each other (2.061–2.062).

The statement 6.4 in the *Tractatus* is succeeded by a number of sentences concerning the world, the meaning of life, death and ethical topics. Therefore it might have other aspects than the one that stands out when it is quoted here. But as it is a comment on 6 ('The general form of a truth-function is $[\bar{p}, \bar{\xi}, N(\bar{\xi})]$. / This is the general form of a proposition') it is most likely to be relevant for the present discussion. When Wittgenstein writes that all propositions are of equal value and cannot form a hierarchy this may be just another way of expressing that they cannot deal with one another. The same theme is touched on in 5.556 which is also quoted here isolated from its connection with statements dealing with another topic.

The assertion that the sense of a proposition cannot be explained by means of other propositions implies that any sentence must be immediately understandable if only one knows the meanings of the words it contains. In a way this is true *per* definition. For if we should happen to perceive a combination of words the sense of which we cannot understand although the meanings of the words are known, then this combination is not a whole containing a sense and therefore not a proposition. Wittgenstein writes in 5.5563: 'In fact, all the propositions of our everyday language, just as they stand, are in perfect logical order. — . . . . .' As the *Tractatus*, in Maslow's words, can, in a certain sense, be characterized as an investigation of 'the necessary prerequisites of an ideal symbolism' (Maslow: *A Study*, p. xv), this statement is a little surprising and it seems to contradict 3.323, 3.324 and 3.143 (*vide* Copi: *Objects, Properties*, p. 147). It does not assert, however, that our 'everyday language' is logically perfect, but only that any proposition is in perfect logical order. That it must be this *qua* proposition is necessary true, or true *per* definition, because otherwise it could not be understood (I will return to this point in chap. II, p. 29). If a proposition did not show its sense clearly, it could never be understood clearly, as its sense according to the thesis of extensionality cannot be explained by means of other propositions. But this does not imply that it meets the demands of an ideal symbolism. A closer examination of its sense may reveal, for instance, that it seemingly has the form of an elementary proposition, but is at the same time a truth-function of several elementary propositions. An analysis of it — on the basis of what Russell (*An Inquiry*, p. 211) calls 'the principle of atomicity' = 2.0201 — will lead, in this case, to the result that the situation described by the proposition can be described more adequately than the proposition does describe it. But *qua* proposition, the proposition must, in any case, have a definite sense and therefore, in a way, be in perfect logical order. Wittgenstein suggests this possibility in 5.156 when dealing with probability: '. . . . (A proposition may well be an incomplete picture of a certain situation, but it is always a complete picture of *something*.) . . . .'

The demands of any theory of meaning, as described above, are in all respects met by the picture theory. According to the picture theory an elementary proposition is a complete picture of a certain state of affairs. The elementary propositions are in all respects independent of each other, and the states of affairs are also independent of each other. The sense of an elementary proposition can be understood without explanation of any kind. The proposition itself shows its sense. It shows what it is a picture of and in this manner all forms of meta-languages are rendered superfluous. There is no need for a description of the relation between the proposition and the state of affairs it depicts.

As I said before, the circumstance that the states of affairs are independent of each other implies that the sense of any proposition is independent of the senses of all others and with this the extensional viewpoint is accomplished not only in regard to the accidental qualities, (truth and falsity), but also to the essential quality (sense) of propositions. However, the assertion that states of affairs are independent of each other, which is necessary if the extensional view of logic is to be maintained, has disagreeable ontological consequences which Wittgenstein proposes without further comments in the passage 1 - 2.063, and the assertion that a proposition shows its sense has disagreeable psychological consequences which are touched upon in the passage 3 - 3.2. The fact that these consequences are not dealt with as exhaustively as one could expect indicates that these introducting parts of the *Tractatus* are those written last, but it is beyond of the scope of this book to develop this historical thesis.

In the literature on the *Tractatus*, the beautiful harmony between the thesis of extensionality and the picture theory is not emphasized. The reason for this is that the picture theory has been interpreted in a manner that brings it into conflict with the thesis of extensionality, which has escaped the notice of all commentators. In my opinion, all of the different interpretations of the picture theory up to this time fall short in not explaining the relation between language and thought indicated in the *Tractatus*. Until this relation is made clear, it is not possible to see the exact connection between Wittgenstein's conception of logic and his theory of meaning. The connection has been noticed (Miss Anscombe even suggests that the two are identical: "Indeed, we should not regard Wittgenstein's theory of the proposition as a *synthesis* of a picture theory and the theory of truth-functions; his picture theory and the theory of truth-functions are one and the same."! (*An Introduction*, p. 81), but she provides no defensible argument for this exaggeration.). The two conceptions cannot be reconciled, however, unless 'thought' is conceived of as a more fundamental concept than 'proposition' (in the ordinary sense of this word) in the *Tractatus*. In chap. II I will attempt to show that Wittgenstein had realized this himself.

In order to prevent misunderstandings, I must here finally point out that Wittgenstein sometimes uses 'proposition' as a designation for elementary propositions only, while at other times 'proposition' stands for truth-function and elementary proposition taken together, and at other times again it stands for molecular propositions alone. One should not therefore be confused when he writes (in 3.341) that some propositions can express the same sense, when he implies in 5.1241 that propositions can contradict each other and when he speaks of 'internal relations' between propositions (in 5.2). The reader who is well-acquainted with the text of the *Tractatus* will know that in 5.2 he is speaking of truth-functions. That these can contradict or imply each other is irrelevant to the views I have proposed in this chapter.

II

THE PICTURE THEORY

a. Introductory remarks.

As mentioned in chapter I the concept of an elementary proposition is, in a way, more fundamental than the other concepts used for the construction of the picture theory, as it is necessitated by the extensional conception of logic, while concepts such as 'object' and 'state of affairs' are necessitated by the concept of an elementary proposition. I believe that Wittgenstein has come to these concepts from his concept of an elementary proposition, although this cannot be verified satisfactorily, and I mention this here in order to indicate the connection between the various theses of the *Tractatus*.

In chapter I it was stated that elementary propositions were independent of each other in regard to truth-values and also to sense. How they can be independent of each other in regard to sense will be explained below. But first of all I will characterize the concept of 'elementary proposition' a little further.

Apart from the quoted statements on elementary propositions the following are essential for the full understanding of the concepts of 'elementary proposition' and 'name':

4.22 An elementary proposition consists of names. It is a nexus, a concatenation, of names.

4.221 It is obvious that the analysis of propositions must bring us to elementary propositions which consist of names in immediate combination.

4.24 Names are the simple symbols: I indicate them by single letters ('*x*', '*y*', '*z*'). I write elementary propositions as functions of names, so that they have the form '*fx*', φ (*x*, *y*)', etc.
Or I indicate them by the letters '*p*', '*q*', '*r*'.

5.55 ... Elementary propositions consist of names...

3.142 Only facts can express a sense, a set of names cannot.

3.202 The simple signs employed in propositions are called names.

3.203 A name means an object. The object is its meaning...

3.22 In a proposition a name is the representative of an object.

3.221 Objects can only be *named*. Signs are their representatives. I can only speak *about* them: I cannot *put them into words*. Propositions can only say *how* things are, not *what* they are.

3.26 A name cannot be dissected any further by means of a definition: it is a primitive sign.

3.3 Only propositions have sense; only in the nexus of a proposition does a name have meaning.

2.0122 ... (It is impossible for words to appear in two different roles: by themselves, and in propositions.)

4.23 It is only in the nexus of an elementary proposition that a name occurs in a proposition.

Elementary propositions are consequently propositions that consist of names only and these names are put together by an 'immediate combination'. Names are conceived of as entities that signify existing things. The possibility of dividing phenomena into things and qualities (or relations) or into 'universals' and 'particulars' is excluded in advance. Even if such distinctions could be made they would not express anything of interest, according to the *Tractatus*. In speaking of things, Wittgenstein seems to be thinking of unalterable entities that make up the substance of any possible world (*vide* 2.021 and 2.024 on which I will comment further along). Nothing but objects form part of a state of affairs, and therefore it is misleading to speak of relations with an ontological status that connect the objects with each other. Nothing can be found that deserves the name of relation. Only objects exist and in immediate connection with each other they make up states of affairs. When a state of affairs is pictured, this is done by forming a configuration of the names of the objects that enter into the state of affairs, a configuration that possesses the same logical form or structure as the state of affairs. I will deal with this matter further on. Here I wish only to stress the point that a logical perfect language according to the *Tractatus* must be one consisting of elementary propositions which in turn consist of names only, each of them signifying an object. Even though Wittgenstein maintains that 'all the propositions of our everyday language, just as they stand, are in perfect logical order. —' (5.5563), he surely would not deny that ordinary language cannot be considered perfect in this sense. When considering propositions such as 'Peter is taller than Paul', 'There is a cat in the garden' and 'Hansel and Grethel take a walk' we notice some words that are not names, such as 'taller than', 'There', 'a', 'in', 'and' and 'take a walk'. It is due to conventions that these words nevertheless form part of our written and spoken language. The possibility exists that a closer analysis of a sentence such as 'Peter is taller than Paul' will reveal that this proposition is compound and can be split up into a number of elementary propositions that do not contain any of the words occurring in the original proposition. None of the words constituting the original proposition can therefore be names if the analysis is correct. Possibly this view lies behind Wittgenstein's remark in 4.002: 'Man possesses the ability to construct languages capable of expressing every sense, without having any idea how each word has meaning or what its meaning is- . . . / It is not humanly possible to gather immediately from it [everyday language] what the logic of language is / . . . The tacit conventions on which the understanding of everyday language depends are enormously complicated.'

But the condition for analyzing ordinary language and showing that the apparent logical form of a proposition of ordinary language is not its real form (cfr. 4.0031: '. . . It was Russell who performed the service of showing that the apparent logical form of a proposition need not be its real one.') is, of course, that the proposition of ordinary language *has* a logical form, that is *has* a sense, that it can be understood immediately, and therefore in a certain sense is 'in perfect logical order'.

Words of ordinary language that appear to be something other than names may have a function, namely the one of helping us to distinguish easily between the various 'pictures' we present to each other when we communicate. In 4.016 Wittgenstein writes: 'In order to understand the essential nature of a proposition, we should consider hieroglyphic script, which depicts the facts that it describes. / An alphabetic script developed out of it without loosing what was essential to depiction.' The reason for replacing hieroglyphic script by alphabetic script is that the latter is the more flexible and elastic. But in order to be so a number of 'enormously complicated tacit conventions' must be understood that find expression in a number of words, tones of voice, gestures etc. that cannot be names according to the picture theory.

According to 3.26 a name cannot be dissected any further by means of a definition. This statement is implied by the demand for a 'definite sense' which must be ascribed to propositions in order that they can be dealt with in logic. If any symbol could be defined by means of other symbols, the question of the meaning of a symbol would lead to an infinite regress. As an elementary proposition only can have a definite sense by virtue of the circumstance that every name in the proposition represents a certain object, there must be primitive signs in order that elementary propositions can possess a sense.

It appears from 3.3 that 'elementary proposition' in a way is a more fundamental concept than the concept of 'name'. It is a widespread opinion, not only in philosophical circles but among psychologists as well, that human beings apprehend language by learning first singular words (by ostensive definitions), and later how these words can be combined into propositions. It seems as if empirical investigations verify this view as children normally learn singular words such as 'daddy' and 'mummy' first of all and not until later (at the age of 1½ or 2 years), do they learn verbs that make it possible for them to form sentences. According to Wittgenstein, however, it is not possible to learn the meanings of words independently of their occurrence in propositions, for 'only in the nexus of a proposition does a name have meaning'. When children in spite of this in some sense or other can learn words such as 'daddy' and 'mummy' before they are able to form sentences we must obviously — according to Wittgenstein — maintain that either they do not understand the meaning of these words or else these words function as sentences that appear to have a form different from the one they really have (cfr. 4.0031).

It is not, of course, clear what is meant by the assertion that children of about 1½ years of age apply words they do not themselves understand. The point is what we read into the word 'understand'. When children that are unable to form sentences say 'mummy', nevertheless, every time their mother appears or when they are afraid, it seems — in any case on the basis of behaviouristic criteria — that they must have associated the sound 'mummy' with the sight of the mother. But it is indeed improbable that they should know that this sound, when applied in other contexts, e. g. when another child is calling his mother, signifies something different from their own mother. If we demand that this has to be the case in order that it can be said properly that they have understood the meaning, then they do not understand any words before they have learnt how words can form parts of propositions.

Therefore Wittgenstein's view cannot be refuted on the basis of psychological considerations of how language is learnt. Independently of these considerations, his statement is that a word has no meaning when viewed in isolation. This is to say that a word such as 'toil' does not mean anything definite when considered separately (cfr. 3.3 and 2.0122). It may cause some associations in the mind of the person who hears it but it cannot be seen from the word itself, to what it should refer. The word does not have any relation to anything different from itself. It does not represent anything unless it appears in a sentence. The same applies to elements of an ordinary picture. A line such as ‿ does not represent anything but in a picture:

it may represent a smiling mouth. It is the whole, the configuration of the elements that make them represent something.

An examination of which sentences a word or a sound can occur in soon reveals that everyday language does not meet the demands of an ideal symbolism. The word 'toil' means something different in the two propositions: 'I toil the whole day' and 'The fisherman repairs his toil'. In order to avoid such homonyms, one could introduce a number of new words and make the rule that a word must represent only one object. But even if language was devoid of homonyms we would still have to adhere to Wittgenstein's view that a name has meaning only in the nexus of a proposition. For names can only represent when they occur as links in a descriptive proposition.[1]

Wittgenstein's conceptions of 'propositional sign' and 'sign' enable us to give a clearer account of this matter. He lets the expression 'propositional sign' stand for the physical appearances of a proposition. In order that a sense is to be communicated it is necessary to apply some material (written signs, sounds or other common phenomena) which can be described in a physical language that does not pay any attention to the sense of the proposition. Thus the expression 'The earth is round' can be conceived of as a proposition that tells us something about the earth and therefore contains names as elements. But on the other hand it can be considered physical material. The distinction between 'proposition' and 'propositional sign' is not new. It is set forth in the *Principia Mathematica*, vol. I (2nd. ed.) where we read at p. 660: 'We must, to begin with, distinguish between a proposition as a fact and a proposition as a vehicle of truth or falsehood. The following series of black marks: "Socrates is mortal," is a fact of geography. The noise which I should make if I were to say "Socrates is mortal" would be a fact of acoustics. The mental occurrence when I entertain the belief "Socrates is mortal" is a fact of psychology. None of these introduces the notion of truth or falsehood, which is, for logic, the essential characteristics of propositions.'

Wittgenstein defines 'propositional sign' in 3.12: 'I call the sign with which we express a thought a propositional sign. — . . .' Thus a propositional sign can be regarded as an articulated field which taken alone does not refer to anything but may be used by a thinking person as a set of names for certain objects. Unfortunately Wittgenstein does not distinguish sharply between the elements of the propositional sign and the elements of the proposition. Elements of a proposition are called names or simple symbols. In 3.21 elements of propositional signs are spoken of as 'simple signs'. Obviously a sign has one status when functioning as a name in a proposition

1. The examples of names and propositions given here are only illustrations to the thoughts; they do not serve as examples of names and propositions as these must be conceived of in the *Tractatus*. This applies to all examples given further on.

and quite another when it only forms part of a physical fact. If we distinguish between 'sign' = 'element of a physical fact or a propositional sign' and 'name' = 'element of a proposition' we might be able to express the circumstance that a name only has a meaning in the nexus of a proposition by saying that names cannot at all occur 'outside' propositions. If something that seems to be a name, for instance 'toil' occurs detached from any linguistic context it is *not* a name, but a mere 'sign' and it can never be more than that. Signs can be combined into propositional signs but still remain signs. A proposition is not established until the propositional sign is used as projective material for a thought. When this is done the signs suddenly become names.

On the basis of these conceptions of the constituents of language, Wittgenstein is forced to accept a specific theory of the nature of what exists.

As I said before, Wittgenstein was forced to assume that some propositions referred to something beyond the domain of language because the sense and truth of any proposition would otherwise depend on the sense and truth of at least one other proposition and thus involve an infinite regress. Furthermore he was forced to assume the existence of primitive signs which as parts of propositions represented something non-linguistic as an account of the definite sense of propositions could not otherwise be given. The demand for a definite sense has, as mentioned above, its source in logic, as a proposition cannot be considered true or false, which is necessary in logic, unless it has a definite sense.

Thus Wittgenstein was led to the assumption that simple non-linguistic elements could be found and that these could form those configurations which we describe by means of propositions.

In the account of these ontological concepts and the concept of 'picture', I will proceed in the following manner. First, I shall try to give a formal stipulation of the concepts, i. e. an analysis intended to define these concepts as clearly as possible without paying any attention to their applications. Next, I will deal with the problem of what Wittgenstein has imagined could satisfy his theory and what *may be able* to satisfy it. In the formal stipulation, I shall temporarily ignore the statements in the *Tractatus* that indicate what Wittgenstein seems to have considered as examples of his fundamental concepts.

b. Formal stipulation of the concepts relating to the picture theory.

As to the concept of an object, we are told in 2.01, though not directly, that it is synonymous with 'entity' and 'thing'. In the *Tractatus* nothing can be found that forbids us to use these words as equivalent. An object is characterized as being something that can form part of state of affairs (2.01:

'A state of affairs (a state of things) is a combination of objects (things).' 2.011: 'It is essential to things that they should be possible constituents of states of affairs'). A state of affairs is characterized as being a connected group of objects (2.01). The two concepts, 'object' and 'state of affairs' seem to be equally fundamental. Both of them are 'defined' in 2.01 and they cannot be understood apart from each other. A state of affairs consists only of objects, or rather, of the configuration of objects (2.0272: 'The configuration of objects produces states of affairs.') It looks as if Wittgenstein has thought that a state of affairs would subsist, even if all of its constituents were substituted with others, if only the configuration of the objects was preserved. I shall deal with this problem further on.

Nothing but objects forms part of the state of affairs. In the same way as names are in immediate connection with each other in elementary propositions, the objects in the state of affairs are connected with each other immediately, i. e. they are not connected with each other by means of anything else. By making this assumption, Wittgenstein avoids infinite regresses of the sort Bradley pointed out in cases where relations were ascribed an ontological existence (*Appearance and Reality*, p. 33). The objects are compared with links in a chain: 2.03 'In a state of affairs objects fit into one another like the links of a chain.' This suggests partly that the objects do not modify each other in the state of affairs and partly that nothing further is needed in order to combine them with each other.

In 2.012 it is said: 'In logic nothing is accidental: if a thing *can* occur in a state of affairs, the possibility of the state of affairs must be written into the thing itself.' This means that the possibility of an object occurring in a state of affairs must in advance 'lie' in the object: 2.0121 '. . . If things can occur in states of affairs, this possibility must be in them from the beginning. . .' The consequence is that objects cannot be 'thought of' or cannot be conceived of when taken alone. They can only be thought of in connection with the possibilities of the states of affairs that they can form part of. At the end of 2.0121 it is said: '. . . Just as we are quite unable to imagine spatial objects outside space or temporal objects outside time, so too there is no object that we can imagine excluded from the possibility of combining with others. / If I can imagine objects combined in states of affairs, I cannot imagine them excluded from the possibility of such combinations.' It is not said whether we are concerned with a logical or a psychological impossibility at this point.

Moreover, it is said that 'If I know an object I also know all its possible occurrences in states of affairs . . .' (2.0123). Since states of affairs, as said before, consist of objects only it must follow that the class of objects contains the possibility of all states of affairs (because every object contains the possibility of any state of affairs it can occur in). If we are right in reading the word 'situation' ('Sachlage') as an equivalent to 'state of affairs' ('Sachverhalt') then it is this 'conclusion' which is expressed in 2.014: 'Objects contain the possibility of all situations.'

In 2.02 we are told that 'Objects make up the substance of the world'. 2.024 tells us that 'Substance is what subsists independently of what is the case'. The world is all that is the case (1). But no matter what world we imagine, it must have something in common with the actual world. This 'something' consists of the objects which constitute the unalterable form of the world (cfr. 2.022 and 2.023).

Since the objects can be regarded in a certain sense as the building material of the world, they cannot be composite (2.021). For the substance has to be something out of which any possible world can be built. If they were composite, they would consist of elements which, taken for themselves, could be used for building a world, which could not have been constructed by means of the original objects. Therefore 'Objects are simple' (2.02).

It is conceivable that the demand, that objects have to be simple, is intimately connected with the demand that propositions have to have a definite sense as mentioned above. This can be illustrated in the following way. Let us say that 'This speck is red' designates a certain speck in the visual field. We can draw the limits for this speck by imagining a system of lines crossing each other parallel to the axes of a rectangular coordinate system laid in the visual field. Wittgenstein suggests this method in *Logical Form*, p. 166 where this drawing occurs:

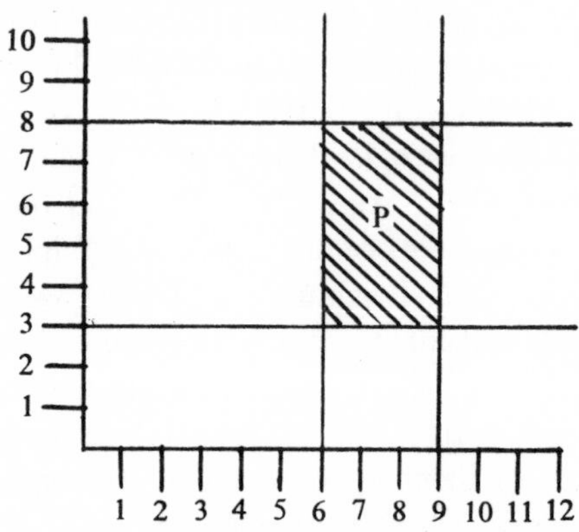

We can then write '[6-9,3-8]*R*' instead of '*P* is red'. Wittgenstein constructed this example in order to show that numbers would occur in any elementary proposition if it was to be formulated correctly. This is a viewpoint which he had apparently developed after the *Tractatus* was written. But the example can be used for a different purpose. Let us say that *P*, as the figure indicates, is composite. In this case the proposition '*P* is red' or '[6-9,3-8] *R*' will be a truth-function because it is a conjunction of a number of propositions about the specks which *P* can be divided into. This conjunction can be written as $p_1 \cdot p_2 \cdot p_3 \cdot p_4 \cdot \ldots p_n$, where p_1 is the proposition describing that a certain speck situated in the area [6-9,3-8] is red, p_2 is the proposition describing that another speck in the same area is red and so on. All the links of this conjunction are propositions that have no definite sense because propositions of the form '*p* is somewhere in the area [6-9,3-8] and *p* is red' is not a univocal description that can be distinguished from any other description. 'Somewhere' can never occur in an exact information. The limits of the conjunction, therefore, will all be indefinite and consequently the sense of '*P* is red' will be indefinite too. In order to give p_1 a definite sense we must indicate the limits of the speck described in p_1. These may be [7-8,4-5]. But please notice that if the subject of the proposition p_1 is a composite speck the whole problem will arise once more. And in this way we can continue, until, at some point, we meet with simple elements. If we never reach this point then '[6-9,3-8] *R*' can never have a definite sense. But as it is a logical necessity that elementary propositions with definite senses can be found, then simple objects must exist.

Even though the described example is to be found in *Logical Form* I believe that it is in accordance with the view of the *Tractatus*. In 4.023 Wittgenstein writes: 'A proposition must restrict reality to two alternatives: yes or no. / In order to do that, *it must describe reality completely*...' (My italics). In 2.1511 and 2.15121 he writes: '*That* is how a picture is attached to reality: it reaches right out to it. / It is laid against reality like a ruler. / Only the end-points of the graduation lines actually *touch* the object that is to be measured.' In *Logical Form* his words are: 'I have said elsewhere that a proposition 'reaches up to reality', and by this I meant that the forms of the entities are contained in the form of the proposition which is about these entities.' (p. 169). And from what follows immediately at that point, it can be seen that a proposition such as '*RPT*' (which is a shortening of '[6-9,3-8] *R*') contains the form of an entity in the sense indicated. It, therefore, is very probable that the illustration from *Logical Form* is an unfolding of the thoughts in 2.1511 - 2.15121.

In spite of his assertion that objects are simple, Wittgenstein speaks of properties of objects. In 2.01231 he writes: 'If I am to know an object, though I need not know its external properties, I must know all its internal properties.' 2.0233 and 2.02331 speak of properties of objects too. It is not clear what is meant by 'internal' and 'external'. In 2.0233 it is held that if two objects have the same logical form, the only distinction between them, apart from their external properties, is that they are different. This seems to indicate that 'logical form' is equivalent to 'internal properties'. Or in other words, it seems to indicate that two objects can have internal properties in common. But we are not told more about these properties. Professor Hartnack has suggested (*Wittgenstein*, p. 31) that 4.123, in which it is said 'A property is internal if it is unthinkable that its object should not possess it ...', might help us here. But though the German version actually has 'Gegenstand' at this place, the subject here is properties of facts (*vide* 4.1221 and the rest of 4.123), and we have no sufficient reason for inferring that what is said here holds good for objects too. I do not think that it can be doubted that 'Gegenstand' in 4.123 — as in 3.2 too — is applied in the colloquial use of the word, corresponding to 'topic'.

To speak of internal properties of objects seems to presuppose that objects can be composite. In the same way 2.014 'Objects contain the possibility of all situations' indicates that objects are composite for nothing simple can contain anything. It is indeed difficult to see how Wittgenstein imagined that 2.014 and 2.01231 could match 2.02 and 2.021. I believe that this question is unanswerable.

I have maintained that the concepts of 'object' and 'state of affairs' are equally fundamental. In 2.0124 it is held that if all objects are given, then at the same time all *possible* states of affairs are also given. Since an object cannot be conceived of in isolation from states of affairs (because a name cannot be thought of apart from sentences), we may reverse 2.0124 and maintain that if all possible states of affairs are given then all objects are also given.

*

As to states of affairs, it is said that they can either exist or not exist (*vide* 2.06, 2.062 and 4.25). I will return to this peculiar statement later; I mention it here only for the sake of the task of giving a clarification of the concept of a 'fact'. This concept seems to be rather difficult to give a reasonable interpretation to, and Wittgenstein surely has not given a clear account of it in the *Tractatus*. The following four possibilities have been suggested as interpretations by experts on the *Tractatus:*

(a) A fact is a group of states of affairs, existing or not existing.
(b) The word 'fact' covers partly a group of states of affairs (existing or not existing) and partly singular states of affairs (existing or not existing).
(c) A fact is a group of existing states of affairs.
(d) A fact is an existing state of affairs.

It will be seen that other possibilities than the ones mentioned can be thought of but as nothing can be found in favour of them in the *Tractatus* I will not consider them here.

Stenius pleads for the possibility (d) (*vide* Stenius: *Wittgenstein's 'Tractatus'*, p. 31) and adduces in favour of it 2, 1.1 taken together with 2.04, 2.05 taken together with 1.12 and also 4.25. Wittgenstein writes in 2: 'What is the case — a fact — is the existence of states of affairs.' In 2.04 he writes: 'The totality of existing states of affairs is the world.', and in 1.1 it is said that 'The world is the totality of facts . . .' Whereas 2 seems to be in favour of (c), 1.1 taken together with 2.04 seems to indicate that the class or totality of existing states of affairs is identical with the class or totality of facts, and this points to (d) as the right interpretation. 1.12 reads: 'For the totality of facts determines what is the case, and also whatever is not the case.' In 2.05 it is asserted that 'The totality of existing states of affairs also determines which states of affairs do not exist.' If we compare these two statements they support (d). Concerning 4.25 which tells us that 'If an elementary proposition is true, the state of affairs exists: if an elementary proposition is false, the state of affairs does not exist.', it must be said that this statement does not contribute to the interpretation, as Stenius believes, unless it is viewed in connection with other parts of the *Tractatus,* as for instance 4.26 in which it is said that 'If all true elementary propositions are listed, the world is completely described' taken together with 1.1: 'The world is the totality of facts . . .' and also 5.43 that tells us that 'Even at first sight it seems scarcely credible that there should follow from one fact p infinitely many *others . . .*' which means to say that a *true* elementary proposition describes a fact.

In his analysis of the concept of 'fact', Stenius also examines the word 'situation' ('Sachlage') and comes to the conclusion that this designates a composition of states of affairs, existing or not existing. If p and q are elementary propositions that describe states of affairs, then $p \cdot q$ is a description of a situation no matter whether p and q are true or not. 2.202 and 2.203 seem to show, however, that 'Sachlage' is sometimes used synonymously with 'Sachverhalt' but this has no importance for the following remarks.

Russell adheres to (b) in his introduction to the *Tractatus*. He writes: 'Facts which are not compounded of other facts are what Mr. Wittgenstein calls Sachverhalte, whereas a fact which may consist of two or more facts is called a Tatsache: thus for example, "Socrates is wise" is a Sachverhalt, as well as a Tatsache, whereas "Socrates is wise and Plato is his pupil" is a Tatsache, but not a Sachverhalt.' (*Introduction,* p. 9). In writing this he probably had a letter in mind which Wittgenstein wrote to him on 19th August, 1919 (*Notebooks,* p. 129) in which appears: '"What is the difference between Tatsache and Sachverhalt?" Sachverhalt is, what corresponds to an Elementarsatz if it is true. Tatsache is what corresponds to the logical product of elementary props when this product is true.' However, Russell in his introduction does not say whether the examples given are true propositions. He therefore represents the view (b), while Wittgenstein in his letter represents (c). As representatives of (a) Weinberg (*An Examination*, p. 38), Barone (*Il Solipsismo*, p. 552) and Anscombe (*An Introduction*, p. 30) can be mentioned.

In Russell's formulation of his interpretation, a small defect can be found as he speaks of facts as something that can be 'compounded of' or 'consist of' states of affairs. In my formulations of the different possibilities, I have avoided these expressions, since according to the *Tractatus* it must be nonsense to speak of combinations of states of affairs at all. $p \cdot q$ does not assert more than that p and q exist simultaneously. The logical constants do not represent anything that has existence, and therefore '·' does not signify any link between p and q, which in some way or other binds the two states of affairs in question together.

In the *Tractatus*, oddly enough, two statements can be found that point to the interpretation (a) as the right one. The two are 2.034 that reads 'The structure of a fact consists of the structures of states of affairs.' and 4.2211 that starts with 'Even if the world is infinitely complex, so that every fact consists of infinitely many states of affairs . . . .' These statements contradict (c) and (d) but make (b) a possible interpretation.

I have the impression that the concepts of 'fact', 'state of affairs' and 'situation' are so blurred in Wittgenstein's exposition that it is not possible to make a satisfactory interpretation of them, [it is typical that he speaks of facts in 5.5423 while in the same situation in *Notebooks* he speaks of states of affairs (*Notebooks*, p. 28)]. On the other hand, the whole matter is not so surprising if it is the case that the ontological introduction to the *Tractatus* has come into existence as a consequence of the demand that elementary propositions have to have a definite sense.

For the present I will for the sake of my exposition adhere to Stenius' interpretation of the concepts in question though I do not think it sufficient, for reasons which should now be clear. It is beyond doubt that Wittgenstein used the word 'Tatsache' in at least two ways but I believe that in connection with the picture theory he always thought of it with the significance indicated in (d). I should like to give a further reason for this assertion. Wittgenstein uses three verbs when speaking of the picturing relation between propositions and what they are about, namely 'darstellen', 'vorstellen' and 'abbilden'. When it is said in German about a picture that it 'abbildet' something, it is usually implied, that this something exists independently of the picture of it. If confronted with a picture of something that never has existed or never could exist in reality, a German person would use instead the words 'vorstellen' and 'darstellen'. In German (and Danish) this distinction is rather sharp. Now, if the interpretation (d) holds good, we should expect Wittgenstein to use the word 'darstellen' in connection with 'Sachverhalt' which signifies something possible and 'abbilden' in connection with 'Tatsache' which signifies something actually existing. This actually appears to be the case. 'Darstellen' occurs in connection with 'Sachverhalt' in 2.201, 3.0321, 4.1 and 4.122, whereas it nowhere occurs together with 'Tatsache'. 'Abbilden' is used in connection with 'Tatsache' in 4.016 and never occurs together with 'Sachverhalt' or 'Sachlage'.

Last but not least, it must not be overlooked that Wittgenstein says of pictures that they are facts (2.141). This indicates partly that some facts, namely pictures, cannot be compounded of or be groups of states of affairs, for a picture only pictures one state of affairs, and partly that 'fact' must to some extent mean the same as 'existing state of affairs', as a picture is not something possible only but always something that exists.

The world is said to be the totality of facts, not of things (1,1). This concept is of no importance in connection with the picture theory, but it has a special interest for Wittgenstein's solipsism and I will deal with it further on. As to the concept of 'reality', Stenius has pointed out that it differs from that of 'world'. It can be seen from 2 and 2.04 that the world is equivalent to the totality of the existing states of affairs. From 2.06 which says that 'The existence and non-existence of states of affairs is reality' it can be seen that reality is a broader concept than world (cfr. Stenius: *Wittgenstein's Tractatus*, pp. 50–51). But here too there is lack of clarity for, as Stenius points out, reality is used in one place for signifying a part of the world as fact, namely in 2.063: 'The sum-total of reality is the world.' (cfr. Stenius' book, p. 35).

There is one more thing to notice concerning the concept of 'world'. In 1.2 it is said that 'The world divides into facts.' This formulation is, unfortunately, ambiguous. We can understand it as the statement that the world in advance, i. e. before it is in any way perceived by anybody, is divided into facts. But it might on the other hand be read as the statement that it is the perceiving subject that puts structure to the amorphous world, so that it divides into facts at the moment he perceives it. In this case the further question can be raised whether the subject could have put another structure to it or whether all subjects perceive the same structure in the world. This way of looking at the matter, which is inspired by Gestalt-psychology, is represented by Stenius (op. cit. pp. 24–25). There are various things in favour of this interpretation. Stenius mentions Wittgenstein's example in 5.5423 where the point is that a part of the world can be structured in at least two ways. As I shall show later, it is beyond doubt that 1.2 is to be understood as a statement of phenomenalism. It is only in relation to a perceiving subject that the world has structure, divides into facts. Wittgenstein's solipsism is closely connected with this thought.

*

I shall now deal with the concept of a 'picture'. The following statements are relevant for the clarification of this concept:

2.11 A picture presents a situation in logical space, the existence and non-existence of states of affairs.
2.12 A picture is a model of reality.
2.13 In a picture objects have the elements of the picture corresponding to them.
2.131 In a picture the elements of the picture are the representatives of objects.
2.14 What constitutes a picture is that its elements are related to one another in a determinate way.
2.141 A picture is a fact.
2.15 The fact that the elements of a picture are related to one another in a determinate way represents that things are related to one another in the same way.
Let us call this connexion of its elements the structure of the picture, and let us call the possibility of this structure the pictorial form of the picture.
2.1514 The pictorial relationship consists of the correlations of the picture's elements with things.
2.16 If a fact is to be a picture, it must have something in common with what it depicts.
2.161 There must be something identical in a picture and what it depicts, to enable the one to be a picture of the other at all.
2.17 What a picture must have in common with reality, in order to be able to depict it — correctly or incorrectly — in the way it does, is its pictorial form.

The translation of Pears and McGuinness is a little incorrect in speaking of 'a picture' everywhere where the German text has 'the picture' ('das Bild'). Contrary to the other concepts of the picture theory the concept of 'picture' is applied consistently in the *Tractatus*. It appears that a picture is a fact (2.141), and as such it consists of objects. The objects are related to one another in the picture in a definite way (2.14) and in order that a picture can picture a fact it is a necessary condition that the objects of the fact are related to one another in the same manner as the objects of the picture. If so, the picture and the pictured fact will have something in common, namely a certain structure or a 'pictorial form' (2.15, 2.16-2.17). It is an essential feature of this view that the picture and the pictured fact can be analysed into the same amount of elements or conceived of as articulated to the same degree, so that a one-one-correspondance can be established between the elements of the picture and the elements of the fact (2.13, 2.131 and 2.1514). An isomorphy of this kind is a necessary condition of picturing in general.

The word 'picture', however, is used in a more extensive way than here indicated. According to Wittgenstein, we may also speak of pictures that are pictures of something which does not exist. As mentioned above Wittgenstein applies the words 'darstellen' and 'vorstellen' in this connection. A picture may present something which does exist or something which does not exist (2.11). In either case it is said to be a 'model' of reality, but in the latter case one cannot say that an isomorphy can be found between the picture and the pictured fact for there *is* no pictured fact. Here, we meet a difficult problem with which I will deal further on in this chapter.

What is said about the concept of 'picture' is transferred to the concept of 'elementary proposition' *via* 3 which reads: 'A logical picture of facts is a thought.' In 3.1 it is held that 'In a proposition a thought finds an expression that can be perceived by the senses', and 3.2 adds in what way a thought can be expressed in a proposition: 'In a proposition a thought can be expressed in such a way that elements of the propositional sign correspond to the objects of the thought.' Consequently, an elementary proposition is a picture of the fact it describes. It therefore must be isomorphic with the fact, and hence it must meet all the demands that are fulfilled by the concept of 'picture'.

*

In connection with the picture theory there is one more concept which Wittgenstein applies, namely 'logical space'. A model of the logical space may look like this:

O O O O O O

Fig. 1 S_1 S_2 S_3 S_4 S_5 – – – – – – – – – S_n

O O O O O O

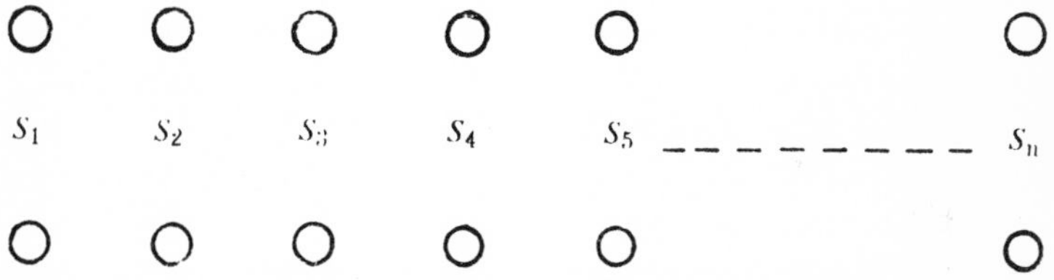

Here S_1, S_2, S_3 . . . etc. each indicate a state of affairs and the series S_1, S_2, S_3 . . . S_n consequently indicates the totality of all states of affairs. The two circles that are placed above and below each state of affair mark the possibilities of existence and non-existence of the states of affairs. Thus, the existence of a state of affairs can be indicated by:

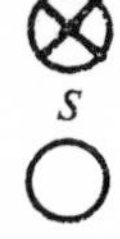

and the non-existence correspondingly:

Fig. 1 can now be viewed as a 'logical space' that gives place for all possible realities. For instance, we may imagine that S_1, S_3, and S_4 exist while S_2 and S_5 do not exist, and correspondingly we can imagine that the further states of affairs in the series either exist or do not exist up to S_n, which in this case does exist. The 'reality', which is hereby 'created', can then be represented by a line:

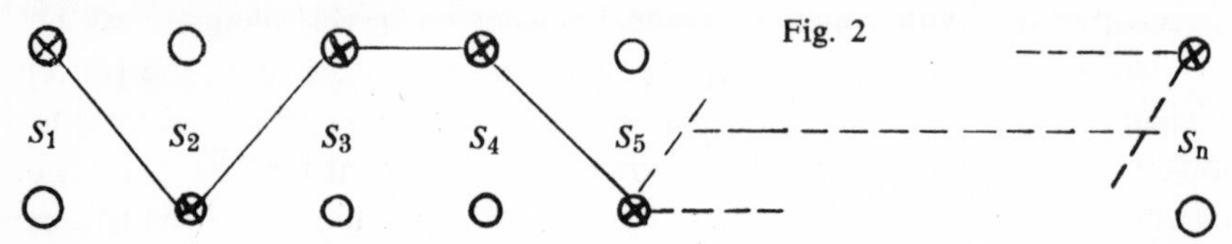

Fig. 2

If we demand in this model that all states of affairs have to be marked as existing or non-existing when a possible reality is indicated, and furthermore maintain that no marking of the existence or non-existence of one state of affairs determines the value of any other state of affairs, and if we finally demand that no state of affairs at one and the same time can both exist and not exist (i. e. that no vertical lines must occur in the figure), then this model meets all the demands of the *Tractatus* concerning 'logical space'.

In 1.13 it is said that 'the facts in logical space are the world.' As the world is the totality of facts (cfr. 1.1), this means that the world is the totality of all states of affairs that exist in the logical space. If we look at fig. 2 we must say that the world here indicated is S_1, S_3, $S_4 \ldots S_n$. The statements 2.11 ('A picture presents a situation in logical space, the existence and non-existence of states of affairs.') and 2.202 ('A picture represents a possible situation in logical space.') are also in agreement with the model given. Likewise, 3.4 ('A proposition determines a place in logical space') becomes clear in connection with this model, whereas 3.42 remains obscure. In 3.42 it is said that: 'A proposition can determine only one place in logical space: nevertheless the whole of logical space must already be given by it. / (Otherwise negation, logical sum, logical product, etc., would introduce more and more new elements — in coordination.) / (The logical scaffolding surrounding a picture determines the logical place. The force of a proposition reaches through the whole of logical space.)' It is clear, however, that if, in our model, we mean by a logical place, a vertical column, a proposition always determines only one place. Furthermore it is evident that any place must be fixed in relation to other places, i. e. to the logical space as a whole, as the word 'place' otherwise loses its meaning. Therefore, a proposition establishes the whole of logical space in establishing a place in it (cfr. 3.42). What Wittgenstein is aiming at in the second part of 3.42, I do not know, but I believe that nothing in this passage contradicts the model. In 4.463 Wittgenstein writes: 'A tautology leaves open to reality the whole —

the infinite whole — of logical space; a contradiction fills the whole of logical space leaving no point of it for reality.' Since any proposition, according to the extensional view of logic, is implied by a contradiction, it is clear that if it is possible to assert a contradiction at all, then one can maintain that any circle in fig. 1 can contain an *X*. In this way the whole of logical space would be filled and no place would be left for reality. On the other hand, the assertion of the tautologies is the assertion of all the possibilities indicated in fig. 1.

Since a state of affairs can be described by means of an elementary proposition, it can be seen that we are able to set up a figure corresponding to fig. 1:

Fig. 3

$$\begin{array}{cccccc} t & t & t & t & t & t \\ p_1 & p_2 & p_3 & p_4 & p_5 \cdots & p_n \\ f & f & f & f & f & f \end{array}$$

where p_1, p_2, $p_3 \ldots p_n$ are elementary propositions and where '*t*' means 'true' and '*f*' means 'false'. From this we see that the logical space is a sort of counterpart to the formal definition of proposition as something that can be either true or false but not both at one and the same time.

By comparing the passages in the *Tractatus* dealing with elementary propositions and those dealing with states of affairs, it can be seen that the 'logical space' is in a way traced from the formal properties of propositions.

We may briefly consider the passages in question. In 4.22, it is said that an elementary proposition is a concatenation of names. Answering to this it is said in 2.01 and 2.0272 that a state of affairs is a concatenation of objects. In 4.221, it is held that the names of a proposition are in immediate combination with one another. Correspondingly it is said in 2.03 that the objects in a state of affairs fit into each other like the links of a chain. In 3.202, names are spoken of as 'simple signs'. The assertion that objects are simple (2.02 and 2.021) corresponds to this. In 3.21, it is asserted that the configuration of objects in a situation corresponds to the configuration of simple signs in the propositional sign. 4.466 says somewhat the same: 'What corresponds to a determinate logical combination of signs is a determinate logical combination of their meanings.' The correspondence between statements about language and statements about reality goes further yet. In 4.23, it is said of names that they can only occur in the nexus of elementary propositions. Answering to this, it is maintained in 2.0121 that objects cannot be imagined apart from the possibility of combinations in states of affairs. In 3.141 and 3.142, it is emphasized that a proposition is more than a medley of words. It is articulated, it has structure. 2.031 reflects this idea when stating that the objects of a state of affairs stand in a determinate relation to one another. Furthermore, it is said in 4.211, 5.134 and 5.152 that elementary propositions are independent of each other. Correspondingly, 2.061 asserts that states of affairs are independent of each other, and as 5.134 asserts that no elementary proposition can be implied by any other, so 2.062 maintains that we cannot infer anything from the existence of one state of affairs about the existence of others.

Apart from all the other statements of the *Tractatus* that indicate, while presenting the picture theory, the nature of the correspondence between language and reality, the statements mentioned above show in what way Wittgenstein imagined reality as a duplicate of language. It seems to be very easy to list the essential features of reality in this way. The enumerated features are necessary features which the reality must possess in order that it can be described at all (and it *has* to be describable, for if logic cannot be applied to anything, propositions have no sense, and therefore no truth-value either, and in this case there can be no logic at all, as pointed out above). What has been said about the picture theory and reality up to now, however, involves a difficulty which seems to be insuperable and which Wittgenstein himself never overcame. It is this difficulty, and apparently only this, which has forced Wittgenstein to form his concepts of 'state of affairs' and 'logical space'.

*

The difficulty lies in that the picture theory, as it is presented in the *Tractatus*, is capable only of explaining where true propositions get their sense from. From the start, Wittgenstein exempts himself from giving any explanation of how an elementary proposition can be *false* and yet have a sense. I am not the first to notice this difficulty. It has been observed by both Anscombe (*vide An Introduction*, chap. IV), Stenius (*vide Wittgenstein's 'Tractatus'* p. 40) and Maslow (*vide A Study*, pp. 75 ff). The problem, however, needs a more detailed study than given until now.

The difficulty appears in the following way. According to Wittgenstein the propositions that serve as arguments in the extensional, truth-functional logic of the *Principia Mathematica* must be independent of each other both in respect of truth-value and of sense. From this it follows that we can never infer that an elementary proposition is true or false on the basis of the knowledge about other elementary propositions, neither by logical, semantical nor empirical analysis. This involves the notion that a negation of an elementary proposition can never, itself, be regarded as an elementary proposition. An expression such as '$\sim p$' must be a truth-function for any value of *p*, for if it was to be an elementary proposition, we could infer from the truth of '*p*' to the falsity of '∼*p*', and this is not allowed. This can be expressed in another way by saying that logical constants do not represent anything (4.0312). For if '∼' was a name of an object, then '∼*p*' would be a configuration of names, as '*p*' is, and consequently it would be an elementary proposition, if '*p*' is an elementary proposition. Now, when an elementary proposition *can* be false, how, then, are we able to distinguish between the two expressions '*p is false*' and '∼*p*'? This is one aspect of the problem which Wittgenstein never succeeded in solving.

The other aspect is the question of what a false proposition describes. According to the picture theory, one name, as is said in 4.0311, stands for one thing, another for another thing, and they are combined with one another, and in this way the whole group — as a living picture — presents a state of affairs. The fact that the picture can describe a fact depends upon the possibility of establishing a univocal correspondence between the elements of the picture and the elements of the pictured fact (The nature of this correspondence will be analysed in chapter III, *a*.). Now, if it happens that when we compare an elementary proposition with reality, the fact which it describes does not exist, then no isomorphic relation can be established between the proposition and the pictured fact, and consequently the proposition cannot be said to picture anything. But in this case it has no sense, since the sense of a proposition is the entity it is about. Hence, the picture theory can be said to imply that only two kinds of propositions, namely true propositions on the one hand and nonsensical propositions on the other, can be found. But this is absurd, because the introduction of the picture theory presupposed that elementary propositions can be endowed with sense, without knowledge of their truth or falsity. If we only have to do with true and nonsensical propositions, we cannot distinguish between truth and sense. Now, where is the way out of this difficulty?

The first problem — what is the difference between (*A*) '*p* is false' and (*B*) '∼*p*' — can only be solved if we distinguish between two kinds of falsity. Normally '∼*p*' is read as 'it is false that *p*' or '*p* is false', and when we read it so no difference can be observed between (*A*) and (*B*). But if there is none, the thesis of extensionality does not hold. For in that case '∼*p*' is an elementary proposition as well as '*p*' and the two propositions will depend on each other.

The first problem — what is the difference between asserting that an elementary proposition is true and negating it — can, as mentioned before, only be solved if we operate with two kinds of falsity. If I maintain that 'There is an ashtray on my desk' and an empirical investigation shows that there is no ashtray to be found on my desk, my conclusion will be that this elementary proposition is false. But this does not mean that it is a negation of another proposition. The kind of falsity I ascribe to it has not been obtained by an operation of negation (this operation is explained in chapter IV, b.). The proposition 'There is an ashtray on my desk' we can negate, i. e. we can form a truth-function with it as an argument, without knowing whether it is the case or not that there is an ashtray on the desk. To state that a proposition does not agree with reality and to negate the same proposition are two entirely different procedures, and we must therefore introduce a sign for each of them. I will use the following notation: If an elementary proposition 'p' describes an existing state of affairs I write this '$p\uparrow$'. If the state of affairs does not exist I write '$p\downarrow$'. In the case of negation the usual notation is applied.

It is clear that Wittgenstein's assertion that logical constants are not representatives implies that we must deny that $\sim p\uparrow = p\downarrow$ and that $\sim p\downarrow = p\uparrow$. For if this was true, the elementary proposition p could be written in a form where it contained the sign of negation as an element and this would mean that this sign represented an object. Moreover we notice that '$\sim$' and '$\downarrow$' indicate something different as '$\sim p$' in Wittgenstein's notation is written as

p	$\sim p$
T	F
F	T

or (FT) (p)

whereas $p\downarrow$ is written (F) (p). That the sign, '$\downarrow$', is a property of a sentence and not a sign of an operation, can be seen from the fact that the expressions $p\uparrow\downarrow$ and $p\downarrow\uparrow$ are self-contradictory, because both of them must be read 'p is the case but not the case' which is impossible. In the same manner it is most likely that the sign-combinations $(p\uparrow)\downarrow$ and $(p\downarrow)\uparrow$ cannot be allowed either, as the signs '$\downarrow$' and '$\uparrow$' can only be applied to something which states *that* something is the case and not to something which states that it is *true* (or false) that something is the case. *That* there is an ashtray on the desk may or may not be in accordance with reality but 'it is true (or false) that 'there is an ashtray on the desk'' can neither be in accordance with reality nor the opposite.

The difference between the two kinds of falsity is concealed by Wittgenstein's notation. Instead of writing:

p	*q*	*pvq*
T	*T*	*T*
F	*T*	*T*
T	*F*	*T*
F	*F*	*F*

one ought to write:

p	*q*	*pvq*
$p\uparrow$	$q\uparrow$	*T*
$p\downarrow$	$q\uparrow$	*T*
$p\uparrow$	$q\downarrow$	*T*
$p\downarrow$	$q\downarrow$	*F*

The circumstance that both *p* and *q* occur among the possible truth-functions that can be constructed on the basis of *p* and *q* (cfr. 5.101) does not contradict this, for (*TFTF*) (*p*,*q*) states an operational value which is produced through the application of operations of negation to *p* (e g. $p|p:|:p|p$) and the truth-values therefore are of a different kind from those resulting from the comparison of *p* with reality. Wittgenstein seems to have noticed that he ought to speak of two kinds of falsity, since he writes in 4.0641: 'The negating proposition determines a logical place *different* from that of the negated proposition. / The negating proposition determines a logical place with the help of the logical place of the negated proposition. For it describes it as lying outside the latter's logical place.' But it remains a problem how he could think that this passage could be reconciled to his remarks on 'logical space'.

When we distinguish between two kinds of falsity, we must speak of two kinds of truth as well. This, however, cannot be seen as clearly, because the logistics of the *Principia Mathematica* are asymmetrical. The propositional logic contains the sign of negation which is prefixed to the negated proposition. But we find no sign in it indicating that a proposition is affirmed. Therefore there is no way of distinguishing between the act of asserting a proposition and the act of asserting that it is true. As far as I know this peculiarity has never been examined in detail. I think it is misleading to disregard it, pleading that whenever we assert a proposition we at the same time assert that it is true. Maslow adheres to this idea when writing:

'While the understanding of a proposition does not require knowledge of its actual truth value, it always involves the formal *truth claim* of the proposition. *The sense of a proposition always tacitly claims its own truth*.... As W. E. Johnson puts it, 'the consideration of the proposition *p* is indistinguishable from the consideration of the proposition *p* as being true'.' (*A Study*, p. 76–77) and he maintains that Wittgenstein expresses this idea in 4.022. But this viewpoint needs a careful basis in argument which has never been worked out in detail. The reader may obtain an impression of the difficulties in Maslow's attitude by reading Jørgensen's *Towards a Theory of Inference* in which a clear-cut distinction between the act of propounding a proposition and the act of ascribing truth or falsity to it is introduced beside the idea that a complete theory of inference necessitates truth-tables not only for negation but for affirmation as well.

For the time being, I will be content with this suggestion of the implications of Wittgenstein's first difficulty concerning the status of false propositions, and will now turn to the other aspect of the problem.

*

Exactly what does an elementary proposition describe? We have observed that an elementary proposition describes an existing state of affairs (= a fact), which is a configuration of objects. In order to be able to describe a state of affairs, it must possess the same structure as the pictured fact. If this is the case a one-one-correspondence of the elements of the proposition to the elements of the fact can be established. If a false elementary proposition could be conceived of as the negation of one or more other elementary propositions, the difficulties could be overcome. But, as we have seen, Wittgenstein's situation was that, somehow or other, he had to explain how it is possible for false propositions to describe something, i. e. have a structure in common with something that does not exist.

It may seem that the difficulty could be overcome in this way: Let us assume that 'The Tower of London is situated in Copenhagen' is a false elementary proposition. It could, then, be imagined that the names contained in this proposition have a meaning and that therefore they are representatives of objects. When the names are combined into this proposition, it could be said, the proposition pictures a certain fact which happens not to exist. The sense of the proposition we understand *via* our knowledge about the meanings of the names. Therefore, we are able to understand the sense of a proposition although it does not have a structure in common with anything.

Wittgenstein follows this path in his attempts to solve the problem but his view is a little more subtle. First of all, it is clear that names do not signify anything when they occur in isolation. They do not have a meaning unless they form part of a proposition (cfr. p. 32). Correspondingly, we cannot imagine or think of an object unless we think of one or another state of affairs in which it occurs (cfr. 2.0121). It cannot possibly be his opinion that, in order that it can be said that we are thinking of an object, we must picture all the known states of affairs, in which the object in question can occur. Later, I shall show in detail why this possibility must be excluded. Here I will only hint at it. According to 3.1 ('In a proposition a thought finds an expression that can be perceived by the senses') a proposition gives expression to a thought. We have good grounds for assuming that a proposition can only express one thought at a time, i. e. that the propositional sign can only be used as 'picturing-material' for one thought at a time. Now, if we perceive a spoken or written proposition, which is formulated clearly, we conceive of it as describing a certain state of affairs and therewith we perceive that the elements of the proposition have meanings. What we do not perceive is that its names each have a meaning by representing an object that can form part of various states of affairs. When we, for example, regard the proposition 'The Tower of London is situated in Copenhagen', this proposition represents *that* the Tower of London is situated in Copenhagen, and not that The Tower of London is situated in London and that no such building can be found in Copenhagen, and that the proposition indicates a relation between the names which cannot be found anywhere. If the latter really was what we did perceive, we would, in many cases, know beforehand, simply by perceiving the sense of the proposition, whether it was true or false. This, however, according to the *Tractatus*, we are never able to know in advance. — In the example given, we must not be disturbed by the fact that we *can* know in advance that the proposition *is* false, for that example is not an elementary proposition. At present, however, I cannot refer to better examples as this presupposes an analysis which will follow below.

Now, if a false proposition really does represent anything, this must mean that it refers to something. This 'something' must subsist in some sense or other while at the same time it cannot be said to exist. The sphere in which it subsists is the logical space. And what exists in logical space is states of affairs. As mentioned above logical space can be conceived as a sort of ontological duplicate of the logical theory of the independence and true-false-poles of elementary propositions.

The only reason for introducing this duplicate is that it enables us to deal with false propositions in the same way as with true or to make only one theory of meaning comprising both categories of propositions.

Maslow (in *A Study*, pp. 75 ff) has given a clear account of the problem how false propositions can have a sense but in my opinion this account starts from untenable premises and I therefore consider it unacceptable. He begins with the assertion that there are only two ways to the solution of the problem: '.... in order to account for the false propositions, we should have to postulate one of the following: (a) the existence of false or unreal facts corresponding to the false proposition .... or (b) two different kinds of relation between the propositions and the facts they represent, one occurring in the case of the true propositions, the other in the case of the false propositions.' (p. 75). The reason that Maslow has not discovered more than these two possibilities is that he does not distinguish between states of affairs and facts. Stenius has tried to solve the problem by accepting Maslow's possibility (b), but this suggestion meets with great difficulties, as I shall point out.

*

The logical space must be conceived as the domain of what is thinkable. That anything is thinkable means, to Wittgenstein, that we can form a picture of it. To form a picture of something is equivalent to establishing a state of affairs in the logical space. This state of affairs, however, does not necessarily have a physical existence. States of affairs can exist as well as non-exist (cfr. 2.06, 2.062, 2.11 and others). But a state of affairs always has a psychological existence in the sense that it is something which the proposition is about. It seems reasonable to call this 'something' mental images but already, in so doing, we meet with difficulties of a psychological character, since it is proved that not all people have or experience such mental images. In a way it is not quite right to speak of 'physical existence' in relation to existing states of affairs (= facts) because this suggests a certain materialistic view. For the present I think it is sufficient to state that Wittgenstein employs three spheres: 1. *The sphere of language*, i. e. the sphere which 'contains' facts that are pictures of something and therefore have a sense, 2. *The logical space*, which is the sphere of the possible or the thinkable and which 'contains' all states of affairs, existing or non-existing, and 3. *The world*, which 'contains' facts and facts only. When a proposition is a picture, it has this quality, in a way, *via* the logical space. For the circumstance that a proposition has sense implies that we can understand it without knowing whether it is true or false, and understanding a proposition means to imagine a state of affairs in the logical space. To perceive that a proposition is true means to perceive or experience in some way or other that the imagined state of affairs exists. Just what is meant by perceiving and imagining, are problems of psychology with which I will deal later. The problem whether states of affairs and/or facts exist independent of a perceiving mind will be dealt with later too. For the time being I accept Wittgenstein's theory as described above as an attempt to endow true and false propositions with the same semantical status. True and false propositions both are about states of affairs, and a state of affairs exists in the sense that it can be spoken of as something consisting of elements, and something that can be correlated with the picture by establishing a one-one-correspondence between the elements of the state of affairs and the picture.

It may be objected here that Wittgenstein must surely contend that states of affairs always exist in the same sense as facts exist. For as it is said in 2.01, 2.0272 and 2.03 that states of affairs consist of objects, and as objects according to 2.021 make up the substance of the world and the substance exists independently of what is the case (2.024), one should think that states of affairs always must exist. The idea seems to be that objects can only occur in states of affairs (though 2.0121 really states no more than that objects can only be imagined in connection with the *possibility* of occurring in states of affairs); how, then, can objects exist unless the states of affairs, in which they occur, necessarily exist? I have not taken note of this objection because it is my opinion that here we have to do with a contradiction in the definitions of the *Tractatus* (which can easily be seen by comparing 2.01, 2.021 and 2.06 and which cannot be removed by any serious interpretation of the book.)

*

In relation to the 'model' mentioned above, it must be said that Stenius, in his book *Wittgenstein's Tractatus'*, has suggested a similar model. Stenius starts his exposition of this by speaking of a 'world' which consists of 5 parallelepipeds (op. cit. p. 39). We may consider one of these:

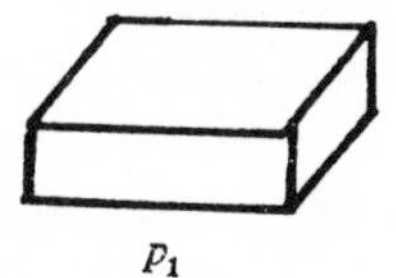

p_1

Stenius maintains that three propositions can be asserted concerning p_1 and they may be, for instance: 'p_1 is 2.3 yds long', 'p_1 is 1.5 yds wide' and 'p_1 is 0.8 yds high'. Since the imagined 'world' consists of 5 parallelepipeds, a description of it must contain in all 15 propositions. When regarding these propositions, we may ask whether they are elementary propositions and whether the model satisfies Wittgenstein's definitions of 'state of affairs' etc. We can see at once, then, that the model can only be used if Wittgenstein's demand that states of affairs are independent of one another is altered to the demand that states of affairs in *different dimensions* are independent of each other. For within one dimension only we can imagine many possibilities that exclude each other, for instance 'p_1 is 2 yds long' and 'p_1 is 118 yds long' etc. If we insist on the claim that states of affairs have to be independent of each other, the model has to be modified and therefore Stenius alters it by restricting the number of possible values in each dimension to two only. Hence the imagined world can be described as consisting of 15 two-valued dimensions. In this system any assertion about a length will automatically be the negation of another proposition. If p_1 can only possess two lengths, 2.3 yds and 4.6 yds, then 'p_1 is 2.3 yds long' will be the negation of 'p_1 is 4.6 yds long' and *vice versa.* We can arbitrarily consider one of the two propositions as a positive assertion and the other as the negation of the positive assertion. This implies that we can only speak of one state of affairs in each dimension. From this we can conclude that 'If the dimensions of the logical space allow for only two values each, these values may be considered as a yes-value and a no-value, which means that only one of the states of affairs in each dimension is considered atomic. A logical space of this kind can therefore be described as one in which all atomic states of affairs are independent of one another,' (op. cit. p. 46). Stenius calls a logical space of this kind a 'yes-and-no-space'.

The reader may object that in the exposition given above I have reached no better result than Stenius. However, I have had two reasons for not proceeding in the way Stenius does. The one is that Stenius obviously makes a detour by starting with an assumption that contradicts Wittgenstein's fundamental concepts. The other is that Stenius' model involves a concept of object which in my opinion should have been explained in detail to the reader. Mr. Povl Dalsgård-Hansen of Copenhagen University has drawn my attention to the fact that Stenius from the beginning must deny that 'p_1 is 2.3 yds long', 'p_1 is 1.5 yds wide' and 'p_1 is 0.8 yds high' are elementary propositions not only for the reason given above but also because the propositions have their subject in common. I shall briefly state this objection in the following way: p_1 designates a certain thing, namely the parallelepiped the sides of which are 2.3, 1.5 and 0.8 yds long, respectively. If now the length of one of the sides is altered we are presented with a new parallelepiped different from p_1. This means to say that if, for instance, we double the length of p_1, then the subjects of the propositions 'p_1 is 1.5 yds wide' and 'p_1 is 0.8 yds high' have to be substituted by another name, since it no longer can be p_1 we are speaking of.

This may be expressed a little more clearly if we apply a terminology introduced by Jørgen Jørgensen (*Towards a Theory of Inference,* pp. 124–27). According to Jørgensen, to assert a proposition is to ascribe a predicate to a subject. By 'subject' he means 'the subject of the statement' and by 'predicate' 'the predicate of the statement'. The name of the subject in the proposition he calls the 'subject-designation' and correspondingly he calls the name of the predicate 'the predicate-designation'. The concept that is formed of a subject, (for instance that a table is a board supported by legs serving the purpose that things can be placed on it .... etc.), he calls 'the concept of the subject' and correspondingly we can speak of 'the concept of the predicate'. Now it can be said that when Stenius applies the same 'subject-designation' in the three mentioned propositions, namely p_1, he not only introduces an interdependence between states of affairs belonging to the same dimension, but also between states of affairs belonging to different dimensions as well. Consequently the 'subject-designation' in the three propositions has to be altered as soon as one of the lengths of the parallelepiped is altered.

It may of course be objected that we can please ourselves on what plane of identity we want to speak when we speak of altering the lengths of the sides. But when speaking of Wittgenstein's picture theory we must not forget that according to him an elementary proposition is a proposition consisting of names that are all 'subject-designations' of certain 'subjects' (which he calls 'objects') and the subjects are simple and therefore unalterable. If a proposition such as (*A*): 'p_1 is 1.5 yds wide' is an elementary proposition this implies that it describes a certain state of affairs which is independent of all other states of affairs. If now the height of p_1 is altered from 0.8 to 100 yds the subject-designation of (*A*) is altered too and p_1 in (*A*) does not any longer designate the same object. The alternative to this is to say that the subject-designation still designates the same object but that this no longer exists. In order to avoid this interdependence between states of affairs belonging to different dimensions, Stenius ought to have described p_1 thus:

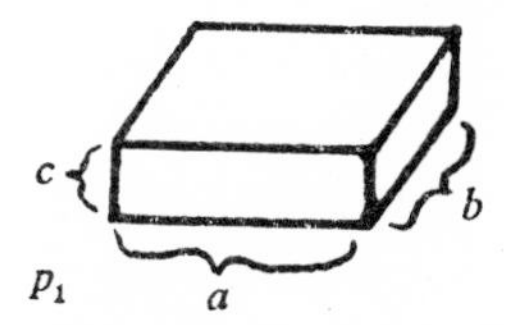

and have written: '*a* is 2.3 yds long', '*b* is 1.5 yds long' and '*c* is 0.8 yds long'. But in this case there would no longer be any point in letting *a*, *b*, and *c* form sides of one and the same parallelepiped. The whole matter might as well have been pictured in this way:

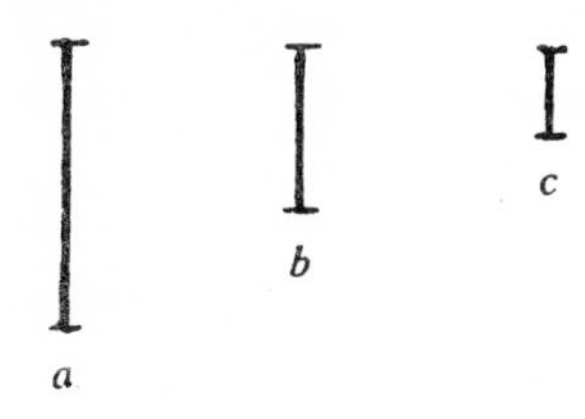

and if in relation to this model we make the restriction that only two values must be possible in each dimension, as Stenius does, we arrive at a model which in all essential respects is similar to the one I have introduced earlier in this chapter.

I here end my formal stipulation of the concepts related to the picture theory. I shall now consider the problem in what way these concepts can be interpreted.

c. Interpretation.

What can serve as instances of the concept of 'object'? If we can find an answer to this question we can easily make out what may serve as examples of states of affairs, facts, names and elementary propositions.

From Wittgenstein's notebooks it can be seen that he first developed the picture theory as a whole and then tried to exemplify it. Certainly he asks already on 3rd September, 1914: 'Is a point in our visual field a *simple object,* a *thing*?' (*Notebooks,* p. 3) and he adds that an answer to questions of this kind apparently can never be found, but it is not until 14th June, 1915 (*Notebooks*, p. 59) that he starts discussing the question, and at this point of time the picture theory has been largely worked out. The discussion that spreads over about 12 pages in the *Notebooks* does not lead to any conclusion. It is impossible to find out from them what Wittgenstein himself regarded as an example of an object, and the text of the *Tractatus* is no more helpful as it does not contain any examples, which are given *as* examples, but only a few hints which cannot support an argumentation.

As said before, we must conceive of objects as something simple. This demand appears to be a consequence of the assertion that objects can only be named and the assertion that elementary propositions are independent of one another. This can be made clear by regarding an example from the *Notebooks* (p. 69) which does not meet these demands. If I say 'This watch is lying on the table', I can make out that this proposition cannot be an elementary proposition. For if the watch contains a wheel W (which it must do *per* definition), then the truth-value of the proposition 'W is lying on (or situated some place above) the table' must be dependent on the truth-value of the first mentioned proposition. In general it can be said that an elementary proposition cannot contain names of spatial complexes, since any statement about the spatial position of a part of the complex will depend on the proposition about the complex as a whole in respect of truth-value. Also it can be said that propositions that contain names of classes, or deal with something that has a duration, or describe something extended in the visual field, cannot be elementary propositions.

In a proposition like 'This watch is lying on the table' the expression 'this watch' is the name of a complex. This shows itself in that other propositions, such as 'The wheel W is situated above the table', are implied by the first one.

Many — insufficient — answers can be given to the question of what can serve as instances of objects. Maslow enumerates several possibilities, but in order not to repeat what others have said before me, I shall, in what follows, examine two possibilities only. For reasons that will become clear, I believe that only these two possibilities can be of interest.

The one possibility may be called a *phenomenalistic atomism.* Objects are conceived of as sense-data which are indivisible in a phenomenalistic sense, something like Ernst Mach's 'Elemente' (*vide The Analysis of Sensations*, pp. 5.22 and 29). Various points suggest that Wittgenstein has very often thought of objects in this way. In 2.013, for instance, he writes that each thing is, as it were, in a space of possible states of affairs, and in 2.0131 this is explained as meaning that a speck in the visual field need not be red but it must have *some* colour, tones must have *some* pitch, objects of the sense of touch *some* degree of hardness, and so on. It looks as if we can say that specks in the visual field are objects. They always must have a colour, but this is not identical with the speck itself which must be conceived of as colourless (cfr. 2.0232: 'In a manner of speaking, objects are colourless.'). Likewise he seems to consider tones and objects of the senses of touch as objects, although it must surely be difficult to distinguish between the qualities of a tone (its pitch, for instance) and the tone itself. In the *Notebooks* also, he is concerned with this interpretation. On page 64, he writes that 'It seems to me perfectly possible that patches in our visual field are simple objects, in that we do not perceive any single point of a patch separately, the visual appearances of stars even seem certainly to be so,' and on page 51, supplements this: 'Does the visual image of a *minimum visible* actually appear to us as indivisible? What has extension is divisible. Are there parts in our visual image that have no extension? E. g., the images of the fixed stars? —'. He has obviously regarded this interpretation as possible and his problem has been whether there is any sense at all in speaking of something as phenomenalistically indivisible or not. At the end of the *Tractatus*, he dissociates himself from the view that specks in the visual field are objects. Here we observe that the problem of interpreting the concept of 'object' is entangled with the problem of the applicability of logic to reality. The well-known passage is this:

6.375 Just as the only necessity that exists is *logical* necessity, so too the only impossibility that exists is *logical* impossibility.

6.3751 For example, the simultaneous presence of two colours at the same place in

> the visual field is impossible, in fact logically impossible, since it is ruled out by the logical structure of colour. Let us think of how this contradiction appears in physics: more or less as follows — a particle cannot have two velocities at the same time; that is to say, it cannot be in two places at the same time; that is to say, particles that are in different places at the same time cannot be identical. (It is clear that the logical product of two elementary propositions can neither be a tautology nor a contradiction. The statement that a point in the visual field has two different colours at the same time is a contradiction.)

In short, the idea in this passage seems to be this. One would think that '*A* is red' could be an example of an elementary proposition (if *A* is an indivisible speck). But the expression '('*A* is red')·('*A* is blue')' is a contradiction. Hence, as it is granted that the logical conjunction of two elementary propositions cannot be a contradiction (nor a tautology), we are compelled to maintain that '*A* is red' cannot be an elementary proposition.

This, however, is a shattering consequence. For, as it is granted in advance in the logistics of *Principia Mathematica* that an elementary proposition can be written as '$f(x)$', this implies that no matter what point we reach in our analysis of reality, we never arrive at anything that can be described as an elementary proposition. The problem is not limited to the question whether '*A* is red' can be regarded as an elementary proposition or not. It is concerned with the whole relation between logic and reality. For if we conclude with the result that even a proposition which describes an indivisible object can be contradicted by other propositions, we must either say that beyond the knowledge of logical possibilities and logical impossibilities, we can experience something which is impossible *a posteriori* (and this would restrict the extensional view of logic seriously), or else we must conclude that something logically impossible can be found which could not have been anticipated because our logic is not refined enough.

According to 6.375 the second possibility is chosen. It is not only physically (or ontologically) impossible for a speck to have two colours simultaneously. Above all, it is logically impossible. The second part of 6.3751 is an attempt to explain what is meant by this. (It is not, as Maslow (*A Study*, p. 33) and Ramsey (*Critical Notice*, p. 473) think, an attempt to 'reduce colour to the physicist's account of it'). That a particle can be in two places at the same time, and that particles that are in different places at the same time can be identical, are logical impossibilities. Probably this should be understood in that our notation is constructed in a way that prevents us from expressing that two different particles are identical without contradicting ourselves, because the circumstance that they are different shows itself in that in order to describe them, we have to apply a different name to each of them, while the circumstance that they are identical implies that the name of one object can be substituted by the name of the other and *vice versa,* whereever we have to do with either of them. But as to propositions about specks of colour, the case seems different and the fact that propositions of this kind form the central theme of *Logical Form* shows, too, that Wittgenstein has felt that a special difficulty was attached to them.

In *Logical Form,* Wittgenstein maintains that his previous view was that propositions such as '*A* is red' were composite, i. e. truth-functions (*Logical Form,* p. 167). It is very probable that he is thinking of *Tractatus,* 6.3751 here. In the *Tractatus* then, he must have believed that the fact that *A* is red could be analysed into a number of elementary facts. This may be true but at the same time it seems as if he has already realized, when 6.3751 was written, that no matter what form of elementary proposition he arrived at in his analysis, another elementary proposition contradicting it could always be found. He has sensed the question whether we can speak of other kinds of possibility and impossibility than the logical, but he has not found an answer to it.

In *Logical Form,* he tries to answer it by admitting that something ontologically impossible can be found. But his next step is to alter logic in such a way that it can anticipate what is ontologically impossible so that this becomes something *logically* impossible. He regards two propositions, '*RPT*' (which is read as 'at the time *T* the place *P* of the visual field is red') and '*BPT*' ('at the time *T* the place *P* of the visual field is blue') and states that both of them are values of the same function: '( )*PT*'. Now the point is that the nature of reality is such that this function can only have one value. 'That which corresponds in reality to the function "( )*PT*" leaves room only for one entity — in the same sense, in fact, in which we say that there is room for one person only in a chair.' (p. 169). The contradiction which results from the conjunction of the two propositions is written:

RPT	*BPT*	
T	*T*	*F*
T	*F*	*F*
F	*T*	*F*
F	*F*	*F*

But Wittgenstein maintains that this notation 'is nonsense, as the top line, "*TTF*" gives the proposition a greater logical multiplicity than that of the actual possibilities.' (p. 170). Obviously, the composite proposition *RPT* · *BPT*, when both propositions are true, is more complex than the state of affairs, ( )*PT* or (*X*)*PT*, and therefore there can be no isomorphy as the picture theory claims it. The top line of the truth-table therefore must be excluded in advance so that only the following conjunctions of the truth-values of *RPT* and *BPT* are allowed:

RPT	*BPT*
T	*F*
F	*T*
F	*F*

That this can be done by introducing a logical-syntactical rule is obvious. Only we must remember, as Wittgenstein remarks, that such rules 'cannot be laid down until we have actually reached the ultimate analysis of the phenomena in question.' This means that a great many of the logical-syntactical rules must be *a posteriori*, and Wittgenstein's concluding remarks in *Logical Form* must therefore be considered as a retreat, as a definite abandonment of the assertion that 'Logic must take care of itself.' (*Notebooks*, p. 2, *Tractatus*, 5.473), the assertion which he steadily adhered to from the day he decided to write a Tractatus until the last page of the book was written.)[1]

No answer was ever given in the *Tractatus* to the question of what could serve as an instance of an elementary proposition, nor in *Logical Form*, but in the *Tractatus*, as well as in that article, Wittgenstein has indicated the path to be followed. Continuous analysis of our visual experiences may lead us to indivisible objects. I shall return to the conditions of such an analysis below.

*

First I shall consider another possibility in interpreting the concept of 'object', namely one presented by Maslow in his book (*A Study*), pp. 38 ff. He writes there: 'It becomes now obvious that, in the view here expounded, it is logically perfectly arbitrary what we shall choose to consider as simple elements and atomic facts; the criterion of simplicity is to be established by ourselves, not found in the world ... The formal definition of a simple symbol is that it must have no parts which are symbols themselves ... what determines the simplicity of the symbol is the definition or the grammar of the symbol. Thus the sign $f(a)$ may be considered either simple or complex, depending on the rules agreed upon. If different rules are valid

1. Moreover Wittgenstein's theory of tautology and contradiction presupposes other a-logical theses, among which is a distinction between various predicate-categories (cfr. Jørgensen's *Towards a Theory of Inference*, pp. 143 ff).

for *f* and for *a*, then the symbol *f*(*a*) is complex; if the rules refer to *f*(*a*) as a simple unit symbol, then it is simple, and *a* is not a separate symbol but merely a typographical curlicue, and may be omitted, if we decide so . . . what a name, that is, a simple symbol, refers to in the world is to be considered as a simple object or element in the world. We can take any object whatsoever in our experience and consider it as an element.' And later he remarks that 'There is no sense in speaking of absolute simples.' (p. 39). Maslow could not have known that this idea had in fact been considered by Wittgenstein when he was preparing the *Tractatus.* In *Notebooks,* it is mentioned as a possibility. On page 59 - 60, he writes:

'What is my fundamental thought when I talk about simple objects? Do not 'complex objects' in the end satisfy just the demands which I apparantly make on the simple ones? If I give this book a name "*N*" and now talk about *N*, is not the relation of *N* to that 'complex object', to those forms and contents, essentially the same as I imagined only between name and simple object? / For N.B.: even if the name "*N*" vanishes on further analysis, still it indicates a single common thing'. And later: 'The question is really this: In order to know the syntactical treatment of a name, must I know the composition of its reference?'

The kernel of this view is that as long as a name can function as a simple sign in a context, the object named can be regarded as simple. If the name actually does function as a simple sign, this means (granted that the other parts of the proposition have a definite meaning) that the proposition has a sense. As mentioned above any proposition *qua* proposition must be a picture of something, and even though the picture does not offer an exhaustive description of a certain fact, it is in a certain sense a complete picture (cfr. 5.156). This circumstance is used as an argument in favour of the aforementioned interpretation. Wittgenstein's words are: 'So a proposition may indeed be an incomplete picture of a certain fact, but it is ALWAYS a *complete picture.* / From this it would now seem as if in a certain sense all names were *genuine* names. Or, as I might also say, as if all objects were in a certain sense simple objects.' (p. 61). But this view involves a difficulty. For if a complex object can be considered indivisible, then some elementary propositions imply others and this does not harmonize with the thesis of extensionality. If, in one connection, we have regarded a speck in the visual field as an indivisible object and have formed a proposition, S_1: 'The speck is situated to the right of the line *L*', and we thereupon analyse the speck and say about a part of it, S_2: 'This coloured point is situated to the right of the line *L*', then it is seen that as the point is part of the speck, $S_1 \supset S_2$. (The example used is from *Notebooks,* p. 64). Hence, S_1 cannot be an elementary proposition. It looks as if Wittgenstein gave up this view because of exactly this consequence, but it is not certain. In *Tractatus* no traces of it can be found. On the contrary the ontological parts at the beginning of the book seem to indicate that objects have to be simple in all respects.

The two views considered here might be compatible with one another. Later I shall show how they can be reconciled. Before this, however, I wish to discuss what we can mean by speaking of indivisible objects.

*

When speaking of objects and of dividing them, we can think of at least two ways of doing this: 1. a phenomenological and 2. a physical. By 'phenomenological' is meant 'how it seems to the senses' and by 'physical' I mean 'independent of the experiencing subject'. A surface experienced by sight may, for instance, be a phenomenologically composite thing. If I am able to distinguish between different parts of it and characterize some of it as 'the right side', some as 'the left side', some as 'top', and some as 'bottom', it must be a composite thing in the phenomenological sense. That a thing is physically composite means that it is divisible by physical methods. Stones, cells, molecules, and atoms are all composite objects, because they can be divided into smaller elements which are describable in physical terms.

Whereas a phenomenologically indivisible thing may be physically compound, the opposite cannot be the case. The smallest thing that can be registered by sight, for instance, will always be physically compound even in the cases where microscopes or other instruments are applied.

As the reader will know, the discussion whether physically indivisible objects exist or not began in ancient Greece, where the atomism of Demokritos and the Aristotelian continuity-view were opposed to each other. He may know too that in our time electrons, protons, neutrons and other particles discovered in atomic physics are simple in a certain physical sense. The discussion of the phenomenologically indivisible object is not so well-known. Nor is it so old, for John Locke was the first to deal with this problem.

Locke comments on the subject in *An Essay Concerning Human Understanding,* Book II, Chap. XV, § 9, in which he writes: 'Every part of duration is duration too; and every part of extension is extension, both of them capable of addition or division *in infinitum.* But *the least portions of either of them, whereof we have clear and distinct ideas*, may perhaps be fittest to be considered by us, as the *simple ideas* of that kind out of which our complex modes of space, extension, and duration are made up . . . Such a small part in duration may be called a *moment* . . . The other, wanting a proper name, I know not whether I may be allowed to call a *sensible point,* meaning thereby the least particle of matter or space we can discern, which is ordinarily about a minute, and to the sharpest eye seldom less than thirty seconds of a circle, whereof the eye is the centre.' (pp. 266 - 267).

Whereas Locke, alongside the phenomenologically indivisible objects, assumes physical bodies that can be divided *ad infinitum* (*An Essay*, Book II, Chap. XXIX, § 16), Berkeley denied the possibility of a physical world on the basis of his *esse est percipi*-principle. But like Locke, he believes that phenomenologically indivisible objects can be found. He writes about this: 'It hath been shown, there are two sorts of objects apprehended by sight; each whereof hath its distinct magnitude, or extension. The one properly tangible . . . the other properly and immediately visible . . . Each of these magnitudes are greater or lesser, according as they contain in them more or fewer points; they being made up of points or minimums. For, whatever may be said of extension in abstract, it is certain, sensible extension is not infinitely divisible. There is a *minimum tangibile,* and a *minimum visibile* beyond which sense cannot perceive. This every one's experience will inform him.' (*A New Theory of Vision*, Section LIV). In Hume's philosophy the same idea occurs and he actually describes a method to be used in order to experience something that has no extension. If one looks at an ink-spot on a piece of paper and views the paper at a great distance, at the moment before he cannot see the spot anymore, as he moves further away, he will have an impression of the spot which is indivisible. (*A Treatise of Human Nature*, p. 35).

As far as I know the best exposition and discussion of the problem whether *minima visibile* can be found is to be found in Edgar Rubin's *Synsoplevede Figurer* (The German edition of this book is called *Visuell wahrgenommene Figuren* (1921). The quotations below are translated from the Danish edition). Rubin enumerates (p. 212) the qualities which, according to Hume, can be ascribed to the indivisible objects or impressions. First, they cannot be divided and they do not consist of parts. Secondly, they have no extension. According to Hume this is a consequence of their indivisibility. Thirdly, they have a colour. This is a necessary condition of the perceiving of them. 'It is not only requisite that these atoms should be coloured or tangible, in order to discover themselves to our senses; it is also necessary we should preserve the idea of their colour or tangibility, in order to comprehend them by our imagination.' (*Treatise*, vol. I, p. 45). Finally Hume, according to Rubin, ascribes one more quality to the *minima* when he writes: 'The first notion of space and extension is derived solely from the senses of sight and feeling; nor is there anything, but what is coloured or tangible, that has parts disposed after such a manner as to convey that idea. When we diminish or increase a relish, it is not after the same manner that we diminish or increase any visible object; . . . Whatever marks the place of its existence, either must be extended, or must be a mathematical point, without parts or composition.'

Rubin has himself made an exact psychological investigation of the *minima visibile*-problem. He gives the following description of his experiments: 'Draw a stripe of indian ink, 2 mm wide, in a straight line on a piece of cardboard and attach the cardboard to a wall so the stripe is vertical. When you stand close to the stripe and look at it, the perceived stripe or line has a distinct width and you can distinguish between right and left within it. If you move away from the stripe you still . . . perceive a clear-cut stripe . . . ; but at last you reach a distance where, after it has been difficult for sometime, it is no longer meaningful to distinguish within the perceived object between a right and a left part.' If the piece of cardboard is attached to the wall so the stripe is horizontal, you will arrive at a similar experience, where it is no longer meaningful to speak of a top and a bottom part of the line. And similarly the experience of a speck on a piece of cardboard at a certain distance becomes an experience of a *minimum visibile* without perceived extension. Rubin's investigations have revealed that there are individual differences as to how small the picture on the retina has to be before points without extension are experienced, apparently due to the size of the cones.

It cannot be doubted that Wittgenstein, when speaking about simple objects, is thinking of phenomenologically, and not physically, indivisible entities. Nowhere in the *Notebooks* or in the *Tractatus* are there suggestions that he has been thinking of physical entities, such as atoms as examples of objects. On the contrary many things — for instance the statements quoted above — reveal that he often followed the phenomenological line in his thought. When he, with his usual lack of knowledge about the history of philosophy, suggests that *minima visibile* may exist, this is, as we have seen not a wrong suggestion. We can, in fact, very well imagine that all our perceptions can be divided until we arrive at some entities that cannot be divided any further. Wittgenstein attempts to prove the existence of such entities in order to discover some form of elementary propositions which are logically independent of each other and therefore satisfy the thesis of extensionality.

As the account above shows, my view is that *Wittgenstein's speculations about whether propositions such as 'this speck is red' are elementary propositions have been very vague and really only give a sketch of how reality is to be analysed in order that 'object' can be interpreted satisfactorily.* In *Logical Form* the analysis is more precise. An incompatibility-principle is suggested in order to explain that elementary propositions can exclude each other without contradicting each other. This is Wittgenstein's last attempt to save the independency of the elementary proposition claimed by the extensional view of logic. Whether this attempt was a success or not I leave to others to judge. For the present I wish only to emphasize that Wittgenstein's discussion of the problem in *Logical Form* is not conclusive.

According to the forementioned supposition that a net of lines could be laid in our visual field so that the extension of a speck could be indicated by numbers, every elementary proposition must contain numbers. 'The occurrence of numbers in the forms of atomic propositions is, in my opinion not merely a feature of a special symbolism, but an essential and, consequently, unavoidable feature of the representation.' (*Logical Form*, p. 166). Unfortunately, however, he does not deal with the problem of how fine a division of the visual field can be made. This problem is of particular interest with regard to the question whether simple objects can be found. It seems as if we could say that if *minima visibile* can be found, their extension can be indicated by help of the coordinates (*vide* the figure p. 36). The indication, however, cannot be established by indicating a difference between two abscissa-values on the one side and two ordinate-values on the other as Wittgenstein does it when symbolizing '*P* is red' by '[6-9,3-8] *R*', *for the coordinate system is itself part of the visual field and consequently consists of minima visibile*. A non-composite speck in the coordinate system can only be indicated by the two specks that correspond to its position and are situated on the axes. The coordinates of a non-composite speck may be: '[7,5]*R*'. If Wittgenstein imagined that the unit of the coordinate system could be chosen arbitrarily small, he would have to admit the possibility of propositions about objects smaller than a *minimum visibile* and this would raise the problem of how it is possible to think of something smaller than the smallest thing which can be perceived by the senses, a problem which indeed would have caused great confusion in his philosophy.

Further problems can be found which were never reached in Wittgenstein's investigations. One of them is caused by the fact that a *minimum visibile* can often be magnified by means of optical instruments. A planet may seem unextended to the naked eye, while through a telescope it appears to be extended. We also know that it would appear larger and larger, the closer we could come to it. And this holds good for specks on paper too. Does this mean that the *minima visibile* we might arrive at, when not using optical instruments, actually are not objects because a further analysis by means of instruments reveals that they are composite?

There is a possible answer to this question which may save Wittgenstein's viewpoint from several difficulties. If I look, with the naked eye, at a speck on a piece of paper and come to the result that it is simple and next look at it through a magnifying-glass and perceive it as composite, I can maintain that it is not 'the same' speck I view in the two situations. I have one experience when looking at the speck with the naked eye and another experience when looking at it through the magnifying glass. From an idealistic or phenomenalistic point of view, it can be questioned whether these two experiences refer to the same thing. If we adhere to an idealistic point of view, we can consistently maintain that all experiences are independent of each other in the sense that two of them are never conditioned by the same external stimulus on the basis that nothing can be known about 'the external world'. This viewpoint, however, implies that experiences have to be demarcated in time as well as in space. If we do not do this it will be difficult to deny that we are concerned with the same speck which at a distance appears to be a *minimum visibile* and at close quarters appears to be composite. Hence, we have to introduce the theory that *minima temporalia* can be found, i. e. time-units which are so small that no shorter moment than such a time-unit can be experienced and maintain that any experience *qua* experience in time is always stretched over at least one *minimum temporale*. In this case we must assume that the world consists of a chain of elementary experiences and that each of these lasts a certain moment which phenomenologically appears to be non-composite. In this way what exists is ascribed a cinematographical character. The theory we arrive at here is, indeed, more cinematographical than the 'cinematographical' viewpoint presented in Russell's *The Ultimate Constituents of Matter* (*Mysticism and Logic*, pp. 123-24).

As said before, Wittgenstein never thought far enough to realize how such problems should be tackled. I am not, therefore, referring to his viewpoints, when I point out that the two conceptions of 'object' which I have considered may be combined. It should, however, be clear that if we regard objects as entities limited in time, we do not contradict ourselves in maintaining that in the example considered we have to do with two different specks or objects. If we consider Wittgenstein's own example (mentioned above, page 61) we may say that while the book *N* is named and spoken of as a non-composite object, it *is* simple to the person perceiving it. If it later appears to be composite then at this later point of time it *is* composite. The point is that we are not speaking about the 'same' object in the two cases. The kernel of this viewpoint is that what can be named has to appear as indivisible in time and space while it is named and experienced.

Perhaps Wittgenstein *en passant* has caught a glimpse of this view since he writes in *Notebooks*, page 70: 'This object is *simple* for *me*.'

It is, indeed, difficult to make out what concept of object fits in best with the other concepts of the *Tractatus*. It looks as if a phenomenalistic continuity-view as I think it is expressed in Jørgensen's *Psykologi på biologisk grundlag* satisfies many of the demands Wittgenstein makes in respect of the concept of object. Jørgensen makes the following remark about objects: 'Strictly speaking no isolated objects can be found and the qualities we perceive the objects to have always depend upon what conditions the objects exist under, for instance, upon temperature, lighting, grade of humidity, pressure-, electrical- and gravitational conditions etc. In a way, any object can be conceived as part of a whole, namely as part of its environment, and its qualities can be 'explained' only by considering its actual environment: 'In themselves' the objects have no qualities for they never exist 'in themselves', i. e. perfectly isolated. The concept of object itself is in fact an abstraction which is formed by our more or less arbitrarily thinking of a part of the field of experience without thinking of other parts .... What we call 'objects' seem to be only the parts of the field of experience which exhibit, under normal conditions, relatively constant qualities, above all a constant form.' At this place in his book, Jørgensen speaks of objects in the sense of 'objective phenomena', but from later parts of his book (*vide* e. g. p. 313) it can be seen that such objective phenomena appear as results of an analysis that has the individual's private experiences as its starting point. If this point is stressed, a phenomenalistic continuity-view can be developed, because in that case objects cannot be conceived of as entities that must exist with a certain form and certain properties, such as sense-data, *minima visibile* or things as conceived of by naive realism, but only as phenomena that appear as demarcated wholes or parts of experience as a result of a structuring of sensations. In a way, a view of this kind fits better into Wittgenstein's text than an atomistic phenomenalism does. First, because it meets the demand that there can be no conception of objects in themselves, but only as parts of states of affairs. Secondly, because it is in accordance with Wittgenstein's view that an object has to be characterized by all the states of affairs of which it can form part, and that the possibilities of these states of affairs must be prejudiced in the object (i. e. in the concept of it). Thirdly, because objects according to this view are simple in the sense that in any combination they will always appear as elements to the perceiving subject, elements that are the smallest conceivable parts of the combination. It can be said that according to this view it is included in the concept of object that objects must be simple because we always reserve the word 'object' or 'element' for those entities that in any given situation are experienced as simple or non-composite.

It is certain, however, that Wittgenstein has never thought of this view as a possibility. In some respects it is contrary to his text, too. His assertion that objects are, roughly speaking, colourless (2.0232) becomes incomprehensible, whereas it remains clear if we take specks in the visual field as instances of objects; and his doctrine that states of affairs are independent of each other cannot become reconciled with the view in question either, unless it is postulated that any object bears the stamp of the state of affairs in which it occurs, so that it can only be characterized in connection with this state of affairs and can never be identical with any element occurring in other states of affairs. In this case it becomes tautologous to maintain that the states of affairs are independent of one another, but at the same time we are precluded from explaining what Wittgenstein was thinking of when he spoke of an object as something that could occur in many states of affairs. My conclusion is, therefore, that this phenomenalistic continuity-view cannot serve as an exemplification of Wittgenstein's conceptions of the world and reality either.

In these considerations of what Wittgenstein could possibly have suggested as an interpretation of his picture theory, I have briefly touched upon the problem of time, and I will conclude this chapter with a reflection on the difficulties Wittgenstein would probably have encountered if he had contemplated this problem.

*

Wittgenstein's picture theory seems to be what I have called a 'cinematographical' theory. By this I mean not only the view that reality must consist of *minima temporalia* but also that these minima are unalterable entities when they occur. This means that an object must be a 'something' that lasts for a moment which appears phenomenologically to last an instant not stretched out in time. In the same way we must speak of a state of affairs which subsists for a moment, and in this moment is unchanging.

A proposition is always a static fact. It is characterized in that its elements, the names, have a certain relation to each other. In regarding the proposition 'The stone flies across the room', we must say that the propositional sign and, consequently, the proposition as well are static phenomena. The state of affairs described by the proposition, however, seems to be a cinematic phenomenon. When a stone flies across a room this implies that the relations which the elements of this state of affairs have to one another continuously alter. How, then, can a static proposition describe a cinematic state of affairs if isomorphy between the two is a necessary condition for establishing a picturing relation?

If by states of affairs we understand 'physical states of affairs', the picture theory cannot hold true. Suppose, that 'The stone flies across the room' describes a physical fact. According to Wittgenstein this proposition must be either an elementary proposition or a truth-function. But it cannot be an elementary proposition because of its being static whereas the fact is cinematical. The names in the proposition have a fixed relation to each other, while the elements of the fact have continuously new relations to each other. If the proposition is a truth-function, it can be split up into a conjunction of propositions of the form: 'At the time t_n the stone is in x_n, y_n, z_n.' But for each of these propositions the same argumentation will hold good, because we cannot assume that space and time consist of a finite number of points. When we say, for instance, that at the time t_2 the stone is in x_2, y_2, z_2, this means that we have performed a measurement with a certain arbitrary exactness. Therefore, we always are concerned with a certain interval of time in which the stone is in a certain interval of space. If our measurement is made more exact, the proposition '$[t_2, x_2, y_2, z_2]$ *P*' must be substituted by a series of new propositions: '$[t_{21}, x_{21}, y_{21}, z_{21}]$ *P*', $[t_{22}, x_{22}, y_{22}, z_{22}]$ *P*' and so on. If we maintain that elementary propositions can be found, in this case we realize that we may proceed *ad infinitum* without ever arriving at them. Consequently, if elementary propositions can be found, there can be found an infinite number of them. But this conclusion we cannot accept, for we have to arrive at a final point in our analysis of propositions such as 'The stone flies across the room' in order that we can endow them with a definite sense (cfr. 4.221 and the discussion above, p. 23).

Hence, *if we accept that Wittgenstein maintains that propositions describing motion are descriptions of physical facts, existing in space and time, we are confronted with two possibilities that are equally unacceptable: 1. In analysing propositions describing motions, we arrive at elementary propositions which each describe their indivisible (and static) part of the motion. This is unacceptable since we should have to adhere to Zeno's view and deny that motion at all exists. 2. In our analysis of propositions describing motions we never can arrive at elementary propositions.* At any step of our analysis, the motion will be described by means of a certain number of propositions which must each be replaced by just as many more as the analysis goes further and so on. *This too is unacceptable* as we cannot, in this case, endow propositions about motion with sense, because the sense of any truth-function depends on its arguments having a definite sense.

Hence, Wittgenstein's picture theory apparently rejects all talk of physical continuity, indivisibility, time, and space.

*

The assertion that elementary propositions *can* be found and that they are necessarily isomorphic pictures of states of affairs forces us to maintain that what is described by an elementary proposition must be something static, something unalterable existing at a certain point of time.

Undoubtedly Wittgenstein himself would have refused to accept this consequence if he had discovered it. He could not have accepted it without rendering his whole philosophy inconsistent. It is difficult to see whether he has noticed at all that whereas facts occur in time, it is pointless to speak of a proposition lasting a certain time. In his exposition of the picture theory no trace of such a distinction can be found. Indeed, 2.027, reads: 'Objects are what are unalterable and subsistent; their configuration is what is changing and unstable.', but this presumably is to be read as a logical-conceptual statement, not as referring to changes in time. In Pears & McGuinness' translation, we read in 4.0311 that the whole group of things, like a *tableau vivant*, presents a state of affairs. The use of the expression 'tableau vivant' strongly suggests a static conception of the concept of picture. For a tableau vivant is, a little paradoxically, a lifeless picture, a static phenomenon. The only living things in it are the persons who perform it, but when we talk of genuine tableaux vivants, the participators have to stand stiff while the curtain is drawn. However, it is worth noticing that Wittgenstein did not use the expression 'tableau vivant' himself but 'lebendes Bild' which might as well mean 'picture, the elements of which may change places in relation to each other'. I do not know who suggested the expression 'tableau vivant' but as several commentators on the *Tractatus* use this expression I think there is a good reason for emphasizing that Wittgenstein never made use of it.

The reference to Hertz's dynamical models (cfr. 4.04) does not help us either, in investigating whether Wittgenstein was aware of the problem in question. It is beyond doubt that Hertz's book *Die Prinzipien der Mechanik* has had an influence on Wittgenstein and at first glance it looks as if it has inspired Wittgenstein to construct the picture theory. In a footnote (*Biographical Sketch*, p. 7) von Wright writes, that 'it would be interesting to know whether Wittgenstein's conception of the proposition as a picture is connected in any way with the Introduction to Heinrich Hertz's *Die Prinzipien der Mechanik*. Wittgenstein knew this work and held it in high esteem. There are traces of the impression that it made on him both in the *Tractatus* and in his later writings.'

Surely, it cannot be precluded that the idea of the proposition as a picture may have come to Wittgenstein by reading Hertz, but the difference between the two thinkers in respect of the concept of a picture is so great that I doubt whether a study of Hertz's view can throw light on the picture theory of the *Tractatus*. By picture, Hertz is thinking of ideas that we may form of the connection between various natural phenomena, connections that cannot be perceived directly and therefore are represented by ideas in our imagination. The entities that the pictures represent he calls 'Gegenstände' (*Die Prinzipien*, p. 2), and he has the view that many pictures can be made of the same 'Gegenstand'. The only pictures which are not possible are those that 'schon einen Widerspruch gegen die Gesetze unseres Denkens in sich tragen, und wir fordern also zunächst, dass alle unsere Bilder logisch zulässige oder kurz zulässige seien.' He furthermore distinguishes 'right' pictures from 'false' ones. A picture is 'right' 'wenn ihre wesentlichen Beziehungen den Beziehungen der äusseren Dinge widersprechen ....' He also distinguishes between expedient and non-expedient pictures: 'Von zwei Bildern desselben Gegenstandes wird dasjenige das zweckmässigere sein, welches mehr wesentliche Beziehungen des Gegenstandes wiederspiegelt als das andere.' Already in these definitions we are far from Wittgenstein's concept of a picture. According to the *Tractatus*, only one picture can represent a state of affairs and therefore it becomes nonsense to speak of more or less expedient pictures. It is, however, very probable that Wittgenstein has been thinking of Hertz while establishing the picture theory. Among other things Hertz writes that 'Ob ein Bild richtig ist oder nicht, kann ebenfalls eindeutig mit ja und nein entschieden werden' (*Die Prinzipien*, p. 3) which strongly recalls Wittgenstein's words: 'Die Wirklichkeit muss durch den Satz auf ja oder nein fixiert sein.' (4.023). In 6.341–6.342, Wittgenstein compares Newtonian mechanics (which he considered apparently, contrary to fact, to be a general world-description) to a net laid down over some black marks on a white sheet, and uses this picture to illustrate that just as we may use arbitrarily many nets to describe the sizes and forms of the marks, so we may use many 'mechanics' besides Newton's as valid world descriptions. This passage also makes one think of Hertz's book. Hertz demonstrates that what we call theorems in mechanics is dependent on an arbitrary choice. Next he shows in what way it is possible to develop different mechanical descriptions (mutually translatable into each other) by using different sets of concepts as fundamental concepts. The different descriptions that can be established in this manner are also called pictures. The usual exposition of mechanics in which space, time, force, and mass, are basic concepts gives us one picture of the world (p. 5). Another picture is obtained if the concept of 'force' is replaced by the concept of 'energy' (p. 17), and furthermore a third possibility can be found: We may be able to eliminate the concept of force and do with time, space, and mass, as fundamental concepts (pp. 29 ff). It is this third possibility that Hertz is particularly concerned with in *Die Prinzipien der Mechanik*. It seems probable that it is alternatives to Newtonian mechanics of this type, that Wittgenstein thought of when he introduced his net-analogy.

Hertz defines a 'dynamic model' in the following way: 'Ein materielles System heisst dynamisches Modell eines zweiten Systems, wenn sich die Zusammenhänge des ersteren durch solche Koordinaten darstellen lassen, dass den Bedingungen genügt ist: 1. dass die Zahl der Koordinaten des ersten Systems gleich der Zahl der Koordinaten des andern Systems ist, 2. dass nach passender Zuordnung der Koordinaten für beide Systeme die gleichen Bedingungsgleichungen bestehen, 3. dass der Ausdruck für die Grösse einer Verrückung in beiden Systemen bei jener Zuordnung der Koordinaten übereinstimme.' (*Die Prinzipien*, p. 197). From this definition Hertz deduces a number of consequences, and he adds two notes to these of which the second is of special interest here: 'Das Verhältnis eines dynamischen Modells zu dem System, als dessen Modell es betrachtet wird, ist dasselbe, wie das Verhältnis der Bilder, welche sich unser Geist von den Dingen bildet, zu diesen Dingen. Betrachten wir nämlich den Zustand des Modells als eine Abbildung des Zustandes des Systems, so sind die Folgen der Abbildung, welche nach den Gesetzen dieser Abbildung eintreten müssen, zugleich die Abbildung der Folgen, welche sich an dem ursprünglichen Gegenstand nach den Gesetzen dieses ursprünglichen Gegenstandes entwickeln müssen. Die Übereinstimmung zwischen Geist und Natur lässt sich also vergleichen mit der Übereinstimmung zwischen zwei Systemen, welche Modelle von einander sind, und wir können uns sogar Rechenschaft ablegen von jener Übereinstimmung, wenn wir annehmen wollen dass der Geist die Fähigkeit habe, wirkliche dynamische Modelle der Dinge zu bilden und mit ihnen zu arbeiten.' (p. 199). If Wittgenstein really did get his idea of the picture theory from Hertz's book, this part of it undoubtedly made the greatest impression on him. For here Hertz indeed does make a sketch of the picture theory, or the idea that an isomorphic relation between mind and nature must be the kernel of all description. But as to the problem of the relation between the 'static' and 'cinematic' in Wittgenstein's theory, this passage gives us no help. We do not know, and, as far as I can see, we shall never find out, whether Wittgenstein realized that his picture theory raised this problem.

Finally, it should be added here that Wittgenstein speaks of processes, ('Vorgänge'), and events, ('Ereignisse'), when dealing with physics (*vide* e. g. 6.3611) and not, as might be expected, of facts or states of affairs. I have found no reason for this, but perhaps he would have maintained that a physical situation which by help of mathematics could be described by a function of the form $y = f(x)$ cannot be split up into a finite number of elementary propositions and that special rules, therefore, are provided in the explanation of the sense of expressions of this sort. But if this is so, a theory of it is missing in the *Tractatus* in any case. And no matter how Wittgenstein would have conceived of the connection between applied mathematics and propositional logic, it is clear that propositional logic can deal with a static universe, only if we adhere to the view that any elementary proposition is an isomorphic picture of a state of affairs.

III

THE PSYCHOLOGICAL ASPECTS OF THE PICTURE THEORY

a. The relation between 'proposition' and 'thought'.

In the preceding chapter the picture theory has been spoken of in rather loose terms. The problems in chapter II have not necessitated a distinct formulation of it, whereas it is strictly necessary, for the sake of the problems that are considered in this chapter, to give a clear-cut exposition of the theory.

The best account of Wittgenstein's concept of isomorphism that I know of is the one found in professor Stenius' book *Wittgenstein's 'Tractatus'*, pp. 91–116. Stenius opens with the following presentation of two systems of objects:

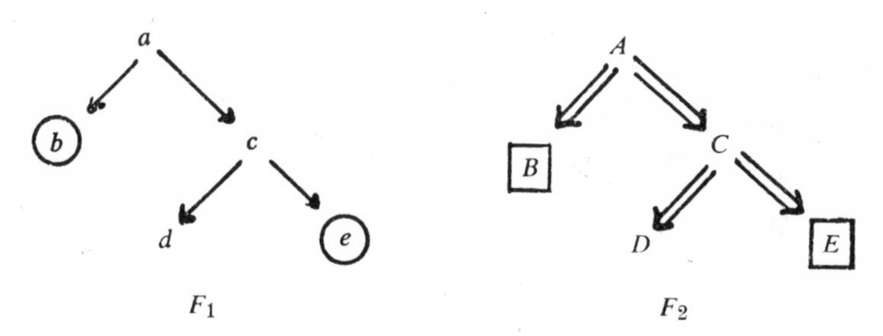

F_1 F_2

The system F_1 consists of 5 persons: *a*, *b*, *c*, *d* and *e*, a father-son relation (indicated by arrows) and a quality, 'intelligence', marked by circles. These elements are ordered so that *a* is the father of *b* and *c*, *c* is the father of *d* and *e* and *b* and *e* are intelligent. The system F_2 consists of 5 officers: *A*, *B*, *C*, *D* and *E*, a relation of 'giving direct orders to' (indicated by arrows) and a quality, 'braveness', marked by squares. These elements are ordered so that *A* gives direct orders to *B* and *C*, *C* gives direct orders to *D* and *E*, and *B* and *E* are brave.

A comparison of the two systems shows that they have what Stenius calls the same 'internal' or 'categorical' structure. By this is meant that in the example given we must make use of three categories: A category of objects, a category of qualities, and a category of relations, and furthermore we must make sure that the two systems contain the same amount of elements in each of these categories. This similarity in categorical structure is, according to Stenius, a necessary condition of a representing relation between the two systems. But it is not a sufficient condition. In the example cited above many unambiguous correspondences between the two systems can be established. If we regard the objects taken alone, we know that two groups, each consisting of 5 elements, can be related to each other so that one element of the one corresponds to one element of the other and *vice versa,* in 5!, i. e. 120 different ways.

In the present example the two systems do not only have the same categorical structure but also the same 'external' structure. Stenius calls the system of elements in F_1, S_1, and the system of elements in F_2, S_2 and asserts that the two systems have the same 'external' structure if the following conditions are fulfilled:

'(a) any object of S_1 has the quality of intelligence in F_1 if, and only if, the *corresponding* object of S_2 has the *corresponding* quality of braveness in F_2;

(b) of two objects in S_1 one is in the relation of 'being father of' to the other in F_1 if, and only if, the *corresponding* relation of 'giving direct orders' holds good in F_2 between the *corresponding* objects of S_2.'

We are not able to state that these conditions are fulfilled unless we have laid down a correspondence, (C_o), between the elements of F_1 and F_2, so that we can tell what is meant by 'corresponding' in the two conditions. Not until then can we say exactly what is to be understood by 'isomorphy'. In order to express ourselves rightly, we must say that the two articulate fields, F_1 and F_2 are isomorphic in respect of the correspondence (C_o).

According to Stenius the concept of isomorphism can in general be defined as follows:

'Given two articulate fields *F* and *G*, the categorical structure of which is the same, and given a one-one correspondence (*C*) between the elements of each category in *F* and *G*, then *F* and *G* are said to be *isomorphic* in respect of (*C*) if, and only if, the following condition is fulfilled:

An elementary state of affairs does or does not exist in F according as the corresponding elementary state of affairs does or does not exist in G.'

In this exposition, it is an important feature that two articulate fields can be said to be isomorphic only in respect to a fixed correspondence between their elements. This correspondence Stenius calls 'the key of isomorphism'. In general any stipulation of which element in the one field corresponds to a certain element of the other is a 'key of correspondence'.

Stenius points out that his terminology deviates noticeably from the usual terminology of mathematics, for in that context we often say that two systems are isomorphic if there is only a key of *some* sort in respect of which they are isomorphic in the above sense, whereas the 'key of correspondence' according to Stenius has to be *fixed* if we are to speak of isomorphy. One may also point out that the mathematical concept of isomorphy only covers finite numbers of elements, while infinite groups of elements cannot be isomorphic but only 'equivalent', as Cantor uses this word (*vide* Bundgaard: *Tallene*, p. 43).

The next point of Stenius' exposition is that when two isomorphic fields are given, the one can be considered a *picture* of the other. If *F* is considered a picture of *G*, then *F* is said to be an isomorphic picture of *G;* the relation between *F* and *G* is called an isomorphic representation and the key of isomorphism is called 'the key of interpretation' (p. 95). Stenius maintains that this concept of a picture fits in with Wittgenstein's concept of a true picture but not with his concept of a picture in general. The reasons for this are in a way the ones I have mentioned above (p. 46 ff.) in the passage about the status of false propositions in the *Tractatus.* In order to make his terminology suit Wittgenstein's text, Stenius must therefore make a correction of his concept of a picture. Consequently this definition is introduced:

'An articulate field F is called a picture (true or false) of the articulate field G if there is a key of interpretation (C) according to which the elements of F are considered to stand for the elements of G. / The picture is said to be true or false according as it is an isomorphic picture of G in respect of (C) or not.'

This implies that a picture must be conceived of as a field about which the question can be raised whether it is an isomorphic picture or not. Stenius urges that this view is in accordance with Wittgenstein's text but a little difficulty is caused by 2.1513 which reads: 'So a picture, conceived in this way, also includes the pictorial relationship, which makes it into a picture.' An articulate field *F* may in respect of one 'key' (*C*) be a picture of *G* and in respect of another key (*C'*) be a picture of *G'*. Shall we now say, Stenius asks, that the same picture (*F*) can be interpreted in two different ways, or should we rather say that we have to do with two different pictures in this case. In order to reconcile his view with 2.1513 Stenius chooses the latter possibility. This means to say that 'the articulate field *F*, as capable of different interpretations, we will call a *picture-field,* using the word *picture* as a name only for those picture-fields to which a fixed key of interpretation is attached.' (*Op. cit.* p. 98).

I should like to criticize three things in Stenius' exposition. First, it seems a little odd to me to distinguish between three categories as Wittgenstein explicitly asserts that a state of affairs consists of objects only and a proposition of names only. Stenius only mentions this point briefly (*op. cit.* p. 97). It would have been natural to put it at the head of the exposition and draw the consequence of Wittgenstein's view by saying that two fields have the same 'internal' structure if they consist of the same amount of elements. Secondly, there is a snag about the fact that Stenius continuously makes propositions about the relation between two fields of which the one is a picture of the other. According to Wittgenstein, propositions of this kind, as we have seen, are inadmissible because they cannot, *qua* meta-linguistic propositions, have a sense, if the thesis of extensionality and the picture theory are valid. I shall return to this point later. Thirdly, an account of what is meant by saying that a key of interpretation is *attached* to an articulate field is missing in Stenius' in other respects very detailed and distinct study.

When Stenius includes a 'fixed key of interpretation' in his concept of a picture, this can be regarded as an *ad hoc*-definition which is introduced with the purpose of complying with 2.1513. But what is the conceptual content of this definition? It must be granted that the key of interpretation is not a part of the articulate field. Stenius obviously does not mean this either. A picture can never contain an element or a region that shows how the picture describes, and how it is to be 'read'. In a picture each element represents an element in the state of affairs described and consequently no element of the picture can describe what the relation is, between the picture and the state of affairs. The same holds good of propositions: an elementary proposition cannot possibly contain a part that gives an explanation of how the proposition is to be read or what it is intended to describe. This certainly is Wittgenstein's opinion which I believe nobody ever could think of objecting to if he considers the picture theory valid.

Now, if the key of interpretation is not a part of the articulate field which represents another articulate field, in what way, then, can it be 'attached' to the field? Stenius gives no answer to this question. From his exposition, however, it can be seen that he considers the key of interpretation to represent a sort of choice made by us. When considering *F* and *G*, we can choose to regard *F* as a picture of *G*. But we can also choose to regard *F* as a picture of *G*'. We are not bound to prefer the one to the other. Our choice manifests itself in that we — mentally — establish certain relations between the elements of *F* and the elements of the represented field. Even if we say with Stenius, that the key of interpretation *per* definition belongs to the picture, this still only consists of elements or objects. Therefore we should, in order to do justice to Stenius, never perhaps speak of 'the picture *F*' but of 'the field *F* conceived of as a picture'. But in either case it is clear that, in presuming that we have an optional choice of key of interpretation, we refer in some way or other to one or more perceiving minds.

The introduction made by Stenius of a key of interpretation is apparently a consequence of the otherwise very plausible interpretation of Wittgenstein's text, but the key is a very unfavourable conception because much of the *Tractatus* speaks against it. I will demonstrate this by working out a new interpretation of Wittgenstein's passages about the picture theory. The kernel of this interpretation will be that the word 'elementary proposition' should actually be substituted by the word 'thought' whereever it occurs in the *Tractatus*.

*

In the *Tractatus* we find some statements concerning the relation between proposition and thought which have been partly overlooked by the commentators on the book. I quote them here together with some related statements:

2.1 We picture facts to ourselves.
3 A logical picture of facts is a thought.
3.1 In a proposition a thought finds an expression that can be perceived by the senses.
3.11 We use the perceptible sign of a proposition (spoken or written, etc.) as a projection of a possible situation.
The method of projection is to think out the sense of the proposition.
3.12 I call the sign with which we express a thought a propositional sign. — And a proposition is a propositional sign in its projective relation to the world.
3.2 In a proposition a thought can be expressed in such a way that elements of the propositional sign correspond to the objects of the thought.
3.5 A propositional sign, applied and thought out, is a thought.
4 A thought is a proposition with a sense.

From these statements, it can be seen, in the first place, that Wittgenstein accepts that some sort of thing, named a thought, can be found. Furthermore it looks as if the concept of 'thought' is more fundamental than the concept of 'proposition'. In 3.1, 'proposition' is spoken of as something secondary to thought. It is merely an expression of the thought. This impression is confirmed by 3.12 and 3.2. It is worth noticing that 4 states that a thought is the same as a proposition or rather that a thought and the proposition expressing it are identical. The apparent pleonasm 'proposition with sense' in 4 presumably must be explained by considering 'senseful' (sinnvoll) as opposed to empty of sense (sinnlos) instead of to non-sensical (unsinnig). (Cfr. 4.461-4.4611 and Weinberg's *An Examination*, p. 187 n). In order to give a full account of the quoted statements I will introduce the following conceptions:

Thought: By this is understood a configuration of *psychical elements.*

Such elements are entities that belong to the stream of consciousness. They can be viewed introspectively only. Sensuous experiences are psychical elements.

Thought-sign: By this is understood (if it *can* be understood at all) the appearance of the thought when it is considered introspectively as it manifests itself, independently of its 'sense'. Maybe it can be viewed only retrospectively.

O-proposition: The ordinary conception of an elementary proposition in the literature on the *Tractatus,* i. e. as a picture that represents something, whether it is thought of, perceived, or in some other way experienced, by a conscious person or not.

W-proposition: By this is understood a configuration of physical elements that are used as substitutes for psychical elements of a thought so that this becomes a public phenomenon.

O-name: Element of an O-proposition.

W-name: Element of a W-proposition.

To these conceptions can be added the better-known: propositional sign, simple sign, state of affairs, and fact. In what follows, I will apply the following notation where I consider it necessary:

p: an arbitrary W-proposition.

'p': the thought expressed by p.

p_m: p's physical appearance, i. e. the propositional sign applied when p is stated.

p_s: the state of affairs described by p.

p_f: the fact described by p.

Probably Wittgenstein, as mentioned before, did not reflect on the relation between proposition and thought until very late in his preparation of the *Tractatus.* It can hardly be doubted that his original view of the nature of propositions was that all propositions are O-propositions. In *Notebooks,* Wittgenstein constantly speaks of propositions only, never of thoughts, in connection with the picture theory, and it is nowhere emphasized that propositions have to be conceived of in a special way in order to be pictures. As also mentioned before, Wittgenstein does not discover that his picture theory has anything to do with the concept of 'thought' until September, 1916, when he writes, 'Now it is becoming clear why I thought that thinking and language were the same. For thinking is a kind of language. For a thought too is, of course, a logical picture of the proposition, and therefore it just is a kind of proposition'. (*Notebooks,* p. 82). The concept of 'thought' is not even mentioned in the rest of the notebooks. This remarkable fact indicates that Wittgenstein's development of the idea of how thought and proposition are related to one another must have taken place between January, 1917, and the summer of 1918, when the *Tractatus* was completed. In this short period Wittgenstein's philosophy has suddenly obtained a new aspect which turns out to be essential, not accidental. In what follows, I will show why 'thought' must be a fundamental concept in the *Tractatus*.

In the *Tractatus*, it seems to be implied that we have reasons for distinguishing between language and thought, even though it seems on the other hand, according to Wittgenstein, as if there is a very great similarity between the two. The words 'thought' and 'language' have already been applied in the preface of the book, in which it is said that the purpose of the book is 'to set a limit to thought, or rather — not to thought, but to the expression of thoughts: for in order to be able to set a limit to thought, we should have to find both sides of the limit thinkable (i. e. we should have to be able to think what cannot be thought). / It will therefore only be in language that the limit can be set, and what lies on the other side of the limit will simply be nonsense.'

Here language is regarded as 'the expression of thoughts', and although a fundamental difference between thought and language is emphasized (namely in respect of drawing a borderline between sense and nonsense), yet it looks as if Wittgenstein assumes a sort of parallelism between thought and language by virtue of which everything that can be said about the structure and application of language holds good for the domain of thought too. Maslow holds this view when he writes: 'Language and thought are inseparable, and an investigation of the formal structure of language thus becomes thought's self-clarification.' (*A Study*, p. xiv). I think that most readers of the *Tractatus* have seen it in this way and consequently have felt that the concept of 'thought' — conceived of as a mental counterpart to 'language' and 'proposition' — has no relevance for interpreting the other concepts of the *Tractatus*. In any case, it is a remarkable fact that no book or article on the *Tractatus* contains more than a few loose remarks on the part played by the concept of 'thought' in Wittgenstein's system. Ever since Bertrand Russell wrote in his introduction to the English version of the *Tractatus* that the book 'is concerned with the conditions which would have to be fulfilled by a logical perfect language' (*Introduction*, p. ix) it has been *comme il faut* to regard the book as a 'Critique of Pure Language' (a label suggested by P. Geach, cfr. Stenius: *Wittgenstein's 'Tractatus'*, p. 220).

I think that this view would have been the correct one if we had had to give a short account of the young Wittgenstein's philosophy in 1916 (although Geach's label becomes pointless, if we consider language and thought to be identical, as the allusion to Kant tends to emphasize the word 'language'), but it does not apply to the text of the *Tractatus*. The picture theory as a whole turns out to be something quite different from what the usual account of it suggests, as soon as we emphasize the concept of 'thought' in Wittgenstein's ideas.

Very few have noticed the part played by the concept of 'thought' in the *Tractatus*. It should, however, be mentioned that von Wright makes a perceptive remark about it in *Logik, filosofi och språk,* p. 141, that reads: 'I think it will be easier to understand Wittgenstein's peculiar view of language as picture, if we notice that by 'proposition' he means something which in colloquial language would be called 'thought', if anything . . . by 'thought' Wittgenstein does not mean anything subjective or psychological (thought-processes). What he means is so to speak 'the content' of the thought, something objective.'

After the following was written I have had the opportunity to read a very interesting paper by Professor Gustav Bergmann (*Stenius on the Tractatus, a Special Review*) in which many reflections on the concept of 'thought' can be found. But as Bergmann's line of thought is very different from my own, I think a comparison between our ideas would be more confusing than illuminating at this point. The same is true of D. S. Shwayder's review of Stenius' book (*Critical Notice, Mind* 1963, pp. 275 - 288), in which some of the problems I deal with here are touched upon.

In what follows, I will first try to show how the picture theory must appear to be, when 'thought' and not 'proposition' is considered the most fundamental concept. I will thereafter make a comparison between my interpretation and the interpretations of other commentators on the subject.

I have mentioned above that the ontological part of the *Tractatus* is probably the part of the book which is written last. In any case, it must have been written later than the last remarks in the *Notebooks*, for in the *Notebooks* we do not meet any of the ideas presented in the first part of the *Tractatus*. Likewise the statements about 'thought' in all probability are written later. When Wittgenstein *discovered* in September 1916 that 'thinking is a kind of language' he could not possibly, at this time, have written the parts of the *Tractatus* dealing with 'thought'. Nevertheless a coordination has been made of all the ideas that have taken form at various points in time. This manifests itself in the arrangement of the introductory parts of the *Tractatus* which nobody has paid attention to. It is to be noticed that in the book we are at first presented with the concepts of 'fact', 'state of affairs', 'object', 'substance' and 'world'. This part which may be called the ontological part spreads over 4 pages in all, from 1 to 2.063. The next part opens with 2.1: 'We picture facts to ourselves', and it deals with the concept of 'picture' and the relation between picture and reality. This part stretches from 2.1 to 2.225 (2½ pages in all). Then the concept of 'thought' is introduced: 3. 'A logical picture of facts is a thought'. In connection with this, we are told what is meant by the word 'thinkable'. This part takes up one page only (from 3 to 3.05). Not until we arrive at 3.1 do we meet with the concept of a proposition: 'In a proposition a thought finds an expression that can be perceived by the senses.' In stating this, Wittgenstein seems to imply that the reader knows what a proposition is. What he tells us is only that the phenomena which we usually call propositions are actually thoughts. The thought *is*, as stated in 4, a proposition with sense.

This order of the theses can hardly be accidental. It looks as if Wittgenstein's idea is that we are not able to explain what a proposition is unless we know what a thought is. And similarly we cannot understand what a thought is unless we are acquainted with the concept of a picture. To me it is obvious that Wittgenstein, when explaining what a picture is, is mainly aiming at explaining 'the thought as a picture', not 'the proposition as a picture' ('proposition' must here be read as 'O-proposition'; if by 'proposition' we mean 'W-proposition' the difference vanishes). I cannot prove that this view is valid but the following exposition will render it plausible.

The relation between language and thought may be explained in this way. A thought is a fact and consequently it has a certain structure. For a thought is a picture (according to 3) and a picture is a fact (according to 2.141). A fact consists of elements, objects arranged in a definite configuration. What sort of elements does a thought consist of? This question Russell asks Wittgenstein in a letter of 1919 which presumably contained a number of questions about obscure passages in the *Tractatus* which Russell at this time possessed in manuscript, and in his reply Wittgenstein lists Russell's questions and his answers to them: '.... ".... But a Gedanke is a Tatsache: what are its constituents and components, and what is their relation to those of the pictured Tatsache?" I don't know *what* the constituents of a thought are but I know *that* it must have such constituents which correspond to the words of language. Again the kind of relation of the constituents of the thought and of the pictured fact is irrelevant. It would be a matter of psychology to find out.' (*Notebooks*, p. 129). 'Does a Gedanke consist of words?" No! But of psychical constituents that have the same sort of relation to reality as words. What those constituents are I don't know.' (*Notebooks*, p. 130).

These remarks are extremely important. Although it is in this same letter that Wittgenstein gets tangled up over the relation between 'Tatsache' and 'Sachverhalt' (*vide* above p. 39), his comments on this matter give the key to a clearer understanding of the text in the *Tractatus*. A thought consists of psychical constituents or elements which form a fixed configuration or logical structure. I have comprised this in my definition of 'thought' above. Wittgenstein makes no attempt to explain what psychical constituents are. We may, however, state that they are objects (for the thought is a picture and a picture is a fact) and, as such, they belong to the substance of the world (cfr. 2.021). Being objects they must be non-composite, but Wittgenstein has not thought over how they are to be defined. Here we meet with great difficulties, as great as those we considered in the previous chapter where the question was what could be understood by phenomenologically indivisible elements. It cannot be doubted, however, that a definition of the elements of thoughts must be established *via* a psychological, introspective investigation. Wittgenstein actually calls them *psychical* constituents. It is remarkable that he also considers the examination of the relation between the psychical constituents of the thought and the objects in the pictured fact to be a *psychological* task and not an epistemological one, as one could be led to think from Russell's demarcation of the problems in his *Introduction* (p. 7).

Wittgenstein was not interested in performing psychological investigations of this kind. He might have thought that the question as to the nature of the elements of thought had no significance for logical and semantical investigations. It is, however, obvious that they cannot be dispensed with. The thought is characterized through its structure, but no structure can exist where no elements can be found. If thoughts exist, psychical elements must exist too. When we think of something the thought may in some way or other appear phenomenologically. But whether it appears visually, audibly, or in some other way, makes no difference. If 5 persons think 'The Eiffel Tower is situated in Paris' they all think the same no matter how different their private images, or what ever they may experience introspectively, are. Wittgenstein apparently takes for granted that something must appear in the imagination no matter what sort of memory images occur (and even if no memory images occur either), and the reason for this may be that it would otherwise be impossible to distinguish one thought from another. That two thoughts are different is revealed in that they have a difference in respect of structure but this is, of course, only possible to check if the presence of elements of thought can be pointed out.

It is a characteristic of the concept of 'thought' that a thought always deals with something different from itself. A thought is a fact, because it consists of objects only. But thoughts are the only facts that point to something different from themselves. A thought is always a thought *of* something. This is an empirical fact. We cannot think without thinking of something. In order to make the thought represent something, we need not do more than think the thought. We need not decide that it has to represent something nor in which way it has to represent. A thought has, *qua* thought, a relation to 'what it is about'. It does not contain an indication of how it represents something, since it consists of psychical elements only. That these elements have a certain relation to one another constitutes the necessary and sufficient condition of the representation of something different from the thought itself.

It seems plausible to me that Wittgenstein was thinking of *the thought* as a picture when he wrote the passage from 2.1 to 2.225. In the first place the passage ends in 3, which states that a logical picture of facts is a thought, and after this Wittgenstein deals with the question of what is to be understood by 'the thinkable'. Secondly, the statements 2.1–2.225 can be made clear without difficulty, if we assume that it is 'thought-pictures' he is thinking of in this passage.

2.1 asserts that we picture facts to ourselves. 2.11 states that a picture presents the existence or non-existence of states of affairs. In 2.12 it is maintained that the picture is a model of reality and 2.13 and 2.131 inform us that the elements of the picture are the representations of objects. These statements are equally understandable whether by 'picture' we think of 'thought' or 'O-proposition'. If by 'picture' we mean an 'O-proposition', however, we already arrive at a difficulty in 2.14. 2.14 reads: 'What constitutes a picture is that its elements are related to one another in a determinate way.' 2.15 reinforces 2.14: 'The fact that the elements of a picture are related to one another in a determinate way represents that things are related to one another in the same way/ . . . .' Here it is clearly stated that a picture consists of elements only and that it is a picture by virtue of the fixed relations of these elements only. If we conceive of 'picture' as the same as 'O-proposition' we are led into the line of thought which Stenius has developed. We are led to distinguish between an 'internal' and an 'external' structure, since an articulated field can be correlated with another possessing the same 'internal' structure in more than one way. Consequently, it is necessary to speak of a key of interpretation in connection with the field, and, instead of 2.14, we should rather say that 'The fact that the elements of a picture are related to one another in a determinate way does not represent anything. It is only in connection with a key of interpretation (which establishes a relation between names and objects), that the elements of a picture represents that things are related to one another in a determinate way.' The reason that Wittgenstein did not formulate 2.15 in this way is not that he forgot to do so. On the contrary he could never have made this formulation without violating the thesis of extensionality and the picture theory. I will show this further on.

If 'picture' is conceived of as 'O-proposition', then 2.14 and 2.15 must be considered as either false or incomplete statements. If, on the contrary, 'picture' is taken to mean 'thought', the statements make sense. They are in full concordance with the fact that a thought, *qua* thought, i. e. in virtue of being a configuration of psychical elements, deals with something different from itself. Whenever we think or have a thought, we inevitably know what the thought pictures or describes. We never have to think of a key of interpretation which indicates how the thought is to be 'read'. In our private experience we never perceive a key of interpretation and we would fall in to logical difficulties if we postulated that there was one. For if one first had to think a thought-sign and in the next place a key of interpretation which could turn this thought-sign into a picture, the question would be what could be understood by the key of interpretation. If it is a thought, it demands a key of interpretation itself in order that we can get to know what it is a thought about and consequently in this case we are involved in an infinite regress.

At the level of language this might appear thus: When we experience a proposition such as 'The Eiffel Tower is situated in Paris' as a picture, this is due to the fact that we correlate the elements of the picture with the elements of the described fact according to a certain key of interpretation. If we are to explain to another person the sense of this proposition, we are compelled to formulate the key of interpretation in language and say something like: 'In the articulate field considered the element, 'The Eiffel Tower', represents so and so, the element, 'Paris', so and so and, 'is situated in', a certain geographical relation.' But when uttering this proposition we really present a new articulate field and this field is not a picture unless we attach a key of interpretation to it. But this new key of interpretation has to be formulated too in order that we can explain to the other person what we are saying at all, and so we get involved in an infinite regress. Stenius seems to avoid this difficulty by a sort of *metabasis eis allo genos*. In his view the articulate field is a sort of propositional-sign, not a thought-sign, and keys of interpretation are sorts of mental entities which he does not go into. If he had spoken of thoughts, instead of propositions, the difficulty would immediately have appeared. And we have no arguments against speaking of thoughts instead of propositions, for, as Wittgenstein says, thought is a language too, and a thought is a picture.

2.141 states that the picture is a fact, and the last part of 2.15 together with 2.151 asserts something about the structure of the picture and its form of representation. These statements are neutral as to the problem whether thought or O-proposition is the more fundamental concept in the *Tractatus*. 2.1511–2.15121 is a very queer passage. It reads: '*That* is how a picture is attached to reality; it reaches right out to it. It is laid against reality like a ruler. Only the end-points of the graduating lines actually *touch* the object that is to be measured.' In *Logical Form* this passage is hinted at: 'I have said elsewhere that a proposition 'reaches up to reality' (in 2.1511 in the first English version of the *Tractatus*) 'and by this I meant that the forms of the entities are contained in the form of the proposition which is about these entities.' This presumably must be taken to mean that a picture only reproduces the logical form of the pictured fact, and not its content, i. e. the objects or the substance. In order that the logical form can be reproduced, the elements of the picture must represent the elements of the fact, but the picture does not tell us anything about the nature of these elements. When we measure something by means of a ruler, the result we obtain is the length of the object. It tells us nothing about the nature of the object. It is presupposed that the ruler and the object exist in some sense or other but their natures are never revealed by any measurement. I mention this only to show that also 2.1511–2.15121 are neutral as to the problem here considered. The expression 'it reaches right out to it' seemingly indicates that in connection with the picture theory we must not speak of projection-lines as when we speak of projections in geometry. The expression is a rather free translation of the German 'es reicht bis zu ihr' which is an expression so obscure that it hardly can be of any interest to try to explain it.

2.1513 is a most essential statement: 'So a picture, conceived in this way, also includes the pictorial relationship, which makes it into a picture.' This statement is supported by 3.13: 'A proposition includes all that the projection includes, but not what is projected. / . . . .' I have mentioned above that it was on account of this very sentence that Stenius redefined his concept of a picture. But the conceptual content of his definition was not clear. If 2.1513 is to be considered as an indication of the fact that by a picture we must understand an articulate field plus a key of interpretation, then not only is 2.1513 a blurred statement, but it also contradicts 2.14 and 2.141. 2.14 asserts, as mentioned above, that what constitutes a picture is that its elements are related to one another in a determinate way, and 2.141 that the picture is a fact. We are really forced to say that if a picture is an articulate field plus a key of interpretation, then the key must be an object, for a fact only consists of objects. 2.1513, however, is a clear statement if we substitute 'thought' for 'picture'. For, as mentioned above, no thought can exist without having a 'pictoriai relationship' even though a thought only consists of elements related to each other in a determinate way. As stated in 2.14, it is this circumstance that endows the picture with its 'pictorial relationship', which consequently is not an extra entity connected with the picture.

The formulation in 2.1514 that 'The pictorial relationship consists of the correlations of the picture's elements with things' does not, as one may think, indicate a distinction between picture-field and key of interpretation. It is not held that the perceiving person must establish a co-ordination between the elements of the picture and the elements of the fact but only that the pictorial relationship consists of the correlations.

The subsequent sentences in the *Tractatus*, as far as 3, give us no further information about the problem here considered.

Naturally, when Wittgenstein conceives of thoughts as pictures, and has this in mind when developing his concept of a picture, the word 'picture' has a special meaning in the *Tractatus*. For it can reasonably be said of pictures as they appear in a newspaper, for example, that they require a key of interpretation in certain cases. It may happen that we see something in the paper which we believe is an ornament until somebody says: 'Look, it's a picture of so and so.' This situation cannot occur when we speak of thoughts as pictures. For a thought has a sense, spontaneously.

*

We now come to the question of what sort of relation can be found between thought and proposition. A thought may picture a certain state of affairs and a proposition may be a picture of the same state of affairs. What exactly is the relation between the thought and the proposition? This question can easily be answered. A thought is a configuration of psychical elements. The essential feature of a thought is the configuration, the logical form, whereas the elements are accidental features that have no interest here. When Wittgenstein writes in 3.1 that in a proposition a thought is expressed so it can be perceived by the senses, this implies that in respect of the essential features, i. e. the logical form, the thought and the proposition are identical as is expressed in 4: 'A thought is a proposition with a sense.' The thought which is experienced introspectively appears in such a way that it can be perceived by the senses in the proposition when the elements of the thought are substituted by the elements of the propositional sign one for one.

Consider this example:

○ × □

Here we see a physical fact which may be structured in such a way that it appears as consisting of three elements, a circle, a cross and a square. Let us say that I now think: 'The book is lying on the table'. This thought is a picture, and it consists of elements which must be characterized as psychical no matter how they appear to me. Now, let us say, that this thought consists of two elements having a determinate relation to each other. If this is the case, the thought can be, so to speak, laid down on the page. I do this by substituting □ for the psychical element representing the table,

○ for the psychical element representing the book, and × for the experienced relation between the two. In this case, the fact, ○ × □, is no longer a mere physical fact. It is, in addition, my thought, 'The book is lying on the table', projected into perceptible things in such a manner that it can be perceived by the senses.

The matter may be illustrated by a situation in a game of chess. The different pieces may be replaced one by one by other pieces different from the original ones. No matter what we substitute for the original pieces, bits of paper, buttons, matches or the like, the situation in the game will be preserved if we agree that the new pieces used really do represent the king, the knight etc. The situation in the game is characterized solely by the configuration of the pieces. The configuration is what is essential, whereas the looks of the pieces and the material they are made of is unessential. They need not even be physical objects for we can play chess without boards and men in the mind only, as is often done by professional players.

In the same way as the pieces in chess can be replaced by other objects, the elements of a thought can be replaced by other elements, for instance physical signs. The elements ○ × □ can be made elements of a thought, and any other articulate fact can be used as a substitute for the psychical constituents of a thought, so long as it has as many elements as the thought. At this point, I should like to draw the reader's attention to 3.2 in which it is said that 'in a proposition a thought can be expressed in such a way that elements of the propositional sign correspond to the objects of the thought'. And in 3.1431, it is said that 'the essence of a propositional sign is very clearly seen if we imagine one composed of spatial objects (such as tables, chairs, and books) instead of written signs'. The spatial arrangement of these things will then express the sense of the proposition. In order to express 'The book is lying on the table' I might as well use a fact such as the rug is lying on the floor as the words we conventionally use. As mentioned above, a proposition is something which only differs from a thought in respect of unessential qualities, namely the nature of the elements. As to the essential quality, the structure, configuration, or logical form, it is identical with the thought, i. e. it *is* the thought. As this is not a common view, I consider it necessary to distinguish between 'O-proposition' and 'W-proposition'. According to the common view O-propositions can be found. But Wittgenstein's view must imply that by 'proposition' we can only mean 'W-proposition'. When we say that a thought and the W-proposition corresponding to it are identical, we must be careful not to maintain that this means that they possess the same structure. For the structure is not a complex of *existing* relations, the structure cannot have any ontological existence. The thought and the W-proposition corresponding to it cannot be said to have the same structure in the sense of 'same' in which we may say that a chair and a table have the same colour. Colours are something we are able to point to in our surroundings. They are qualities which must necessarily exist in order that logical forms can appear. But structures we cannot point to. A structure always appears in connection with something that exists but structures are neither substantial, spatial, temporal or coloured. When a thought is expressed in a proposition, then, what we have to do with, when we regard the propositional sign as something conveying a sense, is the thought *itself* and not the thought presented through the medium of something that has a structure similar to it.

Naturally this relation between thought and proposition is very difficult to describe, if we do not distinguish between 'O-proposition' and 'W-proposition'. I shall once more try to explain it in connection with Wittgenstein's statements quoted in this chapter.

In 3.1, it is held that in a proposition a thought is expressed so that it may be perceived by the senses. This formulation may mislead us to the view that the proposition exists before it is used as a medium for the expression of the thought. This, however, is not the case. If we consider a text such as 'The Eiffel Tower is situated in Paris', and this text is not experienced by anyone as expressing a thought, then it is a mere fact. If it is used for expressing a thought, it suddenly becomes both a propositional sign and a W-proposition ('I call the sign with which we express a thought a propositional sign' (3.12)). While it is used for expressing a thought, the fact is a proposition and must be described as such, which causes some difficulties. The expression of the thought is carried out by replacing the elements of the thought by the elements of the propositional sign. Thus the propositional sign suddenly becomes a picture, a projection of a possible state of affairs. This is described in 3.11: 'We use the perceptible sign of a proposition .... as a projection of a possible situation.' Just after this, Wittgenstein writes: 'The method of projection is to think out the sense of the proposition.' This formulation is a little awkward, but plausible if we regard an example such as 'The Eiffel Tower is situated in Paris'. For according to linguistic conventions we know what should be traditionally projected into — or thought of — this articulate fact; it *could* be used for expressing that 'There is an ashtray on my desk' or that 'The Leaning Tower is situated in Pisa'. We simply can let the sign 'The Eiffel Tower' represent my ashtray, and the sign 'Paris', represent my desk. Conventionally, however, the fact 'The Eiffel Tower is situated in Paris' as it appears on the paper here is used as material of one thought only. This fact has no relation to anything unless somebody thinks that the Eiffel Tower is situated in Paris while looking at the propositional sign which in this case becomes a proposition. The thought that the Eiffel Tower is situated in Paris is the one we always have, conventionally, when we regard the propositional sign in question, and therefore this thought may be called 'the sense of the proposition'. But the propositional sign has to be 'thought out' in order that a projective relation can be established.

A propositional sign which is used or 'thought out' is normally called a 'proposition' in the *Tractatus*. Unfortunately this has led many to think of a proposition as an O-proposition instead of a W-proposition. According to what I have said above, a proposition could really be called a thought as well, and it is to be noticed that Wittgenstein does just this in 3.5: 'A propositional sign, applied and thought out, is a thought.'

It is a consequence of the proposed view that what we cannot think cannot be expressed in language. We cannot form a proposition which gives expression to something unthinkable, because a proposition only comes into existence if it is thought by somebody. This is emphasized in the last paragraph of 5.61: 'We cannot think what we cannot think; so what we cannot think we cannot say either.'

*

In future references to Wittgenstein's picture theory, I shall mean the picture theory conceived of as a thought-picture theory or a W-proposition-picture theory, and not as an O-proposition-picture theory. Undoubtedly Wittgenstein began by constructing an O-proposition-picture theory, and as mentioned above did not until very late shift to proposing a thought-picture theory. This shift solved many problems but, as we shall see, it raised many difficulties at the same time which Wittgenstein never overcame.

The difference between the O-proposition-picture theory, which has found its best formulation in Stenius' book, and the W-proposition-picture theory can briefly be indicated thus:

The O-proposition-picture theory:

1. We picture facts to ourselves (2.1).
2. The logical picture of a fact is a proposition.
3. A thought 'p' and the corresponding proposition p differ from each other in respect of the elements which constitute them.
4. If 'p' has the structure S_1 and p has the structure S_2 it can be said that $S_1 = S_2$.
5. Any proposition is an O-proposition, i. e. any proposition is a picture, or has a sense, no matter whether it is thought or not. p is a picture no matter whether p occurs at the same time as 'p' or not.

6. A proposition is a configuration of objects to which a key of interpretation, which indicates what the objects represent, is attached.

The thought-picture theory.

1. We picture facts to ourselves (2.1).
2. The logical picture of a fact is a thought (cfr. *Tractatus,* 3).
3. A thought 'p' and the corresponding proposition p only differ from each other in respect of the elements which constitute them.
4. 'p' and p exemplify, or manifest one and the same structure.
5. Any proposition is a W-proposition. O-propositions do not exist, i. e. it is nonsense that a proposition is a picture whether it is thought of or not. Whenever p occurs (and not p_m only) this is due to the occurrence of 'p'.
6. A proposition is a configuration of objects. The relations these have to one another show what the proposition pictures.

The divergence between the two theories in respect of 5. may be illustrated by the following example. Let us say that a person utters a number of propositions and at the same time has a number of thoughts. Possibly he sometimes thinks of what he is saying, and at other times thinks of something quite different from the proposition he is actually uttering. The situation may, for instance, be this:

	a ↙		b ↙				d ↙				
propositional signs:	a_m	-	b_m	-	c_m	-	d_m	-	e_m	-	f_m
- - - - - - - -											
thoughts (pictures):	'a'	-	'b'	-	'n'	-	'd'	-	'p'	-	'i'

When sign 'a_m' is uttered simultaneously with the occurrence of thought 'a', a_m becomes a proposition: a. This implies that the thought 'a' at this moment appears as a and that a consequently is a W-proposition. The same is true of b_m and d_m. In the case of c_m the person is not thinking 'c' but another thought 'n' and c_m consequently remains a mere physical fact, a fact of acoustics on a par with an unintended sneeze or cough. Indeed, c_m is not even a propositional sign for we only speak of propositional signs in connection with propositions. If c_m was used for expressing a thought, c_m would in a sense become the thought, but the physical aspects of this thought would be the propositional sign. These features of c_m are repeated in e_m and f_m too in the example considered. The essential point is that propositions can never occur except in connection with a mind. In order that a propositional sign can be turned into a picture it is necessary that a person experiences the sign in a certain way. If I look at a page in a book, I perceive a number of propositional signs. If I start reading the text in the book the propositional signs will become propositions while I am 'reading' them. In reading I successively think the sense of the sentences of the book and follow linguistic conventions while doing this. When my eyes have left a proposition this is again a mere physical fact. *Sense is always connected with what is experienced at the moment. When the propositional signs are not applied, i. e. do not function as substitutes for the psychical elements of the thoughts, they are not pictures of anything but plain facts. According to the O-proposition-picture theory they must, on the contrary, always be pictures solely by virtue of the fact that they have structure in common with the facts they picture.*

I should here like to point out a psychological peculiarity which attaches to the thought as a picture. As mentioned above, a thought *deals with* or *concerns* something other than itself. A thought is always a picture of a state of affairs. This implies that a person thinking 'p' must in some way experience p_s as well. Let us say that p_s is the situation that the flower is yellow. Then 'p' is a picture of this fact. Only 'p' occurs in the mind, not the flower itself, but it is the flower I am thinking of. When asked: What are you thinking of at the moment, the correct answer is: *that* the flower is yellow, or, which is the same, p_s. If p_s, as in this case, is a physical fact, then it consists of physical objects, but if Wittgenstein adheres to phenomenalism, p_s should rather be spoken of as a phenomenon having an objective character. The objects of 'p' represent the objects of p_s. The structure of 'p' however, does not represent the structure of p_s, for the structure of 'p' is a structure in which p_s participates. But what do we mean by saying that 'p' describes p_s? *It cannot be sufficient to say that in 'p' the structure of p_s is reproduced, for the mere reproduction of it does not give us a description of p_s.*

The answer to this question is a psychological one. In Jørgensen's *Psykologi på biologisk grundlag* (pp. 243 ff), a set of concepts can be found which are relevant to this problem. Jørgensen distinguishes between received' and 'symbolized' phenomena. A 'received' phenomenon is something which is only received through one of the senses without being associated with other phenomena by the recipient. A 'symbolized' phenomenon on the other hand, is a phenomenon which points to or refers to something other than itself, and as this peculiarity is not caused by something in the phenomenon itself it must be explained by reference to the attitude of the perceiving person. Consequently a phenomenon can only be a symbol in a person's experience if the person himself, when the phenomenon occurs, is led to think of another phenomenon. It is a psychological fact that one can shift between a 'symbolizing' and a 'receiving' attitude. For instance, when I hear the word 'flower' I may immediately think of the yellow flower, but by an act of will can change my attitude, so that I no longer hear the word 'flower' as a symbol, but as a fact of acoustics. In this case my attitude is 'receiving'. I merely receive the noise 'flower' and perceive it as a series of sounds.

It seems that it is a psychological view of this kind which is implied in Wittgenstein's idea of the thought as a picture. Certainly, he writes that a name can only have a meaning when forming part of a proposition and that in itself it is a meaningless sign, but he seems to think that the elements of the picture are directly representing phenomena so that they provoke a certain symbolizing attitude in the thinking person. This means to say that the elements of the picture are only experienced after closer consideration. What we immediately experience when we think of something is the elements of the imagined state of affairs. This is because we have learnt the meanings of the words (cfr. 4.024-4.026) and therefore automatically think without noticing the elements of the thought.

It is clear, though, that when we are taught the names of various objects we learn nothing about the objects themselves. Objects cannot be described but only named. The picture as a whole does not tell us anything about the elements of the pictured fact. Knowledge of all the facts, which an object can form part of, however, may give us some information about the nature of the object, for as 2.0123 reads: 'If I know an object I also know all its possible occurrences in states of affairs . . .'. This is the way our knowledge of the world is built up. Neither the objects nor the structures of the facts are describable. Structure or logical form can only be shown: 'Propositions can represent the whole of reality, but they cannot represent what they must have in common with reality in order to be able to represent it — logical form. / In order to be able to represent logical form, we should have to be able to station ourselves with propositions somewhere outside logic, that is to say outside the world.' (4.12).

So a thought or a W-proposition shows the structure of a fact or a state of affairs. At the same time, as a result of practice, we perceive in some way or other the elements of the state of affairs whenever the elements of the thought are present. The elements of a thought we only perceive by altering our ordinary attitude in a certain way. Otherwise we actually think of or imagine p_s and not '*p*'.

We are now able to understand a little better why false propositions can be pictures in spite of their falsity. When thinking '*p*' we directly envisage a state of affairs p_s. The thought 'intends' something which is not a part of the empirical 'soul' or ego (this conception will be explained below) in that this something is not identical with the thought itself. Wittgenstein prefers to speak of a logical space which is a sort of fictitious sphere of phenomena containing all those states of affairs we directly imagine or experience when we have thoughts. Even if *'p'* should appear to be false, we experience p_s nevertheless when thinking *'p'*, and the imagined p_s and *'p'* will always have an isomorphic relation to one another. As said before, Wittgenstein's contention that states of affairs consist of objects does not harmonize with his view that objects make up the substance of the world. It would be more reasonable to say that p_s consists of imagined objects in the logical space. Although *'p'* may be false, it can, nevertheless, very well be an isomorphic picture of p_s. It appears to be false only because nothing in the world is similar to the imagined p_s. Thus we can, without contradicting ourselves, speak of false elementary propositions that do not contain a negation-sign. In this case, a false elementary proposition will be on level with a true one. If we think that something is the case the thought immediately puts out feelers, as it were, in the logical space 'feelers of the picture's elements, with which the picture touches reality' (2.1515). When we think of a state of affairs we never meet with elements which correspond with the negation-sign.

Since Stenius has adhered to an O-proposition-picture theory it has been impossible for him to give a satisfying account of the character of false propositions. As mentioned above, an articulate field *F* can, according to Stenius, be conceived of as a picture of an articulate field *G* if a key of interpretation (*C*), according to which the elements of *F* can be regarded as representatives of the elements of *G*, can be found. The picture *F* is called true or false according to whether it is an isomorphic picture of *G* in respect of (*C*) or not (*Wittgenstein's 'Tractatus'*, p. 96). This definition seems to me misleading. It seems perfectly clear that Wittgenstein had the opinion that false propositions are isomorphic pictures of states of affairs. If *F* is a proposition (or rather a propositional sign) and *G* a state of affairs, then *F* either is or is not a picture of *G*. If *F is* a picture of *G* this implies that the elements of *F* one by one represent the elements of *G* and that *F* and *G* have the same structure. The statements 2.13, 2.131, 2.15, 2.16, 2.161, 2.17, 2.2, 2.201, 2.22, 2.223, and many others of the *Tractatus*, unmistakably show this. If Stenius was right the relation mentioned should be taken to mean that *F* is a *true* picture of *G*. But this is impossible. One of Wittgenstein's fundamental ideas is that 'It is impossible to tell from the picture alone whether it is true or false.' (2.224). If *F* is not an isomorphic picture of *G* it is not a picture of *G* at all but of some other state of affairs. If one wants to sustain the view that *F* is a picture of *G* in this case, one might as well say that *F* is a picture of every state of affairs which has the same 'internal' structure as *F*. Stenius has overlooked the fact that a proposition is a picture 'spontaneously', an isomorphic representation of something other than itself, even if this exists perhaps only in a logical space and not as a physical fact. As 4.022 has it: 'A proposition *shows* its sense. / A proposition *shows* how things stand *if* it is true. And it *says that* they do so stand'. How should *F* be able to show how 'things stand' if *F* can be read in different ways according to whether it is true or false. 4.022 claims that a proposition can only be read in one way. It excludes the possibility of reading a proposition in more than one way.

Miss Anscombe also adheres to the O-proposition-picture theory, when she writes: 'Thus there are two distinct features belonging to a picture (in the ordinary sense of 'picture'): first, the relation between the elements of the picture; and second, the correlations of the elements in the picture with things outside the picture; . . . The correlating is not something that the picture itself does; it is something we do . . . Now confining ourselves to pictures, it is also clear that if we 'think the sense of the picture' by correlating its element with actual objects, we can in fact think it in either of *two* ways: namely either as depicting what is the case, or as depicting what isn't the case. That is to say, there are two senses which we can 'think' in connection with the picture. For it is the very same picture we hold up if we wish to say that *it* holds or that *it* doesn't hold.' (*An Introduction,* pp. 68-69). She has not overlooked 2.1513: 'So a picture conceived in this way, also includes the pictorial relationship, which makes it into a picture,' but she maintains that Ogdens translation (which reads: 'According to this conception, the picture must have in addition the depicting relation which makes it into a picture,') can be misleading and is based on a wrong interpretation made by Ramsey. Ramsey wrote in his *Foundations of Mathematics,* p. 271 that the elements 'are coordinated with the objects by the representing relation which belongs to the picture', but according to Anscombe 'this interpretation throws Wittgenstein's quite straightforward idea into obscurity; the sentence has no such obscurity for educated native speakers of German.' It seems that Miss Anscombe has felt a difficulty at this point but tried unsuccessfully to exorcise it.

Miss Anscombe makes the same mistake as Stenius, perhaps in a more crude version. She considers Wittgenstein's example in the *Notebooks,* p. 7:

and writes: 'if I have correlated the right-hand figure with a man *A*, and the left-hand figure with a man *B*, then I can hold the picture up and say: 'This is how things are.' But I can just as well hold the picture up and say: 'This is how things aren't.'

This view of the matter is extremely inconsistent with the thesis of extensionality. The picture may be rendered by the proposition '*A* is fencing with *B*'. But a compound expression such as 'This is how things are: *A* is fencing with *B*' is, according to Wittgenstein, neither a truth-function nor an elementary proposition, no more than the expression,' '*A* is fencing with B' is true', is. When Wittgenstein states that a proposition shows how things stand *if* it is true, then to hold the proposition up and say 'This is how things aren't' amounts to saying $p\uparrow\downarrow$, and this is, as shown above, a sign-combination which cannot be allowed according to the picture theory.

Apparently Anscombe, like Stenius, thinks that it is possible to form propositions with sense about the relation between the picture and the pictured state of affairs. It should be understood that the essential point of the picture theory is that this cannot be done, and that any sentence can be understood without further explanation. This is why propositions are compared with pictures (one of the first comparisons Wittgenstein makes is with the demonstration of traffic accidents in the court in Paris by means of dolls, *vide Notebooks*, p. 7). If a theory of meaning of this sort could not have been established, Wittgenstein would have been forced to give up his extensional view of logic. For according to this no proposition can deal with any other. It is not a valid objection to this that Wittgenstein himself writes about the relation between the picture and the pictured fact. For, firstly, he has carefully avoided all talk of laws of projection and keys of interpretation. Secondly, the statements in the *Tractatus* are not propositions but pseudo-propositions or elucidations (Erläuterungen) which are neither true nor false but nonsensical (cfr. 4.112 and 6.54). The statements of the *Tractatus* are, as I will explain in detail further on, a kind of acoustic means of making the reader understand how everything concerning logic and semantics is to be conceived of. One might compare them with certain movements a person has to do in order to perceive a certain thing. If a man in the street asks me where the University of Copenhagen is I may, instead of explaining it to him, take his hand and lead him to the university. In this way I lead him to a result, to perceive something, without forming any propositions. It must be noticed that the elucidations of the *Tractatus* are never characterized as propositions which must be known in order to understand the picture theory. On the contrary a person might very well have recognized the picture theory as valid without ever having had it explained to him for it is a theory which has to be *seen* or *perceived* and not deduced from certain premisses. None of the statements of the *Tractatus* form part of an argumentation in favour of the picture theory for it does not really rest on any arguments, according to Wittgenstein. This it would do, however, if one was forced to speak of laws of projection in connection with the relation between a proposition and the pictured fact, for the propositions about these matters would have to be true in some sense or other if the picture theory was to be valid. But, as I hope I have pointed out clearly, this they could never be if it *was* valid.

b. Wittgenstein's concept of 'mind'.

When speaking of thoughts it is reasonable to class them in a sphere different from what we call 'the external world', no matter whether we regard this as having an objective existence or not. For in the sensuous experience we do not meet with thoughts, but only with facts. Since the days of Descartes it has been customary to place thoughts in a substance called the mind and as Wittgenstein follows traditional pathways in his way of thinking about ontological and psychological matters, it seems natural to ask how he conceives of the mind.

Stenius has pointed out (*Wittgenstein's 'Tractatus'*, pp. 220-21) that in reading the *Tractatus* it is essential to distinguish between two 'subjects' or 'egos', namely between what in the following will be named respectively *an empirical ego* and *a metaphysical subject*. The evidence for this is the third part of 5.641 which runs as follows: 'The philosophical self is not the human being, not the human body, or the human soul, with which psychology deals, but rather the metaphysical subject, the limit of the world — not a part of it.' Here the two egos are mentioned side by side, 'the human soul, with which psychology deals' corresponding to what Stenius calls the empirical ego. As I have shown above Wittgenstein makes use of the concept of 'thought', and the question is whether thoughts occur in the empirical ego or in some way or other form part of the metaphysical subject. As far as I can see, the answer must be that thoughts belong to the domain of the empirical ego or, to put it in another way, constitute the empirical ego. I have mentioned before that Wittgenstein in a letter to Russell writes that a thought consists of 'psychical constituents'. In 5.641, 'the human soul' is spoken of as the soul 'with which psychology deals', and from this we can see that the constituents of the thought belong to the material of psychology.

Wittgenstein definitely never imagined that thoughts 'belonged to' or 'formed part of' the metaphysical subject. For this is unambiguously characterized as non-composite. 'The subject does not belong to the world: rather it is a limit of the world.' is said in 5.632. This characteristic is repeated in 5.641, and in 5.64 it is said that 'the self of solipsism shrinks to a point without extension' (In chapter V, *a*. I will give reasons why this self must be the metaphysical subject). If the metaphysical subject does not belong to the world, clearly it cannot contain thoughts. For thoughts are pictures (3) and pictures are facts (2.141) and the world is made up of *all* the facts that can be found (cfr. 1, 1.1 and 1.11). Furthermore, thoughts, like other facts, must be compound whereas the metaphysical subject is simple. How could something simple possibly contain something which is not simple? Finally Wittgenstein himself states that the subject neither thinks nor has ideas: 'There is no such thing as the subject that thinks or entertains ideas.' (5.641). From the second part of 5.631 it can be seen that he is speaking here of the metaphysical subject, the subject which does not belong to the world.

I therefore do not agree with Stenius when he writes: 'For Wittgenstein too, the form of experience is 'subjective' in the transcendental sense, the metaphysical subject being the 'subject' which uses and understands language, and which must be distinguished from the empirical subject, which is part of the world describable in language.' To 'use and understand language' is, as pointed out above, to think. The metaphysical subject does not think in the sense that it forms thoughts independent of experience. Because thoughts are facts, they must belong to the world, and as we never meet with them in our sensuous experience they must form parts of the empirical ego, the subject-matter of psychology.

The two egos are fundamentally different. The empirical ego thinks and entertains ideas. The metaphysical subject does neither. The empirical ego is a part of the world (5.641). The metaphysical subject does not belong to the world but is a limit of the world (5.632). The empirical ego is complex, a combination of elements, whereas the metaphysical subject is simple.

In *Notebooks,* some attempts at the formulations in the *Tractatus* dealing with the metaphysical subject can be found. A determination of it begins on pp. 72-73. Here the subject or the I (the two designations are synonymous whereever Wittgenstein applies them) is contrasted to the world: 'I know that this world exists. That I am placed in it like my eye in its visual field.' Some remarks about the will can also be found. On page 74 the point that the I is something different from the world is emphasized: 'There are two godheads: the world and my independent I.' On page 79 it is maintained, as in 5.632, that the I is a limit of the world, and, shortly after, that 'The subject is not a part of the world but a presupposition of its existence . . .' On page 80 it is said that 'The I is not an object. / I objectively confront every object. But not the I.' And it is 'concluded': 'So there really is a way in which there can and must be mention of the I in a *non-psychological sense* in philosophy.' On page 79 the subject is characterized, as in 5.632, as a limit of the world and on page 82 the first formulation of 5.641 is presented: 'The philosophical I is not the human being, not the human body or *the human soul with the psychological properties,* but the metaphysical subject, the boundary (not a part) of the world . . .' The corresponding passage in 5.641 reads: 'The philosophical self (Pears and McGuinness prefer to translate 'Ich' into 'self') is not the human being, not the human body, or *the human soul, with which psychology deals,* but rather the metaphysical subject, the limit of the world — not a part of it. (My italics. They mark what is different in the two texts in the German version). From this it clearly appears that Wittgenstein speaks of an empirical ego as the subject-matter of psychology. The metaphysical subject lies beyond this and, as mentioned, it neither thinks nor entertains ideas. In *Notebooks* he even says that it cannot have knowledge: 'It is true that the knowing subject is not in the world, that there is no knowing subject.' (p. 86). It is difficult to see what knowing means in this connection. Later I will try to show that in a certain sense the metaphysical subject can comprehend something but that it cannot 'think' (in the *Tractatus*-sense of this word). Here Wittgenstein seems to conceive of the subject as only a willing subject. On page 80 he writes: 'The thinking subject is surely mere illusion. But the willing subject exists.' On page 87 he writes: 'The subject is the willing subject' and in other places too, (e. g. p. 79), the subject is characterized thus.

But the circumstance that the subject is a willing subject does not mean that it must belong to the world. 6.373 reads: 'The world is independent of my will.' and in 6.374 this is explained in the following way: 'Even if all that we wish for were to happen, still this would only be a favour granted by fate, so to speak: for there is no *logical* connexion between the will and the world, which would guarantee it, and the supposed physical connexion itself is surely not something that we could will.' (The last part is an inadequate rendering of 'könnten wir doch nicht selbst wieder wollen.'). The view expressed here is connected with the Humean scepticism advanced in 6.37: 'There is no compulsion making one thing happen because another has happened. The only necessity that exists is *logical necessity.*' The idea here is that if we can find no sufficient reason why one physical event should follow another, we cannot guarantee what sort of physical event will be the consequence of an act of will. This circumstance has paradoxical consequences in connection with ethics. If I adhere to Hume's scepticism, I must admit that I can never guarantee that I am able to do a good or a bad deed. Let us say that I take a walk and suddenly see a child drowning in a lake. Even though I *wish* to help the child, it may happen that my act of will leads to quite other actions than those intended and expected (for the same reasons for which one billiard ball's impact on the other in Hume's example may be followed by any imaginable event). It is possible that my wish to help the child will result in the act of throwing stones at is. Only if a *logical* connection between the act of will and action could be found, could I be sure that my decision about helping the child will lead to the action of helping it. But a logical connection cannot possibly be found (because, according to Wittgenstein, all states of affairs are logically independent of each other), so one can indeed only hope that the actions he wishes to perform actually occur. If I wish to help a distressed child, I may hope that the events in the physical world accidentally follow each other in such a way that my body tries to save the child. If they do, this circumstance is truly a 'favour granted by fate'.

This is the reason why, in Wittgenstein's opinion, we cannot speak of good and bad, or right and wrong actions. Ethical predicates only concern the will independently of its connection with the world. When in our daily life we speak of 'a good deed', the deed is logically purely accidental since no sufficient reason for it can be found. It is possible to speak of something ethically necessary only if we hereby refer to the will as a *prima causa* which is not dependent on anything other than itself. In this case the will must lie 'outside' the world, beyond the constant conjunction of events. Consequently it becomes irrelevant to introduce hypothetical imperatives (cfr. 6.422). But when ethical judgments can only concern the will, and when this as a feature of the metaphysical subject lies outside the world, it follows that ethical judgments cannot be formulated. For only propositions which describe a state of affairs in the world can have sense. No elementary proposition can describe the will for it is neither an object nor a state of affairs. As a consequence of the picture theory we are precluded from saying anything about the will or anything else which is 'outside', — or, as Wittgenstein occasionally says, 'higher than' — the world. 6.42 expresses this: 'And so it is impossible for there to be propositions of ethics. / Propositions can express nothing of what is higher.' In 6.421 it is said that 'It is clear that ethics cannot be put into words. / Ethics is transcendental.' and 6.423 reads: 'It is impossible to speak about the will in so far as it is the subject of ethical attributes. / And the will as a phenomenon is of interest only to psychology.'

Obviously Wittgenstein is influenced at this point by Schopenhauer (whom he mentions in the *Notebooks*, p. 79). But I do not think that the obscure remarks on the willing subject in the *Notebooks* can be explained by looking for their background in Schopenhauer's philosophy. Actually it is only the problems and the subject-matter of their reflections that Wittgenstein and Schopenhauer have in common. Schopenhauer regards the body as the product and instrument of the will, whereas Wittgenstein regards it as independent of the will. Moreover, we find no suggestions of the idea that the will is the 'Ding an sich', in Wittgenstein's reasons for the peculiar theory of the willing subject. Possibly he has only aimed at explaining where propositions concerning ethical, aesthetic and religious problems are to be placed, after we have seen that only the propositions of natural science can have sense, according to the picture theory. They cannot be elementary propositions but in an everyday sense they have some sort of 'content', and the question is then what sort of existence the things they deal with can have. On the other hand Wittgenstein may have begun by reflecting on Schopenhauer's philosophy and have arrived hereby at a personal view about a willing, metaphysical subject. I mention this here because I shall later examine Wittgenstein's reasons for introducing a metaphysical subject. Besides the motives I will consider then, the speculations about the will have some importance although their origins cannot be found.

We must not be distracted by the fact that Wittgenstein writes in 5.631 that the metaphysical subject does not exist. The last paragraph of 5.631 reads: 'If I wrote a book called *The World as I found it,* I should have to include a report on my body, and should have to say which parts were subordinate to my will, and which were not, etc., this being a method of isolating the subject, or rather of showing that in an important sense there is no subject; for it alone could *not* be mentioned in that book. —' The idea surely is that if a person starts investigating which parts of the body are subordinate to his will, he will — in succession — realize that not one single action can be said to be a necessary consequence of a decision or act of will. Consequently he must come to the result that everything in the world is independent of his will (6.373). But even though the willing subject becomes in this way isolated from all events in the world, and therefore must lie 'outside' the world, it still exists in a special sense. It is only in 'an important sense' that the subject does not exist. I will return to the problem in what sense it can be said to exist. It is not appropriate to analyse Wittgenstein's text, and especially his use of the word 'mine' in 5.6 and 5.63, on the basis of the supposition that Wittgenstein denies the existence of the ego, as, for instance, Barone does (*vide Il neopositivismo logico,* p. 112).

I have mentioned that Wittgenstein's conceptions of thought and picture imply that the metaphysical subject cannot think; thoughts cannot 'belong to' the metaphysical subject as long as they are conceived of as facts, for the world is *the totality* of facts (cfr. 1.1 and 1.11). I have also mentioned that Stenius believes that the metaphysical subject does think (that it is the subject which uses and understands language). A similar view can be found in Jaakko Hintikka's article *On Wittgenstein's 'solipsism'*. Hintikka, like Stenius, distinguishes between the empirical ego and the metaphysical subject, but in my opinion he is mistaken in his characterization of the metaphysical subject as 'a complex not unlike a totality of propositions'

(p. 90). Later he writes: 'Perhaps a more natural way of saying that Wittgenstein identified the metaphysical subject with a totality of propositions would be to say that he identified it with a totality of *thoughts*' (p. 90), but otherwise he maintains that it makes no difference whether one speaks of thoughts or propositions. Hintikka founds his view on an analysis of 5.541–5.5421 to which I will return. Unfortunately he does not test his conception of the metaphysical subject by means of the paragraphs from the *Tractatus* quoted above in which Wittgenstein speaks of the subject as something simple, a point without extension. He seems to have mistaken the problem of the relation between the limits of the subject and the limits of language for the problem of the relation between the language and the subject themselves. It may be true that 'the only way of drawing the limits of the metaphysical subject seems to be to identify them with the limits of my language' (p. 90) (I will examine this problem in detail in chapter V), but from this it cannot be inferred that the metaphysical subject can be identified with 'the totality of one's language' (p. 91). Later I will show that the problem is much more complicated. On page 91, Hintikka writes: 'This is the basis of Wittgenstein's 'solipsism'. Having identified the metaphysical subject with the totality of one's language and the limits of language with the limits of the world, he could say that the limits of the (metaphysical) subject are the limits of the world. 'I am my world."' But the world is complex and, therefore, so is language. How, then, can Hintikka give an explanation of Wittgenstein's idea, which occurs in more than one place, that the metaphysical subject is simple, unextended?

On similar lines, Maslow characterizes the metaphysical subject as the formal limit of language (*A Study*, p. 149). Maslow believes — as does Stenius — that the subject plays the same part as Kant's 'transcendental apperception' (cfr. *Kritik der reinen Vernunft*, A 107–108). This is a very controversial view which I will deal with in the chapter about Wittgenstein's solipsism. According to Maslow the subject cannot be an entity. Therefore it must be some sort of pseudo-concept, as Weinberg also thinks (*An Examination*, p. 201). So here he dissociates himself from the view that the I is complex, because it is naturally nonsense to discuss whether a formal determination is complex or not.

One *could* ask whether Wittgenstein had serious reasons for denying that the metaphysical subject is able to think. I think it is very probable that he had. That it had to be simple is no reason. Why should we not be able to assume that the metaphysical subject in some sense or other was complex? But reasons of quite another sort can be found and although I will consider them further on, I should like to mention one of them here: in order to determine whether an elementary proposition is true or false we must compare it with reality (or, more correctly, with the world). If the state of affairs described in the proposition exists, the proposition is true. If not, it is false. When a proposition is compared with reality there must exist something which compares the two entities in question. For the picture cannot compare itself with reality. If we assume that the metaphysical subject thinks, i. e. 'pictures facts to itself' (and we must have in mind here that thought or W-proposition — and not O-proposition — is what is to be compared with reality), then we are obliged to maintain either that the subject itself compares its thoughts with reality or else that there is something above or beyond it which compares thoughts with reality. If we say that the subject itself compares the thoughts it has with reality, this can be understood in two ways: either it consists of more than thoughts or else one thought can compare another (for instance the one that occurs just before it) with reality. If we accept the first of these two possibilities, we thereby maintain that the metaphysical subject is more than the thoughts, that besides these it consists of an essential part. If we accept the second possibility we contradict the thesis of extensionality which excludes the fact that one thought (or W-proposition) deals with another. If we on the other hand maintain that something above or beyond the metaphysical subject can be found and this new entity can compare the subject's thoughts with reality, then this entity cannot think or entertain ideas, because we would otherwise become involved in an infinite regress.

Wittgenstein said about the metaphysical subject that it was not a thinking subject. Hereby the thoughts are classed with the empirical ego. His choice between the mentioned possibilities results in that the empirical ego forms pictures of states of affairs, i. e. thinks. The metaphysical subject compares these thoughts with reality in order to determine whether they are true or false. But the metaphysical subject does not think. If it did, the existence of a supermetaphysical subject has to be assumed, or else we could not compare the thoughts of the metaphysical subject with their subject-matter. Since the metaphysical subject does not think and the thoughts of the empirical ego cannot deal with one another all forms of meta-language are precluded, and this impossibility of a meta-language is already inferred from the thesis of extensionality. Whether Wittgenstein assumed on these grounds that a metaphysical subject must exist is, as far as I can see, an insoluble question. I wish only to point out that the metaphysical subject cannot possibly think or entertain ideas, if the unity in Wittgenstein's system is to be preserved. But it is clear that, in a certain sense, it *has* knowledge, because to compare propositions with reality and decide whether they are true or false is to receive knowledge. But the kind of knowledge the subject can obtain is, as I will show further on, always of something which can only be shown and consequently can never be described (cfr. 4.1212: 'What *can* be shown, *cannot* be said').

*

According to what I have said, Wittgenstein's theory of the relation between language and thought, and the theory of mind implied by this, must have developed relatively late, namely between January, 1917, and some time in 1918 when the *Tractatus* was completed. I presume that Wittgenstein never got to the bottom of these problems but was content with a sketchy view of them. It seems as if he realized that the concept of thought was indispensable for the establishment of a theory of meaning. In *The Blue Book* we have an indication that he was acquainted with this view. He starts there by discussing exactly the problems discussed here and he considers some views which fit hand-in-glove into the conceptions in the *Tractatus*. We may regard the following passage: 'We are tempted to think that the action of language consists of two parts; an inorganic part, the handling of signs, and an organic part, which we may call understanding these signs, meaning them, interpreting them, thinking. These latter activities seem to take place in a queer kind of medium, the mind; and the mechanism of the mind, the nature of which, it seems, we don't quite understand, can bring about effects which no material mechanism could. Thus e. g. a thought (which is such a mental process) can agree or disagree with reality; I am able to think of a man who isn't present; I am able to imagine him, 'mean him' in a remark which I make about him, even if he is thousands of miles away or dead.' (pp. 3 - 4). Later he writes: 'Without a sense, or without the thought, a proposition would be an utterly dead and trivial thing. And further it seems clear that no adding of inorganic signs can make the proposition live. And the conclusion which one draws from this is that what must be added to the dead signs in order to make a live proposition is something immaterial, with properties different from all mere signs.' (p. 4), and furthermore: 'It seems at first sight that that which gives to thinking its peculiar character is that it is a train of mental states, and it seems that what is queer and difficult to understand about thinking is the processes which happen in the medium of the mind, processes possible only in this medium.' (p. 5).

Here we are presented with one of the most convincing reasons for preferring the thought-picture theory to the O-proposition-picture theory. Without thoughts, propositions would be dead and trivial things. They would be no more than inorganic signs on paper, and no matter what inorganic signs we added to them (for instance Frege's judgment-stroke or the expression 'It is true that . . .') they would still remain dead things which did not picture anything. Not until we think the sense of the proposition do the dead signs obtain a projective relation to some further thing (cfr. 3.11). I have shown that this view is expressed in the *Tractatus*. It inevitably implies a dualistic view: thoughts must be entities which are fundamentally different from inorganic signs. Therefore they cannot be classed with the physical world for in this we meet only with 'inorganic' signs. Consequently they must exist in 'a queer kind of medium, the mind'. It is this medium which in the *Tractatus* is called 'the human soul, with which psychology deals' and which I call 'the empirical ego'. It must necessarily have some qualities which cannot be ascribed to material or physical objects. 'The mechanism of the mind .... can bring about effects which no material mechanism could.' The essential thing which the empirical ego has in preference to the dead signs is the possibility of making pictures of states of affairs. The picture theory maintains that an elementary proposition is a picture. A proposition, however, cannot, so to speak, single-handed be a picture of anything (O-propositions cannot be found). Hence something above or beyond the propositions which is able to picture something must exist. This 'something' is thoughts. Contrary to what in everyday language we call 'propositions', thoughts can, as Wittgenstein says in *The Blue Book* 'agree or disagree with reality'. They can do this, as I said, in virtue of their pointing to something different from themselves. I am able to think of a person who is not present, to imagine him or 'mean him'. Here no new signs are needed, neither organic nor inorganic, in order that the thought can become a picture of something. A thought is *qua* thought a picture which into the bargain includes the pictorial relationship (cfr. 2.1513). In virtue of this those entities which we normally call propositions can be made into pictures of something by letting the elements of the propositional sign replace the elements of the thought.

The introduction of the concept of 'thought' in the picture theory necessitates a theory of the mind for 'thinking is the processes which happen in the medium of the mind, processes possible only in this medium.' Wittgenstein has also felt that this theory becomes 'queer and difficult', and probably this is the main reason why we hear no more about the empirical ego in the *Tractatus* than we do. In *The Blue Book* Wittgenstein settles with his former view. All that he says here consists of examples showing which problems the picture theory causes, and from the beginning we are told that the way the dead signs of language obtain a meaning does not consist in their having a connection with thoughts but in using them in a certain way (like using tools, chess pieces, etc. in a certain way). 'But if we had to name anything which is the life of the sign, we should have to say that it was its *use*', writes Wittgenstein on page 4, immediately after the paragraph about thoughts as pictures. Later on in *The Blue Book* the question what it is to think is one of the main themes of the book.

*

Some readers of this book may ask whether Wittgenstein in his remarks on the concept of thought is indebted to Frege. At first glance, this seems to be possible. In the preface of the *Tractatus* Wittgenstein mentions that he has read Frege's 'great works' and some have maintained that the *Tractatus* can only be fully understood in the light of Frege's writings. For instance Miss Anscombe writes: 'Wittgenstein's *Tractatus* has captured the interest and excited the admiration of many, yet almost all that has been published about it has been wildly irrelevant. If this has had any one cause, that cause has been the neglect of Frege and of the new direction that he gave to philosophy.' (*An Introduction*, p. 12).

At the risk of being 'wildly irrelevant' I would maintain, however, that Wittgenstein's concept of a thought has nothing to do with Frege's viewpoints. On the contrary Wittgenstein's view of the relation between language and thought suggests that he had only fragmentary knowledge of Frege's 'great works'. In many small articles from the period 1892 - 1923, Frege deals with the concept of thought and says things about it so definite that one would expect Wittgenstein's viewpoints to contain an attitude to Frege's, if he had read these articles. Indeed, the most essential of Frege's papers on 'thought' are published too late to have any influence on the development of Wittgenstein's ideas. I am here thinking of the articles *Der Gedanke* (1918), *Die Verneinung* (1919) and *Gedankengefüge* (1923). But in a number of previous papers Frege has essential remarks on the concept of 'thought'.

In *On Sense and Reference* Frege maintains that a thought is the sense (Sinn) of a proposition, and that a thought is not 'the subjective performance of thinking but its objective content, which is capable of being the common property of several thinkers.' (p. 62). Already, in his review of Husserl's *Philosophie der Arithmetik* of 1894, Frege suggests this view: '. . . . one and the same thought can be grasped by many men. The constituents of the thought, and *a fortiori* things themselves, must be distinguished from the images that accompany in some mind the act of grasping the thought — images that each man forms of things.' (p. 79). There is a great gap between this view and the one in the *Tractatus*. According to Wittgenstein the thought is a picture and consequently something subjective. According to Frege the thought is what the proposition describes and consequently it is something objective. And the gap between the views of the two authors becomes even greater if we consider Frege's *Die Verneinung* which Wittgenstein could have known in manuscript before he accomplished the *Tractatus*. In *Die Vernei-*

nung (*Negation*) Frege writes (p. 128): '... negation ... is part of a thought and as such, like the thought itself, it needs no owner, must not be regarded as a content of consciousness.' In the *Tractatus* it is considered impossible for the sign of negation to form part of a thought. The sign indicates only an operation done by a person. In *Der Gedanke*, which Wittgenstein may also have read in manuscript, Frege elaborates his concept of 'thought' without dispensing with his previous remarks on it. Nor in this article do we find any viewpoints resembling ideas of the *Tractatus*. And *vice versa* in the *Tractatus* we do not find any hint about the complex of problems which Frege attacks in *Der Gedanke*.

My conclusion is, therefore, that Wittgenstein in his reflections on the concept of 'thought' is in no way influenced by Frege. As mentioned above, it looks as if Wittgenstein has discovered independently that his concept of a proposition presupposes a concept of 'thought' in the way he describes in *The Blue Book*. It is also worth noticing that in *The Blue Book* he does not refer to Frege either. When he speaks of Frege's 'great works' he must primarily be thinking of the logical-mathematical writings from the period 1879 - 93.

c. Wittgenstein's explanation of propositions of the form 'A says p'.

In her book *An Introduction to Wittgenstein's Tractatus*, Miss Anscombe enumerates the problems which have to be settled if we accept that Wittgenstein's picture theory is a general theory of meaning. She lists the following types of propositions which all have to be examined: 'Laws of inference, and, generally, logical truths. / Statements that one proposition implies another. / Generality — i. e. propositions containing 'all' and 'some'. / Propositions giving logical classifications of terms and expressions ... / Propositions that are important in the foundations of mathematics such as 'a is the successor of b'. / Statements about the possibility, impossibility, necessity, and certainty of particular states of affairs. / Statements of identity. / Propositions apparantly expressing functions of propositions, such as 'it is good that *p*', or '*p* is possible', '*p* is necessary' or again '*A* believes *p*' or '*A* conceives *p*'; and perhaps even statements about e. g. the beauty of pictures. / Propositions stating probabilities. / Propositions of mathematics. / Propositions stating laws of nature. / Propositions about space and time. / Egocentric propositions. / Propositions about the world as a whole, about God and the meaning of life.' As will be understood from the first chapter in this book, it is the thesis of extensionality rather than the picture theory which necessitates an explanation of these types of propositions. For on the face of it they are all in conflict with that thesis. None of them seem to be truth-functions.

In the discussions caused by the *Principia Mathematica* and the *Tractatus*, some types of propositions have attracted the attention more than others. These are the rules of inference, the general propositional forms [$(Ex)f(x)$ and $(x)f(x)$], the statements of identity and probability, and the propositions of the type '*A* believes *p*'. In the following, I will deal only with the last kind of proposition.

It can easily be seen that Russell and Whitehead believed that only the general propositions and propositions of the type '*A* believes *p*' were of particular interest. In some early works Russell advanced a theory about propositions of the type '*A* believes *p*' which were said to express so-called 'propositional attitudes'. In the first edition of the *Principia Mathematica*, he had arrived at the view that propositions of this kind could not be considered truth-functions, and the extensional view of language was consequently limited, to comprise only mathematics and mathematical logic. At the time of the second edition of the book, no greater clarity had been obtained, but, strange to say, Wittgenstein's theory of these propositions in the *Tractatus* is accepted although the authors of the *Principia* obviously have not understood this theory at all. In this edition the thesis of extensionality is regarded as a possible improvement of logistics. The reason why an improvement is desirable is that the so-called 'axiom of reducibility' in the first edition functions as a seemingly indispensable axiom although it has in part an ontological character and in part seems quite unreasonable. According to this axiom if an arbitrary function fx is given, then a formally equivalent predicative function can always be found. This means that in the case that fx is true the equivalent predicative function will be true too, and if fx is false, the predicative function will be false. Clearly this axiom is not evident, and when we consider its application it seems less evident than the other axioms in the book. (*vide Principia Mathematica*, lst. ed. Vol. I, pp. 59–62 and pp. 173–74). As early as the first edition, it is discussed whether this axiom could be rendered superfluous by proceeding in another way when establishing the whole system of logic, (for example, the assumption that classes exist should be sufficient for this purpose). The authors observe that the axiom is only given proof of pragmatically, and that it has no other consequences than those which have necessitated it. In the second edition, Wittgenstein's thesis of extensionality is regarded as a viewpoint which renders the axiom superfluous. It will lead us too far to try to explain how Russell and Whitehead thought this possible. But as it is said in the second edition this possibility 'requires us to maintain that "*A* believes *p*" is not a function of *p*. How this is possible is shown in *Tractatus Logico-Philosophicus*' and the authors refer to 5.54 ff as well as to Russell's introduction to the book. Nothing is said in explanation of the other types of propositions which Anscombe mentions. The authors apparently thought that the only difficulty which needed an explanation was the one connected with propositions of the type, '*A* believes *p*', and, '*p* is about *A*', and in Appendix *C*, pp. 659–66, it is explained that these propositions do not conflict with the thesis of extensionality.

However, Wittgenstein's own explanation of propositions expressing 'propositional attitudes' is more than obscure and what he actually maintained concerning this topic has often been disputed. Further on I will first give an account of what others have said about Wittgenstein's view and next show what interpretation we are led to on basis of the thought-picture theory proposed above. The paragraphs that are relevant here are the following ones:

5.54 In the general propositional form propositions occur in other propositions only as bases of truth-operations.

5.541 At first sight it looks as if it were also possible for one proposition to occur in another in a different way.

Particularly with certain forms of proposition in psychology, such as '*A* believes that *p* is the case' and '*A* has the thought *p*', etc.

For if these are considered superficially, it looks as if the proposition *p* stood in some kind of relation to an object *A*.

(And in modern theory of knowledge (Russell, Moore, etc.) these propositions have actually been construed in this way.)

5.542 It is clear, however, that '*A* believes that *p*', '*A* has the thought *p*', and '*A* says *p*' are of the form '"*p*" says *p*': and this does not involve a correlation of a fact with an object, but rather the correlation of facts by means of the correlation of their objects.

5.5421 This shows too that there is no such thing as the soul — the subject, etc. — as it is conceived in the superficial psychology of the present day.

Indeed a composite soul would no longer be a soul.

5.5422 The correct explanation of the form of the proposition, '*A* makes the judgement *p*' must show that it is impossible for a judgement to be a piece of nonsense. (Russell's theory does not satisfy this requirement.)

According to Russell, who was the first to attempt an explanation of this passage, the idea is that propositions of the form '*A* believes that *p*', '*A* believes *p*' and '*A* says *p*' are disguised expressions of a determination of the relation between the proposition conceived of as a fact (i. e. as a propositional sign) and the fact which the proposition describes. 'The real point is that in believing, desiring, etc. what is logically fundamental is the relation of a proposition *considered as a fact*, to the fact which makes it true or false, and that this relation of two facts is reducible to a relation of their constituents.' (p. xx). This view is followed up in the second edition of the *Principia Mathematica:*

'Suppose "*p*" is "Socrates is Greek". A word is a class of similar noises.

Thus a person who asserts "Socrates is Greek" is a person who makes, in rapid succession, three noises, of which the first is a member of the class "Socrates", the second a member of the class "is" and the third a member of the class "Greek". This series of events is part of the series of events which constitutes the person. If A is the series of events constituting the person, α is the class of noises "Socrates", β the class "is" and γ the class "Greek", then "A asserts that Socrates is Greek" is ....

$$(\exists x, y, z).\ x \varepsilon \alpha.\ y \varepsilon \beta.\ z \varepsilon \gamma.\ x \downarrow y \dot{u} x \downarrow z \dot{u} y \downarrow z c A.$$

The authors maintain that this clearly shows that p is not a truth-functional argument in 'A asserts p'. In spite of the fact that detailed arguments are missing, the authors hold the view that all propositions indicating 'propossitional attitudes' are not truth-functions because the propositions occurring in them are regarded only as propositional signs, and not as real propositions (pp. 661–66).

This opinion is accepted by the majority of the commentators on the *Tractatus*. Weinberg, for instance, adheres to it in *An Examination*, pp. 59 ff, although he adds that it rests upon Wittgenstein's view that 'there is no subject in the metaphysical sense of a simple personal entity.' Unfortunately neither Russell nor Weinberg have carefully analysed Wittgenstein's text. According to 5.5421 it should follow from 5.542 that a soul or subject as 'it is conceived in the superficial psychology of the present day' cannot be found. Russell's interpretation, however, has no consequences concerning the concept of a subject. That 'A says p' must be rendered 'the propositional sign p_m is correlated with the fact p_f' does not show that the soul or subject exists nor the opposite, nor does it imply anything concerning the nature of the subject, whether it is simple or complex etc. It is an astonishing fact that neither Russell nor the adherents to his view have noticed this. Furthermore we are not told how it is possible to give the propositions 'A believes p', 'A has the thought p' and 'A says p', different as they are, the same form.

Maslow's account is a little more detailed than Russell's and Weinberg's. He maintains (in *A Study*, pp. 108 ff) that 'A says p' 'is about Mr. A making certain noises 'p', and *not* about the proposition p.' Hence, 'A says p' is a description of a behaviouristic fact, i. e. of something a person does (This view is suggested by Russell in *The Analysis of Mind*, chap. XII). In 'A says p', p occurs only as a propositional sign. According to Maslow the right explanation of 5.542 therefore is: 'On the intensional interpretation of the type of propositions 'A says p', the object A was coordinated by some such relation as believing, thinking, saying, and so forth, with the proposition p. Now we coordinate the fact 'A says p' with the fact of A's saying 'p'.' (p. 109). Maslow illustrates this point in this manner:

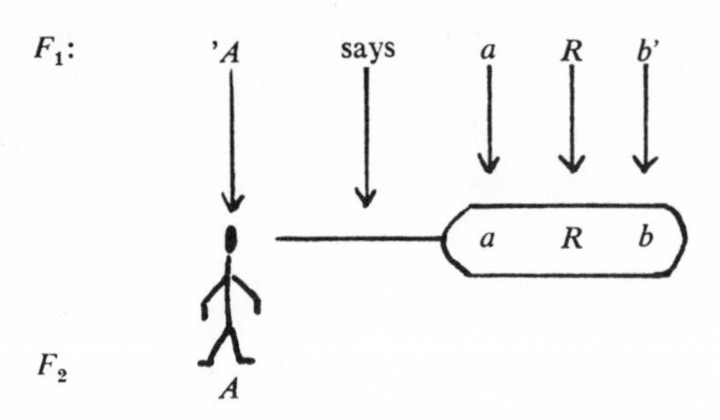

Here F_1 and F_2 are coordinated in that their elements are coordinated. From this we can see, says Maslow, that no such thing as a soul is involved here, exactly as stated in 5.5421.

In Maslow's account, however, there are many shortcomings. First of all the fact that no soul is involved in the figure does not prove that the soul does not exist. But this is what is maintained in 5.5421 on the basis of 5.542. Secondly, it seems as if Maslow thinks that "*p*' says *p*' expresses some sort of isomorphy between F_1 and F_2. But in the figure *p* is the same as *aRb* and therefore the fact that 'F_1 and F_2 are isomorphic' cannot be represented by "*p*' says *p*'. (Here and further on I prefer the notation "*p*' says *p*' *to* '"*p*" says *p*' as Pears and McGuinness make use of, because I think it the best to follow the German version in these matters). How, according to Maslow, are we to paraphrase the expression "*p*' says *p*'? There is no answer to this question.

In Maslow's, as well as in Russell's and Weinberg's interpretation, the point is that the proposition *p* cannot occur in the proposition '*A* says *p*', but that only propositional signs can occur in sentences of this type. If *p* could occur as a proposition in the sentence '*A* says *p*', we could be forced to say either that '*A* says *p*' is a truth-function, dependent on the truth-value of *p*, which is an absurdity (because any proposition with the same truth-value as *p* in this case could be substituted for *p*) or that the thesis of extensionality is invalid, because it implies that no proposition can form part of a complex expression without affecting the truth-value of the complex. It is reasonable to suppose that Wittgenstein was trying to show that '*A* says *p*' was not a molecular proposition, and I believe it a rash assertion of Barone to say that Wittgenstein tries to show that *p* is a truth-function of '*p*' in the expression "*p*' says *p*'. Barone thinks that 'Wittgenstein's investigation aims at showing that these propositions, i. e. propositions such as '*A* believes *p*' like all molecular propositions are truth-functions of elementary propositions.' (*Il Solipsismo*, p. 161). 'The subject', Barone says, 'is a fact and like all other facts it can be pictured by a proposition, for instance *p*, the sense and truth of which can always be determined on empirical grounds

From this it follows that the second proposition in the complex proposition "*p*' says *p*' is a truth-function of the first proposition.' I have not been able to find any sufficient ground for accepting this explanation.

Of other explanations of 5.542, Ramsey's may be mentioned. Ramsey states (*Critical Notice,* p. 469) that Wittgenstein expresses himself in a 'rather obscure' way but thinks that in 5.542 he explicitly reduces the whole question to the following: 'What is it for a proposition token to have a certain sense?' This formulation exactly covers my own account below but Ramsey is not able to say anything distinct about what Wittgenstein meant. However, it can be seen (p. 471) that he thinks that the question must be answered by giving an account of how a propositional sign is correlated with the described fact.

The explanation offered by G. E. M. Anscombe is at the same time subtle and obscure. It is her view that 'The expression schematically represented by ' "*p*" ' (she here applies the notation used by Pears and McGuinness), which in a concrete case would consist of an actual proposition in quotation marks, is to be taken as a way of describing the arrangement of signs that constitutes the proposition. '"*p*" says that *p*' thus admits of various interpretations; e. g.: 'That in "*a*Rb" "*a*" is written in italics and "*b*" in Roman says that *a*Rb' might be the way we *interpreted* '"*a*Rb" says that *a*Rb'.' (p. 89). Therefore, what Wittgenstein expresses in "*p*' says *p*' must be the way the propositional sign must be read and so "*p*' says *p*' should be a 'genuine proposition' in the sense applied in the *Tractatus*. This interpretation has the same defects as the others: it gives no explanation of the alleged fact that 5.5421 is a consequence of 5.542, nor an explanation of 5.5421. Anscombe's version lacks documentation of any kind. She maintains that what she writes, Wittgenstein meant, but she does not support her assertions.

I will now try to show in what way the passage 5.54-5.5422 must be read according to the thought-picture theory developed above. If we start by considering 5.542 we may ask what *A* signifies. Clearly *A* refers to a person that believes, thinks, or says something. But if we limit ourselves to 5.542 only, it is an open question whether *A* represents a body or a mind. 5.5421, however, indicates that *A* refers to the empirical ego of the person that says *p*. I do not know what Wittgenstein is referring to by the label 'contemporary superficial psychology', and unless he has made some hitherto unpublished notes on the matter I think it will be very difficult to discover. But it is clear from 5.5421 that the superficial psychology, he is thinking of, maintains that in the world we do find souls that are simple and yet are able to think and entertain ideas. For an adherent to the superficial psychology, it would be right to maintain that '*A* says *p*' is a coordination of a fact in the Wittgensteinian sense, namely the propositional sign *p* (which really should be written: p_m), and an object, namely the thinking soul which, because it is simple, must be called an object. According to Wittgenstein a 'superficial psychologist' would say that ' *A* says *p*' is a correlation of a fact with an object, as said in 5.542. Wittgenstein maintains that '*A* says *p*' expresses a 'correlation of facts by means of the correlation of their objects.' If he is not dealing with the question of what *A* represents here, but is only saying something about the correspondence between the proposition (or the propositional sign) and the pictured fact, as Russell and others think, it is difficult to understand in what way this is to imply something about the nature of the subject. But if he *is* dealing with the question of what *A* represents, it is obvious that he thinks that *A* in this connection represents a fact which is just as complex as the proposition *p*.

Contrary to the superficial psychological view, Wittgenstein maintains that in '*A* says *p*' we have to do with a coordination of two facts *via* a coordination of the objects of which they are put together. And in this view is included, as can be seen from 5.5421, the notion that the thing which is called the soul or the subject in the superficial psychology is really complex and therefore no longer *is* a soul, if by 'soul' we think of something simple as the superficial psychologists obviously do. From this we can infer that in 5.542 Wittgenstein is thinking of a composite soul, and according to my previous discussion this soul must be the empirical ego, since the metaphysical subject is characterized as something simple. The empirical ego thinks, and apparently this means no more than that it is a sequence of thoughts ('a train of mental states' (*The Blue Book*, p. 5)). If we refer to the empirical ego at a certain point of time we do not refer to it as to a certain substance which can be named, but only to the thought which is now present, not as a state of something but as a link in the train of thoughts which we call the empirical ego. What *A* refers to in '*A* says *p*' is therefore not the empirical ego as such (for actually nothing named the empirical ego can ever be found, because only facts and objects exist) but the thought occurring 'in' the domain of the empirical ego at the moment when *p* is uttered. The thought is a fact and it is correlated with the proposition *p* which also is a fact *via* the coordinations of their elements. In order that the thought can be coordinated to the proposition, the two entities must be equally complex. Consequently the empirical ego must, as said before, be complex at any point of time.

I have previously shown in what way a propositional sign can be rendered as a picture of something. What happens is that a thought which is a picture of something is expressed, perceptible to the senses, in the propositional sign by replacing the elements of the thought by the elements of the propositional sign. If, for instance, I think that 'there is an ashtray on the desk', I can turn this thought from a private experience into a phenomenon which can be perceived by others by choosing any fact consisting of the same amount of elements as the thought, and thereupon replacing the elements of the thought one by one by the elements of the fact. The fact then becomes a W-proposition.

In connection with this it was pointed out that as a consequence of Wittgenstein's view, a propositional sign, when uttered, remained a propositional sign if it was not thought out, i. e. if the sense of the proposition was not thought of. If, for instance, I utter p_m while thinking 'q', then p_m is not a picture but a mere physical fact. In order that p_m can become a picture of a state of affairs I must think 'p' while uttering p_m (cfr. 3.11). (It is of course presupposed here that p_m and q do not have the same structure. If they have, p_m naturally can be used for expressing q). If the person A says p_m while thinking something other than 'p', for example 'q', then p_m remains a propositional sign or a fact which does not picture anything. The obscurity in Wittgenstein's text is caused by the fact that he does not distinguish between a proposition (i. e. a W-proposition) and a propositional sign in his notation. If we do so, the content of 5.542 can be stated clearly.

When a person utters a proposition these are the possibilities given:

a_1: A utters p_m and at the same time thinks 'p'.

a_2: A utters p_m but does not think 'p' while uttering p_m.

Since A, as mentioned above, does not refer to the person's body but to A's empirical ego — which must be conceived of as the thought occurring 'in' the domain of the empirical ego, while A utters p_m — then a_1 and a_2 must be formulated in this way:

a_{11}: 'p' says p_m, and A at the same time thinks 'p'.

a_{21}: 'q' says p_m but A does not think 'p' while uttering p_m.

Obviously these statements are misleading because A has to be identified with the actual thought occurring 'in' the empirical ego. Their correct form must be:

a_{12}: 'p' says p_m.

a_{22}: 'q' says p_m.

In the first case in which the person thinks 'p' while saying p_m, p_m will become p, i. e. the propositional sign will become a picture or a proposition. In the latter case the propositional sign is not affected in any way. In the first case A actually says p. In the second case he only utters p_m. a_{12} should therefore be altered to:

a_{13}: 'p' says p.

This is the formulation we meet with in 5.542. a_{22} cannot be written in this way. If A says p_m and simultaneously thinks 'q', the situation can be expressed in such a way (on the condition that we can get to know what other persons think) that two propositions about the behaviour of *A* can be made, the one describing what he is uttering and the other what he is thinking. But after all it is nonsense to say that "*q*' says p_m' as '*q*' of course says nothing. a_{13}, however, is not a nonsense. For here the word 'says' obtains a meaning different from the usual one. Its meaning is here: turns p_m into a picture of something.

From this it follows that "p' says p' is a pseudo-proposition. It neither is a truth-function nor an elementary proposition but on the contrary an account of in what way an elementary proposition (or a W-proposition) obtains its sense. Consequently it is on a par with the other statements in the *Tractatus* that introduce the picture theory. These statements are not descriptions but elucidations (this will be explained in detail in chapter IV, part *c*.). "*p*' says *p*' really belongs to what can only be *shown* but never *said* and statements of this kind therefore, like statements of identity or logical inference, cannot be in conflict with the thesis of extensionality. For we have knowledge of the things which can only be shown in quite a different way from that in which we have knowledge of things which can be described, as we shall see in the next chapter. The thesis of extensionality applies only to what can be thought of and said, i. e. what can be expressed in language. Statements about identity, logical inference, and — as we have now seen — the way elementary propositions obtain their sense are all pseudo-propositions which aim at pointing to the things that can only be shown.

In the case where *A* says *p* while not thinking '*p*', the situation must, as mentioned above, be described by means of a proposition concerning the thought of *A* (in fact it is only the thought-sign which is describable), and a proposition about *A*'s behavior and utterances. Here we are not in conflict with the thesis of extensionality as we are only dealing with empirical propositions. But in this case we ought to write '*A* says p_m, and it seems as if Wittgenstein has ignored this when formulating 5.542. He only deals with the case where *A* thinks '*p*' and thereby turns *p* into a W-proposition. The examples considered are '*A* believes that *p* is the case', '*A* believes that *p*', '*A* has the thought *p*', and '*A* says *p*', and they all come under the case of a_1. In addition they all express the same, which can be seen from the analysis given above. The fact that '*A* says *p*' implies the fact that '*A* has the thought *p*', because if he says *p*, then *p* must be a W-proposition which it only is in the case where *A* thinks '*p*' simultaneously. Furthermore, to think '*p*' is tantamount to believing *p* or to believing that p_s exists. This follows from the fact that a proposition (or a thought) not only describes how things stand if it is true but in addition says that they *do* so stand (cfr. 4.022). It is simply impossible to think of something without believing that it is the case. According to the picture theory 'to think', 'to say' and 'to believe' are synonymous expressions. The reader will readily observe how one would be in conflict with the thesis of extensionality by distinguishing between these expressions. Expressions such as '*A* wishes for *p*' and '*A* hopes that *p* is the case', however, Wittgenstein passes by in silence. Probably he shrank from the difficulties which these sentences cause and preferred not to mention them at all.

For the sake of clarity I will paraphrase 5.542. According to what has been said up to now the passage must read: 'It is clear, however, that "*A* believes that *p*", "*A* has the thought *p*" and "*A* says *p*" are of the form "'*p*' says *p*": and here we do not have a correlation of a propositional sign *p* (which should really be written p_m) and an object *A*, which some superficial psychologists conceive as the person *A*'s non-composite soul or subject, but a correlation of two facts, namely the propositional sign *p* and the thought '*p*', which when occurring 'in' *A*'s empirical ego turns the propositional sign *p* into the proposition *p*. The two facts are correlated by means of a correlation of their objects.'

That there are two facts, which are coordinated with each other, shows that 'there is no such thing as the soul — the subject, etc. — as it is conceived in the superficial psychology of the present day. / Indeed a composite soul would no longer be a soul.' (5.5421). But the 'soul' in question *must* be 'composite' for every single thought is composite. Therefore the superficial psychologists who regard it as simple are wrong.

I believe that this interpretation is superior to the ones described at the beginning of this section partly because it takes 5.5421 into consideration, which the others do not, and partly because it explains all the types of propositions mentioned in 5.541 and 5.542. Moreover it is in all respects in accordance with my interpretation of the picture theory and finally it is consistent with the attempts at formulating 5.542 which can be found in the *Notebooks*. In *Notes dictated to G. E. Moore* we read that 'The relation of "I believe *p*" to "*p*" can be compared to the relation of '"*p*" says (besagt) *p*' to *p*: it is just as impossible that I should be a simple as that "*p*" should be.' (*Notebooks*, p. 118). Here it is actually stated that the thinking or judging subject is complex. But in other respects this assertion is blurred. I believe that the first part of it should be read: 'The relation of 'I believe *p*' to 'p_s can be compared to the relation of "*p*' says (besagt) *p*' to 'p_s'. It is clear, though, that Wittgenstein entertains an idea of replacing the I by the thought '*p*' even though he does not take up the problem again until some years later. And it is of interest that he writes '*besagt*' at this point of time and not 'sagt' as 5.542 has it. For, as mentioned above, it is not in the usual sense of the word 'says', that "*p*' says *p*'. By saying "*p*' *besagt p*' we can better express what we have to say according to my interpretation: that '*p*' does not say *p*, but that '*p*' indicates or means *p*.

Already in the *Notes on Logic*, Wittgenstein deals with propositions such as '*A* says *p*', but at that time he is not able to give an explanation of their logical form. We must notice, however, that he writes: 'The proposition "*A* judges (that) *p*" consists of the proper name *A*, the proposition *p* with its two poles, and *A*'s being related to both these poles in a certain way. This is obviously not a relation in the ordinary sense.' (*Notebooks*, p. 96). From this we can see that what he attempts to throw light on is the relation between *A* and *p* and not — as Russell and others think — the relation between p_m and p_s. This is why the whole problem appears to be difficult, for he realizes from the outset that the relation between *A* and *p* is not a relation 'in the ordinary sense'.

It remains to explain 5.5422 in the light of the suggested interpretation. According to 5.5422 the right explanation of the form of the proposition '*A* makes the judgment *p*' should show that it is impossible to 'judge a nonsense'. In an article to be published in *Mind* (*Tractatus 5.542*) I have mentioned $p \cdot \sim p$ as an instance of a nonsense and shown that on the basis of my interpretation of 5.542 it is impossible to maintain or judge $p \cdot \sim p$, because a person can only think one of the links of this conjunction at a certain point of time so that the other part remains a propositional sign because it is not thought of. In short, the idea is that it is possible to utter $p_m \cdot \sim p_m$ but that if '*p*' is thought of one cannot at the same time think $\sim p$. Consequently if we think '*p*' the uttered proposition is $p \cdot \sim p_m$. If we think '$\sim p$' we cannot simultaneously think '*p*'. In this case the uttered proposition therefore is $p_m \cdot \sim p$. As we can never simultaneously think '*p*' and '$\sim p$', it is impossible to maintain or judge $p \cdot \sim p$. Consequently it is impossible to 'judge a nonsense'. However, since this article was written, I have noticed that Wittgenstein in his *Notes on Logic* in connection with his ideas about '*A* judges *p*' gives an example of a nonsense ('Unsinn') when writing: 'Every right theory of judgment must make it impossible for me to judge that "this table penholders the book" (Russell's theory does not satisfy this requirement).' (*Notebooks*, p. 96). If this is what Wittgenstein was thinking of when he wrote 5.5422, it must be observed that according to my interpretation one can only possibly judge a nonsense if one can think a nonsense. This, however, is impossible. According to 3, thoughts are pictures and pictures have 'sense' (cfr. 2.12 and 2.221). We can only think of something which is possible. To picture something possible is to form something which has a sense. We cannot think of something which is not possible for this would mean to have a thought the sense of which was nonsensical. Whether we are concerned with a psychological or a logical-syntactical problem here, Wittgenstein does not tell us. He does not give any precepts concerning logical syntax which prohibits combinations such as 'This table penholders the book'. If we limit ourselves to psychological investigations, we might find that the expression is a nonsense because we cannot form a picture of, cannot think, that a table penholders a book. In this case we must say that 5.542 shows us that it is impossible to judge a nonsense.

It has been urged that the eventual truth of 5.542 implies that it should be impossible to tell a lie. According to my interpretation it is possible to lie, and surely Wittgenstein meant so too. A person can tell a lie by uttering one propositional sign, p_m for instance, while thinking of something other than 'p'. What he utters, then, is only a propositional sign. Another person B may *per* convention think 'p' when hearing p_m and thus conceive of p_m as a proposition p. He then may believe that A also is thinking 'p' and in this way he is deceived by A.

Furthermore I should like to say that my interpretation takes 5.5423 into consideration as little as do the others. In this paragraph Wittgenstein says: 'To perceive a complex means to perceive that its constituents are related to one another in such and such a way.' After this it is said that a cube can be seen in two ways and that therefore two different facts can be perceived according to which way we look at the cube. As far as I can see, 5.5423 has no direct connection with the passage 5.54-5.5422. According to the numbering system of the *Tractatus* it should be a comment on 5.542 but even if some sort of connection between the two statements could be found (one *could* say, for instance, that 5.5423 elaborates the problem which arises when a propositional sign is used for expressing two thoughts, — this is possible if the two thoughts each consist of the same number of elements as the propositional sign, — a problem which will be dealt with further on) I am inclined to think that the numbering here, as in many other parts of the *Tractatus*, is misleading. I refer the reader to the appendix concerning principles of interpretation.

Finally, it must be noticed that Wittgenstein in his remark about 'Russell's theory' in 5.5422 very likely alludes to Russell's article *On the Nature of Truth* (*Proceedings of the Aristotelian Society 1906-07*). (Russell suggests this himself in the *Introduction*, p. xix). In this article Russell maintains that a 'belief' cannot be 'validly regarded as a single state of mind'. 'That is', he writes, 'if we believe (say) that A is B, we shall have the ideas of A and of B and these ideas will be related in a certain manner; but we shall not have a single complex idea which can be described as the idea of "A is B"' (p. 46). This view is, according to my interpretation, contrary to the view presented in the *Tractatus*. According to Wittgenstein the thought or the elementary proposition is the smallest bit of language which can have a sense. The thought '*A* is *B*' cannot consist of other thoughts unless these have a structure. But structure can only exist if at least two elements are connected with each other and therefore '*A* is *B*' cannot be put together of an idea of *A* and an idea of *B*. A belief such as '*A* is *B*' is, as shown above, in Wittgenstein's opinion a 'single state of mind' which cannot be divided into smaller parts. When he says of Russell's theory that it does not show 'that it is impossible for a judgment to be a piece of nonsense' he is consistent to his view. For if a thought or a belief could be regarded as a combination of beliefs about its parts, nothing would prevent us from thinking or believing that 'this table penholders the book'. According to Wittgenstein's theory, however, this expression is nonsense because it does not describe a possible state of affairs. Even if the corresponding psychical elements can be put together in the empirical ego they do not form a picture of anything or establish a possibility in logical space. Hence the elements do not constitute a thought.

IV

SOME CONSEQUENCES OF THE THESIS OF EXTENSIONALITY AND THE PICTURE THEORY

a. Formal concepts and logical truth.

It is an immediate consequence of the picture theory — no matter whether it is conceived as an O-proposition-picture theory or a thought-picture theory — that it is impossible to establish a meta-language, i. e. a senseful system of signs besides the language comprising elementary propositions and truth-functions. In a way this is, as mentioned, implied by the thesis of extensionality, as 'senseful propositions' according to this thesis are truth-functions only (elementary propositions are truth-functions of themselves). *But on the basis of the picture theory it can be shown clearly that a meta-language not only is impossible to establish but that it is moreover superfluous. This is one of Wittgenstein's most essential points.* According to the thesis of extensionality and the picture theory he is forced to acknowledge only one language — we may call it 'the object-language' — and it may therefore seem that, because of this, he is prevented from knowing more than that which can be described in the propositions of natural science. But in virtue of his distinction between what can be said and what can only be shown, he tries to 'save' the sort of knowledge which the logical empiricists some years later classed with the sphere of meta-language. What can be said, can, according to Wittgenstein, be expressed in elementary propositions and only by means of them. What can be shown can never be described in language, but by the application of a univocal logical notation it can show itself in language to the perceiving subject.

The thesis about the impossibility of a meta-language and about what can be shown only and not said has many aspects. In the following I will call attention to some of these.

Previously I have stressed the point that one of the most important implications of the thesis of extensionality is that one proposition cannot deal with another. In a sense, therefore, it is absurd to give an account of the picture theory as I have done. In such an account one is forced to speak of propositions when explaining their relations to reality, and consequently the propositions spoken of occur in the account in a way which is not truth-functional. I say that this is absurd *in a sense*. Later I will show that it is not quite as absurd as it first appears. On the face of it, it is absurd that Wittgenstein has written the *Tractatus*. For in this book we are presented with a number of statements which can neither be elementary propositions nor truth-functions and yet deal with something, namely propositions. This is altogether in conflict with the ideas of the book. But, as the reader will know, Wittgenstein ends his book with the declaration that all the statements in it are nonsensical (6.54). However, the fact that the statements of the *Tractatus* are nonsensical in the light of the picture theory does not imply that they have no function at all. I will return to this point.

We must keep in view that according to Wittgenstein a full understanding of the picture theory implies that everything said about it must be considered pseudo-propositions. In accordance with our usual conceptions of understanding and knowledge, what we know or understand can always be expressed in propositions (because it can be thought of). The peculiar character of Wittgenstein's picture theory makes it necessary for him to introduce a new kind of understanding or insight which cannot be formulated in any way (and therefore cannot be thought of either), but which, nevertheless, is knowledge or insight. This indescribable insight is possible because something which cannot be said can be shown.

This famous doctrine of Wittgenstein's that there will always be something that can be shown and what can be shown cannot be said (4.1212) appears in many ways in the *Tractatus*. The logical form of an elementary proposition, for instance, is something which is shown and can never be described. If another proposition was to describe the logical form of a proposition *p*, it could only do this by participating in the logical form of *p*. The 'description', then, would amount only to a transformation of *p*. The essential feature of a proposition, its logical form, cannot be described, but it nevertheless can be perceived. It shows itself just as its common structure with the described state of affairs shows itself. Also we can perceive that two propositions '*f*(*a*)' and '*g*(*a*)' deal with the same object (cfr. 4.1211), but we are excluded from expressing this experience in a proposition because it would be a violation of the thesis of extensionality to say '*f*(*a*) and *g*(*a*) both deal with *a*'. That they do so, however, we can *see* simply by perceiving that *a* occurs in both propositions. Moreover we can perceive that one truth-function is implied by another although we cannot make a senseful formulation about this, and finally we are able to see that two mathematical expressions are identical (e. g. $3 + 5 = 8$) although we cannot describe this identity-relation. The sign of identity we can dispense with in a perfect logical notation (cfr. 5.533), for all equations are pseudo-propositions (cfr. 5.534).

As far as I can see, Wittgenstein's view is consistent. If propositions and thoughts really are configurations of elements and if propositions cannot have a sense unless they have a certain structure, then it seems impossible that a meta-language describing the relation between language and reality can be established. It is, of course, possible to say something about the nature of a propositional sign, but no more can be said of the sense of a proposition than the proposition itself expresses. And if a meta-language cannot be established this fact implies that all the words used for giving an account of the picture theory are not names. According to the picture theory a word is always a name of an object, but the word 'object' does not represent an object. The impossibility of a meta-language precludes that this word could ever be a name. We may argue the other way around too, and state that as 'object' does not signify an object, it is impossible to form propositions containing this word. This implies that it is equally impossible to form propositions about the relation between name and object.

Using Gilbert Ryle's terminology (cfr. *The Concept of Mind*, p. 16) we may call it a category-mistake to believe that the word 'object' is a name. If it has sense to say that various objects exist, it is a category-mistake to believe that besides these something can be found which must be labelled 'object'. To say that in the world we are presented with chairs, tables, books, pencils and objects is a nonsense if we have granted in advance that chairs, tables, books and pencils *are* objects.

Wittgenstein calls generic terms such as 'object' 'formal concepts'. In 4.126 he writes: '. . . . When something falls under a formal concept as one of its objects, this cannot be expressed by means of a proposition. Instead it is shown in the very sign for this object. (A name shows that it signifies an object, a sign for a number that it signifies a number, etc.) / Formal concepts cannot, in fact, be represented by means of a function, as concepts proper can. / For their characteristics, formal properties, are not expressed by means of functions. / The expression for a formal property is a feature of certain symbols. / So the sign for the characteristics of a formal concept is a distinctive feature of all symbols whose meanings fall under the concept. / So the expression for a formal concept is a propositional variable in which this distinctive feature alone is constant.' Here Wittgenstein, for once, expresses himself with a clarity which renders further explanations superfluous. If we consider, for instance, the statement 'This pencil is an object' we can clearly see that it cannot have sense, for if it could each name in it would represent an object. Now if this was so the pictured fact should consist of both a pencil and an object. But if it did the statement considered could never be true because the pencil and the object, being two different things, cannot be identical. Moreover, the assumption that the word 'object' referred to an object would exclude the possibility of anything falling under the concept 'object' or, to put it in another way, 'object' could not be a concept. Consequently the expression 'This pencil is an object' is a combination of words which do not all represent objects and therefore *per* definition it is not a proposition.

If we consider 'object' a concept, the word 'object' must, as Wittgenstein has it, be equal to a characteristic feature of all the symbols falling under this concept. If the words 'The ashtray *A*', 'The book *B*' and 'The chair *C*' all are names of certain objects the word 'object' must indicate something which is a common characteristic of these names. This feature, however, we cannot perceive just by regarding the names. Probably Wittgenstein thought that it would show in a perfect logical notation. The fact that the names are symbols of objects would show itself in that all of them can be values of the function $f(x)$. The indication of the possible values of a function of this kind would form a part of the logical syntax of language if it could be formulated. The characteristic feature which the names have in common cannot be described. This is a consequence of the fact that names, according to the picture theory, are 'simple signs' which cannot be dissected by any sort of analysis (cfr. 3.201 and 3.26).

In $f(x)$ 'x' consequently is, as Wittgenstein writes in 4.1272, 'the proper sign for the pseudo-concept *object*.' '$f(x)$', however, is a logical form devoid of sense. It cannot be endowed with a sense and what it shows is only the logical-syntactical structure of all possible subject-predicate propositions. It shows the common feature of all the facts that are described by letting x and f successively have all possible values, but it does not describe anything. The signs of the logical notation all signify nothing. They indicate pseudo-concepts and in order that pseudo-propositions do not arise they must not be mistaken for names. '.... So one cannot say, for example, 'There are objects', as one might say, 'There are books'. And it is just as impossible to say, 'There are 100 objects', or, 'There are $\aleph_0$ objects'. / And it is non-sensical to speak of the *total number of objects* ....' The picture theory, however, cannot be formulated unless we apply pseudo-concepts as names. Hence, the picture theory, being the only possible theory of meaning, must abolish the possibility of its own formulation.

Besides 'object', we find 'complex', 'fact', 'function', and 'number', mentioned as examples of formal concepts in 4.1272. In addition to these, 'picture', 'proposition', 'name', 'thought', 'state of affairs', and 'symbol', can be listed as formal concepts too. It is necessary to know of these concepts in order to grasp the picture theory. Therefore there must be knowledge which cannot be formulated but only shown — if the picture theory is valid.

Wittgenstein's simple account of logical inference gives us a strong impression of the view that in human knowledge a great part can never be described but only shown.

If we arrange the survey of truth-functions developed on the basis of two propositions only, presented in 5.101, thus:

	p	q	$p \supset p . q \supset q$	$\sim(p . q)$	$q \supset p$	$p \supset q$	$p \vee q$	$\sim q$	$\sim p$	$p . \sim q : \vee : q . \sim p$	$p \equiv q$	p	q	$\sim p . \sim q$	$p . \sim q$	$\sim p . q$	$p . q$	$p . \sim p . q . \sim q$
A	T	T	T	F	T	T	T	F	F	F	T	T	T	F	F	F	T	F
B	F	T	T	T	F	T	T	F	T	T	F	F	T	F	F	T	F	F
C	T	F	T	T	T	F	T	T	F	T	F	T	F	F	T	F	F	F
D	F	F	T	T	T	T	F	T	T	F	T	F	F	T	F	F	F	F

we can grasp Wittgenstein's theory of logical inference without difficulty. In this table we are presented with all the possible truth-functions which contain only p and q as arguments. Probably Wittgenstein has introduced the truth-table notation in order to demonstrate as lucidly as possible what can be shown and what can be said. The thing he intends to show here is that the rules which we apply when making inferences need not be formulated. Naturally he wishes to show this as according to the thesis of extensionality they *cannot* be formulated in senseful propositions. Statements of the type: 'If we know that p is true and if we know that $p \supset q$ is true, then we know that q is true' are inadmissible. For here neither p nor $p \supset q$ nor q occur in a truth-functional way. One could also say that the picture theory demands that the statement is either a truth-function or a nonsense. If the statement had a sense this would imply that p, $p \supset q$, and q, were names, but this would be against the way 'name' and 'proposition' are defined in the picture theory. Wittgenstein is compelled to conclude that laws of inference can not be formulated.

When Wittgenstein wrote the *Tractatus* the idea of distinguishing between an object-language and a meta-language had not yet been developed. The idea was not actually advanced until Russell suggested it in his introduction to the *Tractatus* (p. xxii). But Wittgenstein apparently thought of this distinction a long time before and rejected it. Indeed, the logical parts of the *Tractatus* appear to be an attempt to exclude all forms of meta-language. The statements dealing with logical inference are detailed objections to the idea of a meta-language. As mentioned above, the ground for rejecting this idea was above all the thesis of extensionality but it must be noticed that Wittgenstein had other grounds too. For instance, it is probable that he rejected the possibility of formulating laws of inference because he was convinced that it implied an infinite regress. At any rate, according to G. E. Moore, he advanced this argument in his lectures 1930-33. Moore writes: 'He also, shortly afterwards, gave some further explanation of what he had meant by saying that if a rule were needed to justify the statement that one proposition follows (logically) from another, we should need an infinite series. He said that if a rule r, were needed to justify an inference from p to q, q would follow from the conjunction of p and r, so that we would need a fresh rule to justify the inference from this conjunction to q and so on *ad infinitum*. Hence, he said, 'an inference can only be justified by what we see, and added that 'this holds throughout Mathematics'.' (Moore: *Wittgenstein's Lectures*, pp. 294-95).

By regarding the table above, we can easily demonstrate Wittgenstein's theory of inference. In 5.11 he writes: 'If all the truth-grounds that are common to a number of propositions are at the same time truth-grounds of a certain proposition, then we say that the truth of that proposition follows from the truth of the others.' and 5.12 reads: 'In particular, the truth of a proposition '*p*' follows from the truth of another proposition '*q*', if all the truth-grounds of the latter are truth-grounds of the former.' If, for instance, $p \cdot q$ is true this implies that pvq is also true. For, in the matrix of pvq, a '*T*' occurs in the same row as the '*T*' in the matrix of $p \cdot q$ occurs in. To put it in another way we can say that if $p \cdot q$ is true then A (the top row of the table) is realized (A, B, C, and D, indicate the possible 'worlds' described by means of p and q), and if A is realized, then pvq is true. Therefore to maintain $p \cdot q$ is at the same time to maintain pvq. That the truth of pvq follows from the truth of $p \cdot q$ we can see from the structure of the truth-functions (cfr. 5.13). The structure shows itself in the matrixes and from these we can directly see the relation between $p \cdot q$ and pvq. The relation between these two truth-functions is internal which means that we cannot even imagine that it does not exist. Just as two colours must have an internal relation to each other (i. e. the one must be lighter or darker than the other or they must be equally light, cfr. 4.123), so $p \cdot q$ and pvq in virtue of their structure are connected with each other by means of an internal relation.

This means that if these truth-functions exist the relation inevitably holds between them. It is not necessary to establish a relation between them (cfr. 5.131: 'If the truth of one proposition follows from the truth of others, this finds expression in relations in which the forms of the propositions stand to one another; nor is it necessary for us to set up these relations between them, by combining them with one another in a single proposition; on the contrary, the relations are internal, and their existence is an immediate result of the existence of the propositions.') Internal relations are not accidental features. They 'exist' because all truth-functions can be developed by successive applications of one operation only, namely the operation of negation (I shall return to this further on). This operation is an application of Sheffer's stroke, (which is given the matrix (*FFFT*) (*p*, *q*)), and if all truth-functions in the table were written solely by means of the stroke, the relations between the truth-functions could be seen from the propositional signs alone (cfr. G. E. Moore: *Wittgenstein's Lectures*, p. 295). This view seems to be suggested in the formulation of 5.1311 where it is exemplified in respect of $\sim p$ and pvq, as the relation between these two functions, when written '$p|p$' and '$p|q \cdot | \cdot p|q$' respectively, corresponds to the internal relation which can be found between two terms of a series of forms (cfr. 4.1273).

A more complicated example of the assertion in 5.11 is this: If we maintain that $\sim(p \cdot q)$ is true, we maintain that either *B*, *C*, or *D*, is realized. If we maintain that pvq is true, we maintain that either *A*, *B*, or *C*, is realized. If we simultaneously maintain $\sim(p \cdot q)$ and pvq, this implies that either *B* or *C* is realized, and no more than this. From this it follows that $p \cdot \sim q.v.\sim p \cdot q$ is true because the matrix of this truth-function has a '*T*' in the rows *B* and *C*. Consequently $p \cdot \sim q.v.\sim p \cdot q$ is implied by $\sim(p \cdot q) .\therefore. pvq$. Similarly the validity of *modus ponens*, which is presented in *Principia Mathematica* (1. ed. vol. I, p. 9) as a rule of inference, can be seen from the table. For if p is true, then either *A* or *C* is realized and if $p \supset q$ is true, then either *A*, *B*, or *D*, is realized. Consequently only *A* can be the case if both of them are true. But if *A* is the case, q is true. Hence, *it shows itself* that $p .\therefore. p \supset q. \supset .q$.

If the internal relations were not established as soon as the truth-functions are developed, it would be necessary to *relate* the functions to each other in order to demonstrate that some of them could be inferred from others. It would then be absolutely necessary to introduce a metalinguistic sign indicating whether two truth-functions were related to each other or not. Here we see that different ideas form a synthesis in Wittgenstein's philosophy. The rejection of all forms of meta-language implies that no relation can be established between two truth-functions one of which follows from the other. Therefore the relation must be there beforehand. In order to be sure of this we must know of some certain operation by means of which all truth-functions can be generated. This operation is the operation of negation. The possibility of defining all logical constants by means of one, Sheffer's stroke, saves us from violating the thesis of extensionality and the picture-theory.

As a consequence of 5.131 and 5.1311 Wittgenstein in 5.132 can write: 'If p follows from q, I can make an inference from q to p, deduce p from q. / The nature of the inference can be gathered only from the two propositions. / They themselves are the only possible justification of the inference. / 'Laws of inference', which are supposed to justify inferences, as in the works of Frege and Russell, have no sense, and would be superfluous.' Just as in the development of the picture theory, the claim of the thesis of extensionality that one proposition must not deal with another, is taken into account. The picture theory is based on the idea that the sense of a proposition must be gathered from the proposition itself independently of all other propositions. Here we meet with a parallel to this idea: 'The nature of the inference can be gathered only from the two propositions.' Nothing but these must be necessary for this purpose.

From this account of Wittgenstein's theory of inference it can be seen that it is misleading to say that we infer one proposition from another. We should rather say that we discover the relation which holds in advance between the considered propositions. 'All deductions are made *a priori*' ('geschieht a priori'), it is said in 5.133. It may be questioned whether the content of the propositions has any 'objective' existence, but clearly Wittgenstein had the opinion that the relations which hold between the propositions are as 'objective' as the propositions themselves.

From the table it can be seen that no two truth-functions are related to each other in such a way that the truth of the one implies the truth of the other and *vice versa*. This would only be possible if both of them had the same matrix, but if this was the case they would simply be two manifestations of one and the same truth-function (cfr. 5.141). Likewise, it can be seen that the tautology follows from any truth-function (because it only contains T's in the matrix), whereas the contradiction implies all other truth-functions because it contains no T's. Because all the propositions of logic are tautologies, it is clear that logic never can determine what is the case and what is not the case.

In this chapter, when I have constantly written that a truth-function 'follows from' or is 'implied by' another, naturally the statements I make must be pseudo-propositions if the picture theory is valid. The fact that one truth-function is implied by another is something which shows itself. Therefore it cannot be described at all. The relation between two or more truth-functions therefore cannot be represented in any logical notation. Maslow has pointed out that Wittgenstein cannot mean by 'follows from' what Russell reads into his material implication (*vide* chap. I). The fact that p implies q cannot be written $p \supset q$. The material implication is, as Maslow writes, nothing but truth-function n° 4 in the table and 'it may happen to hold even when both p and q are atomic, as well as when either or both of them are molecular. '$p \supset q$ tautologically' means 'q follows from p' and it holds only when there is some formal relation between p and q, such that 'the truth grounds of p are contained in those of q'; p in '$p \supset q$ tautologically' must be molecular, except in the limiting case where we infer p from itself.' (pp. 124-25) According to Maslow, Wittgenstein must mean by 'follows from': '$p \supset q$ tautologically'. This is indisputable, but it is an offence against Wittgenstein's claim of the impossibility of a meta-language to indicate this relation, '$p\ T\supset\ q$', as Maslow does, (the sign $T\supset$ is composed of T and $\supset$). In an ordinary account of Wittgenstein's theory, signs of this sort are admissible but we must never forget that according to Wittgenstein they are meaningless simply because expressions such as $p T\supset q$ are neither elementary propositions nor truth-functions.

*

According to what has previously been pointed out, it seems reasonable to say that by a proof in logic and mathematics Wittgenstein must understand a demonstration of a certain fact. 6.1262 reads: 'Proof in logic is merely a mechanical expedient to facilitate the recognition of tautologies in complicated cases.' ("ein mechanisches Hilfsmittel zum leichteren Erkennen der Tautologie, wo sie kompliziert ist."). He seems to have realized, what now is generally accepted (*vide* e. g. Nagel & Newman: *Gödel's Proof*, p. 18), that such a thing as a geometrical representation of a logical inference, which we often use when demonstrating syllogisms by means of Euler's circles, or such a thing as a comparison of truth-tables which we undertake and conceive of as a representation of a calculation by means of the symbols of logistics cannot be considered a proof but only a reproduction of something already known by means of other symbols than the usual ones. None of these lines of action takes precedence over the others. No matter what line of action we follow, what we do is only an 'unfolding' or 'unveiling' of something which is tautologous. In the most simple cases we can immediately see that an expression is a tautology. Thus Wittgenstein shows in 6.1203 how we can see in a simple way that $\sim(p \cdot \sim p)$ is a tautology. Because of the clarity of this passage I will not give an account of it here, but only stress the point of it, which is that all tautologies can be written in a way so their truth can be gathered from a consideration of the propositional sign only (cfr. 6.113: 'It is the peculiar mark of logical propositions that one can recognize that they are true from the symbol alone, and this fact contains in itself the whole philosophy of logic . . .'). In the cases where the tautologies are expressed in a way so complicated that we cannot immediately recognize their truth a lengthy and detailed representation must be elaborated in order that the tautologous character can become clear. In these cases we normally speak of 'proofs' but by a proof we cannot understand something containing more evidence than the notation itself gives us. As soon as we have established an adequate notation (by this Wittgenstein generally thinks of the symbol-language of the *Principia Mathematica*) the logical truths, the tautologies, are automatically given. They are not postulated anymore than the notation is. 6.1223 reads: 'Now it becomes clear why people have often felt as if it were for us to 'postulate' the 'truth of logic'. The reason is that we can postulate them in so far as we can postulate an adequate notation.' And at the end of 6.124 it is said that 'logic is not a field in which *we* express what we wish with the help of signs, but rather one in which the nature of the natural and inevitable signs speaks for itself. If we know the logical syntax of any sign-language, then we have already been given all the propositions of logic.'

This conception of proof can be illustrated in the following way. If a piece of paper is folded a certain number of times it can be difficult to see whether we have to do with one or with more than one piece of paper. If a piece of paper is folded once only we can see this directly, but in the more complicated cases we must investigate the situation simply by unfolding the paper. To prove that the piece of paper is folded, say, eight times we must unfold it while counting how many times it is folded. The proof is here a sort of mechanical process ending with a *demonstratio ad oculos*. We cannot read more than this into the word 'proof'. In order to see whether an expression is a tautology or not, no more than a mechanical process is needed. (In Wittgenstein's *Foundations of Mathematics*, III, 17 - 21, IV, 51, and V, 51, we are presented with this view again.) For, as is said in 6.127: '. . . . / Every tautology itself shows that it is a tautology.' A superior rule for deciding whether an expression is a tautology or not is not necessary (cfr. 6.123).

From what has been said, it can be gathered that the propositions of logic, the tautologies, belong with that which 'shows itself'. Miss Anscombe, however, distinguishes between logical truths and 'the things that are 'shewn'' (*Introduction*, p. 163) on the basis that tautologies can be said even if they are empty of sense, whereas an attempt to say what can only be shown results in a *nonsensical* expression. But this distinction can hardly be legitimate. When we say, for instance, '$p \vee \sim p$', indeed we *say* a tautology but we do not say *that* it is a tautology. For this can only be shown. An expression such as "$pv{\sim}p$' is a tautology' would be a nonsense. From this it is seen that the tautologies come under what can only be shown.

In order to complete this account of Wittgenstein's theory of inference it must be observed that 'if p follows from q, the sense of 'p' is contained in the sense of 'q'' (5.122). Even though the relation between two truth-functions is indicated solely by means of their truth-values it inevitably represents at the same time a relation between their sense. This is connected with the fact that only truth-functions which are generated on basis of the same elementary propositions are related to one another. For example, '$p \cdot q$' and 'pvq' are both generated by operations applied to p and q and therefore they both refer to the same states of affairs. It is clear that the sense of 'pvq' is contained in the sense of '$p \cdot q$' because the proposition 'pvq' leaves more of logical space open to reality than does '$p \cdot q$'. '$p \cdot q$' contains more sense than pvq.

*

It is in accordance with the account presented here when Wittgenstein writes in 4.442: '.... (Frege's 'judgement-stroke' '$\vdash$' is logically quite meaningless: in the works of Frege (and Russell) it simply indicates that these authors hold the propositions marked with this sign to be true. Thus '$\vdash$' is no more a component part of a proposition than is, for instance, the proposition's number. It is quite impossible for a proposition to state that it itself is true.) / ....' For as to tautologies what Wittgenstein attempted to show was exactly that their truth shows itself in the propositional sign (cfr. 6.1203). Perhaps it is not immediately clear that '$pv{\sim}p$' is a tautology, but if this proposition is written in the manner described in 6.1203, its tautological character can be observed from a consideration of the propositional sign only.

The judgment-stroke was introduced by Frege in order to make a distinction between a judgment and a thought. 'I make a distinction between *judgment* and *thought* and understand by *judgment* the acknowledgment of the truth of a *thought*. I shall call the ideographic representation of a judgment by means of the sign '$\vdash$' an 'ideographic theorem' or more shortly a 'theorem'.' (*Grundgesetze*, Geach & Black: *Philosophical Writings*, p. 156). This distinction was accepted in the *Principia Mathemathica* in which it was held that the judgment-stroke is 'required for distinguishing a complete proposition, which we assert, from any subordinate propositions contained in it but not asserted.' (1. ed. pp. 8–9). In the *Principia* the stroke is placed in front of every postulate and theorem. The main reason for Wittgenstein considering the stroke superfluous is probably that the tautological character of the propositions of logic is a feature of the logical notation applied and therefore must exist whether the propositions are asserted or not. Already in *Notes on Logic* he had criticized the application of the stroke and maintained that only 'unasserted propositions' can be found (*Notebooks*, p. 96). But he had other motives than this one. In 4.442 it is said that '⊢' is not more a component part of a proposition than is, for instance, the proposition's number. The judgment-stroke cannot do more to a proposition than the number can and this in no way affects the proposition. I should like to draw the reader's attention once again to the first chapter of *The Blue Book*. Wittgenstein writes here: 'Without a sense, or without the thought, a proposition would be an utterly dead and trivial thing. And further it seems clear that no adding of inorganic signs can make the proposition live.' (p. 4). The idea must be that if the O-proposition-picture theory is valid then propositions must for ever remain utterly dead things which not even a judgment-stroke can make alive.

If the thought-picture theory is valid, not only is the judgment-stroke superfluous but in addition impossible to apply. Because first of all a thought is a configuration of elements each representing an object. Since no object corresponds to the judgment-stroke this cannot be an element of a thought. Secondly, the thought *qua* thought is a picture of something. Nothing extra (therefore not a judgment-stroke either) is provided in order that a picturing relation can be established. Consequently we cannot think something without asserting it. There is no difference, therefore, between '*A* believes *p*' and '*A* says *p*' or between '*A* has the thought *p*' and '*A* makes the judgment *p*'. From 5.542 and 5.5422 we see that Wittgenstein in fact does not distinguish between these forms. To think *p* is the same as asserting that *p* is the case. This can clearly be seen from 4.022: 'A proposition *shows* its sense. / A proposition *shows* how things stand *if* it is true. And it *says that* they do so stand.' It is not the person saying the proposition but the proposition itself that says that some things are related to each other in a certain way.

The reader may understand that I strongly disagree with Stenius when he writes (*Wittgenstein's 'Tractatus*', p. 161): 'In effect 4.022 assigns two different tasks to a sentence: the task of *depicting* a state of affairs and the task of *asserting* that this state of affairs exists. And though Wittgenstein does not pay any attention to this circumstance in the Tractatus, the comparison of a sentence with an ordinary picture .... shows that these two factors must be separated also in indicatives: a *picture* does not in itself assert anything, it can be used for different purposes and is therefore not a 'sentence' but merely a sentence-radical.' To me it is completely incomprehensible that Stenius can maintain that a picture does not in itself assert anything when it is asserted in 4.022 that it '*says that* they do so stand.' (And we must notice that nothing in the *Tractatus* disavows this assertion.)

On the other hand we are forced to adhere to Stenius' view if we conceive of the picture theory as an O-proposition-picture theory.

As mentioned above, the judgment-stroke in the *Principia Mathematica* is used for distinguishing between an asserted proposition and a proposition which is only mentioned. According to Wittgenstein we must say that a proposition such as '*p* occurs on this page' (in which *p* according to Russell and Whitehead is mentioned but not asserted) can never contain the proposition *p*. If *p* in this connection was conceived of as a proposition with sense, the example considered would be a violation of the thesis of extensionality, because it is not a truth-function. According to 3.143 it is out of the question that *p* is a name. In the example considered, *p* can only be conceived of as a propositional sign and we know this in advance if we know the rules of language that show themselves. Therefore in such cases, Wittgenstein does not need a judgment-stroke to mark the difference between a proposition and a propositional sign either.

b. The operation of negation and 'the general form of a proposition'.

In the passages 5.5–5.51 and 6–6.01 Wittgenstein propounds his theory of how all truth-functions can be generated by successive applications of one certain operation. This operation is, as mentioned above, an application of Sheffer's stroke. As will be known the stroke has been applied differently in the course of time, i. e. the matrix for $p|q$ has been ascribed different values. In the second edition of the *Principia Mathematica* (vol. I, p. xvi), for instance, the matrix of $p|q$ is $(FTTT)\ (p, q)$, whereas in the *Tractatus* it is $(FFFT)\ (p, q)$. No matter whether one or the other of these matrixes is preferred, it is possible — as Jean Nicod has shown in *A reduction in the number of the primitive propositions of logic, Proc. Camb. Phil. Soc. Vol. xix* — to define all other truth-functions such as negation, disjunction, conjunction and implication solely by means of Sheffer's stroke. Using Whitehead and Russell's version of the stroke, we define $\sim p\ .=p|p$ Df and $p \vee q\ .=.\sim p|\sim q$ Df. Using Wittgenstein's, $\sim p$ is defined in the same way but $p \vee q\ .=.\ p|q|p|q$ Df.

In what follows it is implied that $p|q$ has the matrix $(FFFT)\ (p, q)$. With an arbitrary number of elementary propositions as a basis, the truth-function can be written $(-----T)\ (\xi, \ldots.)$, where the brackets to the right indicate an arbitrary number of elementary propositions and the brackets to the left the denial of them all, since the matrix in the brackets to the left only has '*T*' as value in the case where all the elementary propositions are false, and has '*F*' in all other cases. Wittgenstein writes in 5.5: 'Every truth-function is a result of successive applications to elementary propositions of the operation $(-----T)\ (\xi, \ldots.)$. This operation negates all the propositions in the righthand pair of brackets, and I call it the negation of those propositions.'

I will now describe how the various truth-functions which can be constructed out of two elementary propositions can be generated. For the sake of clarity I number the different truth-functions:

p,	*q*	*1*	*2*	*3*	*4*	*5*	*6*	*7*	*8*	*9*	*10*	*11*	*12*	*13*	*14*	*15*	*16*
T	*T*	*T*	*F*	*T*	*T*	*T*	*F*	*F*	*F*	*T*	*T*	*T*	*F*	*F*	*F*	*T*	*F*
F	*T*	*T*	*T*	*F*	*T*	*T*	*F*	*T*	*T*	*F*	*F*	*T*	*F*	*F*	*T*	*F*	*F*
T	*F*	*T*	*T*	*T*	*F*	*T*	*T*	*F*	*T*	*F*	*T*	*F*	*F*	*T*	*F*	*F*	*F*
F	*F*	*T*	*T*	*T*	*T*	*F*	*T*	*T*	*F*	*T*	*F*	*F*	*T*	*F*	*F*	*F*	*F*

These 16 truth-functions can be generated in many ways. Here I shall choose one way which is in accordance with Wittgenstein's idea. We start by negating the two propositions p, q. According to Wittgenstein this has number 12 which can be written $p|q$ or $\sim p \cdot \sim q$ as a result. As far as I can see there is a mistake in this first step. When we negate p, q we do not arrive at $\sim p \cdot \sim q$ but at $\sim p, \sim q$. In order to arrive at $p|q$ we must presuppose that p and q are connected with one another in some way. This connection, of course, cannot be a conjunction for the negation of $p \cdot q$ is $\sim(p \cdot q)$ and not $\sim p \cdot \sim q$. However, if p and q are negated separately we arrive at $\sim p, \sim q$. To conjugate these two results, as Wittgenstein does, is not permissible.

After having arrived at the result $\sim p \cdot \sim q$ we can in turn negate this proposition. Since $\sim p \cdot \sim q$ (number 12) can be written $N(p, q)$, the negation of this proposition must be written as $N(N(p, q))$. Since the matrix of $N(p, q)$ is $(FFFT)(p, q)$, the matrix of $N(N(p, q))$ must be $(TTTF)(p, q)$ which is truth-function number 5 in the table. This result also represents the mistake mentioned above. For if the negation of p, q is $N(p, q)$ then the negation of $N(p, q)$ must be p, q. (In his notes to his Swedish translation of the *Tractatus* Wedberg hints at this fact (p. 136).) Instead we arrive at number 5 (pvq), if we follow Wittgenstein's ideas. My conclusion is that Wittgenstein has made two serious mistakes. First, he has not observed that p, q is not a truth-function and that therefore it cannot be negated as a whole. Secondly, he has overlooked the fact that the expression $N(N(p, q))$ is equivalent to p, q and not to pvq.

By negating $N(p, q)$, p a new truth-function can be generated according to the *Tractatus*. $N(N(p, q), p)$ has the matrix $(FTFF)(p, q)$ which is number 14 in the table. Again the question can be raised how we are able to consider and negate $N(p, q)$ and p as a whole. Furthermore it can be asked what the philosophical consequences are of the idea of selecting arbitrarily two propositions and negating. I shall return to this question below but first I wish to give an account of the way in which all 16 truth-functions are generated.

First, two propositions are given: p, q. By applying the operation $N(\ )$ once we obtain:

$N(p, q)$ matrix: $(FFFT)(p, q)$. No. 12.

By negating No. 12 we arrive at:

$N(12)$ matrix: $(TTTF)(p, q)$. No. 5.

If we apply the operation to No. 12 and 5 as a whole, we obtain:

$N(12.5)$ matrix: $(FFFF)(p, q)$. No. 16.

By applying the operation $N(\ )$ to this result we arrive at:

$N(16)$ matrix: $(TTTT)(p, q)$. No. 1.

The development may continue in this way:

$N(16, p)$	matrix:	$(FTFT)(p, q)$.	No.	7.
$N(7)$	" :	$(TFTF)(p, q)$.	"	10.
$N(16, q)$	" :	$(FFTT)(p, q)$.	"	6.
$N(6)$	" :	$(TTFF)(p, q)$.	"	11.
$N(12, p)$	" :	$(FTFF)(p, q)$.	"	14.
$N(14)$	" :	$(TFTT)(p, q)$.	"	3.
$N(12, q)$	" :	$(FFTF)(p, q)$.	"	13.
$N(13)$	" :	$(TTFT)(p, q)$.	"	4.
$N(7,6)$	" :	$(TFFF)(p, q)$.	"	15.
$N(15)$	" :	$(FTTT)(p, q)$.	"	2.
$N(14,13)$	" :	$(TFFT)(p, q)$.	"	9.
$N(9)$	" :	$(FTTF)(p, q)$.	"	8.

The notation used here is a simplification. For instance, in order that the propositional sign can show how it is generated, No. 11 should be written thus:

$$N[N(N(N(p, q), N(N(p, q)))\ q)]$$

For the sake of clarity, I dispense with this notation. It will be noticed that the amount of propositions is increased each time we apply the operation. In the survey below I have shown how the original number of propositions is successively supplemented by the first ten applications of the operation. The italicized elements in a totality of propositions are the ones that are selected and negated as a whole in order to generate the next truth-function in the series. In order to move from γ to δ one must, for example, select 12 and 5 and apply the operation $N(\ )$ to these elements taken together.

α: *p*, *q*.	ζ: p, q, 12, 5, 16, 1, *7*.
β: p, q, *12*.	η: *p*, q, 12, 5, *16*, 1, 7, 10.
γ: p, q, *12*, *5*.	ϑ: p, q, 12, 5, 16, 1, 7, 10, *6*.
δ: p, q, 12, 5, *16*.	ι: *p*, q, *12*, 5, 16, 1, 7, 10, 6, 11.
ε: *p*, q, 12, 5, *16*, 1.	$\varkappa$: p, q, 12, 5, 16, 1, 7, 10, 6, 11, *14*.

etc.

From this we see that at each step in the development of the truth-functions we must perform a *selection* of elements from the totality of propositions existing at this step. Wittgenstein has apparently not thought about this peculiarity. On the contrary he seems to have thought that it did not exist. For in 5.5 he writes that 'Every function is a result of successive applications to elementary propositions of the operation '(- - - - - *T*) (ξ, ...)' . .' If this was true, we should be able to produce δ out of γ by applying the operation $N(\ )$ to p, q, 12, and 5, as a whole. This, however, cannot be done. In order to obtain the class of propositions δ we must select 12 and 5 from γ and negate them. We therefore cannot generate all the truth-functions by applying only (- - - - - *T*) (ξ, ...).

The consequence is that the series of truth-functions cannot be ordered in a formal series such as Wittgenstein speaks of in 5.2521 and 5.2522. This passage reads:

5.2521 If an operation is applied repeatedly to its own results, I speak of successive applications of it. ('O'O'O'a' is the result of three successive applications of the operation 'O'ξ' to 'a'.)

. . . .

5.2522 Accordingly I use the sign '[a, x, O'x]' for the general term of the series of forms a, O'a, O'O'a, ... This bracketed expression is a variable: the first term of the bracketed expression is the beginning of the series of forms, the second is the form of a term x arbitrarily selected from the series, and the third is the form of the term that immediately follows x in the series.

In accordance with this definition the general form of a proposition is presented in 6: 'The general form of a truth-function is $[\bar{p}, \bar{\xi}, N(\bar{\xi})]$. / This is the general form of a proposition.' Usually it is maintained (*vide* Jørgensen: *Logical Empiricism*, p. 24, and Weinberg: *An Examination*, p. 75) that this statement must be explained in the following way. Any proposition can be generated by selecting a sub-class (ξ) out of the totality of elementary propositions (p) and applying the operation of the negation to this sub-class ($N(\xi)$). In the case of α (on the basis of which matrix 12 is generated) the notation is satisfying. But at all other steps, for instance when we proceed from η to ϑ it is misleading. For here p should represent not only p, q but also the six truth-functions already produced, and ξ must consist of p and No. 16. If the selection of ξ, which is different at each step, is included in the definition of the operation of negation we must admit that at each step from α to $\varkappa$ we are presented with a new kind of operation. For at each step we actually have to select some specific elements out of the given totality of propositions in order to develop a new truth-function and *no rule for the way the selection must be made can be found*. Wittgenstein, however, does not include the procedure of selection in his definition. According to his view, it must therefore be right to say that any proposition has the form $[\bar{p}, \bar{\xi}, N(\bar{\xi})]$, if by p we think of both elementary propositions and the truth-functions which must exist in order that a certain proposition can be generated. But the question about the nature of the procedure of selection is left unanswered. Is it a logical, a mechanical selection, or does it presuppose a subject which intuitively or reflectively selects the propositions which must be negated if a certain truth-function is to be generated? I will return to this question further on.

The alleged fact that a truth-function can be generated out of others by means of an operation and that all truth-functions are connected with each other in virtue of the operation of negation provides an understanding of the assertion, dealt with above, that if two truth-functions are given, the relation between them is given too. Since 14, for instance, can be produced by N(10, 12) it is obvious that if 14 is true, then 10 and 12 must be false. For this relation is established by means of the operation alone. It really only expresses that the operation has been applied.

*

Wittgenstein has two motives for developing the general form of a proposition by means of the operation $N(\quad)$. The one is, as mentioned above, that by doing this we are able to explain why internal relations between truth-functions generated out of the same class of elementary propositions must hold. The other is that a rational justification of the picture theory presupposes the establishment of a general form of a proposition. As we have seen, the picture theory is the only possible theory of meaning which fits into Wittgenstein's extensional view of logic. Since the principles of logic can be proved to be valid *a priori*, because they are tautologies, it must be capable of proof that no future experiences can invalidate them. This implies that we can never meet with a proposition which violates the thesis of extensionality. But if we can be sure of this all propositions must have something in common, and as this common feature cannot be anything concerning the content of the proposition (because the sense of an elementary proposition is independent of the sense of any other elementary proposition), it must be a strictly formal feature. Wittgenstein hints on this in the *Notebooks:* 'If the most general form of proposition could not be given, then there would have to come a moment where we suddenly had a new experience, so to speak a logical one. / That is of course impossible.' (p. 75). The thesis of extensionality implies that a general form of a proposition can be found. If we could not find one this would show that a contradiction or in any case an insufficiency was attached to both the thesis of extensionality and the picture theory. Later on in the *Notebooks* Wittgenstein expresses this very clearly: 'The fact that it is possible to erect the general form of proposition means nothing but: every possible form of proposition must be FORESEEABLE. / And *that* means: We can never come upon a form of proposition of which we could say: it could not have been foreseen that there was such a thing as this. / . . . / Thus it must be possible to erect the general form of proposition, because the possible forms of proposition must be *a priori*. Because the possible forms of proposition are *a priori*, the general form of proposition exists.' (p. 89). In January, 1917, he still had not arrived at a formal characteristic of the general form. It belongs to the parts of the *Tractatus* which were developed latest.

The general form of a proposition indicates the external structure of any proposition. By this I understand the properties which any proposition must possess in order to function as an argument of a truth-function in contradistinction to the internal structure of a proposition which is specific for each proposition and equivalent to its sense. $[\bar{p}, \bar{\xi}, N(\bar{\xi})]$ indicates the structure a proposition *qua* proposition must possess. It is not surprising that Wittgenstein has placed the statement about the general form as one of the seven main theses in the *Tractatus,* because to understand this general form is equivalent to understanding logic as a whole. The general form of a proposition as written in 6 explains to us how any proposition can be generated by applying the operation $N(\ )$ and this operation is all that we need in order to create the whole multiplicity of logic. Even elementary propositions fit into the general form, for an elementary proposition can be conceived of as the result of no applications of the operation to itself, or of two or four or six and so on.

The internal structure of a proposition is casual, as is the existence of a state of affairs. The external structure or the general form is at one and the same time the structure of the world and the structure of language. It represents the scaffolding of the world (cfr. 6.124) or, to put it differently, represents the features of the world which are mirrored in the structure of language (cfr. 6.13: 'Logic is not a body of doctrine, but a mirror-image of the world. / Logic is transcendental.')

I shall once more recall one of the fundamental statements in the

Tractatus namely 4.0312: 'The possibility of propositions is based on the principle that objects have signs as their representative. / My fundamental idea is that the 'logical constants' are not representatives; that there can be no representatives of the *logic* of facts.' The point stressed here is that the logical constants are not names in line with the elements of an elementary proposition. Only names represent. The difference between names and logical constants can be indicated in that we are concerned with names only in connection with what can be said, whereas we are concerned with logical constants only in connection with what is shown. In a way the general form of a proposition is the only logical constant in our language in virtue of the fact that to understand it one has to know the function of Sheffer's stroke. Wittgenstein mentions this in 5.47: '... / One could say that the sole logical constant was what *all* propositions, by their very nature, had in common with one another. / But that is the general propositional form.' And 5.472 reads: 'The description of the most general propositional form is the description of the one and only general primitive sign in logic.'

Although logical constants do not represent anything, a sign such as '$\sim$' indicates something, namely, that we have applied an operation of negation to the proposition which the sign precedes. As we have seen, this was not the same as stating that the proposition is false, for $p \downarrow$ and $\sim p$ are two entirely different expressions. In the same way signs such as '$\supset$', 'v', and '$\cdot$', indicate that a certain number of operations have been applied successively to the propositions connected by them. To maintain $p \supset q$ therefore can never be to assert that two events are causally connected with each other. To maintain $p \supset q$ is to maintain $(p \cdot q) v (p \cdot \sim q) v (\sim p \cdot \sim q)$. If the logical constants *did* represent something real, then '$\supset$' would represent a causal nexus between p and q, but as they only indicate operations it follows that we can never formulate any hypothesis about a necessary connection between the described facts. We are *a priori* debarred from introducing causal laws (cfr. 6.37).

What happens precisely when we negate something? Does $\sim p$ indicate that we know the sense of p but that we simultaneously think to ourselves that p_s does not exist? This seems impossible. According to the *Tractatus* to think is to form pictures, and therefore to believe that something is true or false cannot be described as mental activity. If it can, we must grant that propositions such as '*A* believes *p*' are genuine propositions for it is possible, then, to distinguish between a thought and a thought about this thought. To put it another way, if I can simultaneously think p and think (or believe) that p is false then the thought that p is false cannot belong to p (for if so we must admit that logical constants represent something). But if 'p is false' is not a part of p it is a thought about p and this contradicts both the picture theory and the thesis of extensionality. To believe that something is true or false therefore cannot be a mental activity. Rather it must, if we adhere to the views of the *Tractatus,* be conceived of as an action or an act of perception. Just as the knowledge that one truth-function tautologically implies another can be gathered from the perceiving of their matrixes, so the act of 'believing' that a proposition is false can be executed by writing:

p	$N(p)$
T	F
F	T

which is a mere physical manipulation, and perceiving this table. To manipulate and to perceive is to gain knowledge of something although what is perceived cannot be put into words. To say $p \supset q$ is to think p and to think q and in addition to indicate that three operations have been performed as $p \supset q$ is equal to $N[N(N(p,q)q)]$. Whether Wittgenstein would allow us to say that these operations could have been performed mentally, and not mechanically by means of pencil and paper, I do not know. It is not my intention to defend his view but simply to show the direction it must follow. I believe that what I have suggested here is supported by his view of philosophical communication which I will now attempt to make clear.

c. Philosophical communication.

Previously I have referred to the problem raised by Wittgenstein's conclusion that no meta-language can ever be established. According to the picture theory only an object-language, in which each word represents an object, can be found. Any combination of signs containing elements which do not represent anything is nonsensical and can never be more than a mere physical fact. Since all statements about the picture theory must necessarily contain words such as 'object', 'fact', 'picture' etc. which cannot be names of anything, these statements are nonsensical, and since no statements of the *Tractatus* are either elementary propositions or truth-functions every statement of the *Tractatus* must be nonsensical if the picture theory is valid. This, however, does not imply that they are without a function, for this, of course, they have since it is through reading them that we understand the picture theory and thereby learn that they are nonsensical. But how can they have a function without having a sense? The *Tractatus* does not give us a clear answer to this.

Wittgenstein himself realized that the situation was paradoxical in that in revealing the conditions of communication we find that all that we say of this is without sense. He states this most clearly at the end of his book: 6.53 'The correct method in philosophy would really be the following: to say nothing except what can be said, i. e. propositions of natural science — i. e. something that has nothing to do with philosophy — and then, whenever someone else wanted to say something metaphysical, to demonstrate to him that he had failed to give a meaning to certain signs in his propositions. Although it would not be satisfying to the other person — he would not have the feeling that we were teaching him philosophy — *this* method would be the only strict one.' And the book ends with the famous passage: 6.54 'My propositions serve as elucidations in the following way: anyone who understands me eventually recognizes them as nonsensical, when he has used them — as steps — to climb up beyond them. (He must, so to speak, throw away the ladder after he has climbed up it.) / He must transcend these propositions, and then he will see the world aright. 7 'What we cannot speak about we must consign to silence.'

Wittgenstein marks off the natural sciences in contrast to philosophy. Every elementary proposition states that something in the field of experience is ordered in a certain way and therefore belongs to one of the natural sciences but must mean something above or below the natural sciences (4.111). Hence, philosophy cannot consist of elementary propositions and this means that no philosophical view can be pictured in language. In 4.112, philosophy is defined: 'Philosophy aims at the logical clarification of thoughts. / Philosophy is not a body of doctrine but an activity. / A philosophical work consists essentially of elucidations. / Philosophy does not result in 'philosophical propositions', but rather in the clarification of propositions. / Without philosophy thoughts are, as it were, cloudy and indistinct: its task is to make them clear and to give them sharp boundaries.' And 4.115 reads: 'It will signify what cannot be said, by presenting clearly what can be said.' In this way philosophy becomes a sort of 'critique of language' (4.0031).

Wittgenstein suggests that the statements of the *Tractatus* should be called elucidations (Erläuterungen). So elucidations can be defined as formations of words which form part of an activity the aim of which is to teach us what can be said and what cannot be said. But they are not propositions or pictures. To maintain that they were would lead to inextricable difficulties.

This paradox has often been hinted at. Russell had already written in his introduction to the *Tractatus* that 'What causes hesitation is the fact that, after all, Mr. Wittgenstein manages to say a good deal about what cannot be said, thus suggesting to the sceptical reader that possibly there may be some loophole through a hierarchy of languages, or by some other exit.'

(*Introduction,* p. xxi). And in the introduction to the Italian version of the book, Colombo lists the problem as an aporia and claims that it is insoluble. He first quotes Russell's remark and then writes: 'Indeed, if the only propositions which can be given a correct formulation are those expressing facts, i. e. the propositions of science, it is clear what we must think about the propositions of the *Tractatus* which are not at all, not even approximately, scientific assertions . . . / Only two possibilities remain. Either we accept the possibility that the logical form, which is the presupposition of a symbolism and a language, can, in turn, be made the object of another language different from the first, or we deny that these assertions which are constructed contrary to the rules of the symbolism have a sense.' ('E invero: se le uniche proposizioni che si possone formulare correttamente sono quelle che esprimono dei fatti, cioè le proposizioni della scienza, appare chiaro che cosa si debba pensare delle proposizioni del *Tractatus* che non sono affatto, o quase, asserzioni scientifiche . . . / Non ci sono che due vie aperte: o ammettere la possibilità che quella forma logica che è il presupposto di un simbolismo e di un linguaggio possa divenire a sua volta l'oggetto di un altro linguaggio diverso dal primo, o negare che quelle asserzioni costruite contro le regole del simbolismo abbiano un senso.' (pp. 108-9)). He mentions that Wittgenstein tries to choose the second possibility and that the *Tractatus* consequently becomes nonsensical, while at the same time he openly violates his most treasured maxim namely statement 7 (p. 109). Also Carnap has pointed out that Wittgenstein's philosophy is self-destructive if meta-linguistic propositions are prohibited (*vide Logical Syntax*, pp. 282 ff.).

Contrary to these commentators, Maslow's attitude is a more reserved one. He thinks that Russell in his critique misunderstands Wittgenstein 'because in the *Tractatus* Wittgenstein has in mind not any one particular symbolic system within the setting of another and larger one, but the fundamental principles of all possible symbolism; and in our discourse we cannot put ourselves entirely outside all symbolism, simply because that would put us outside all discourse. And as to Russell's uneasiness . . . Wittgenstein would possibly say that it was due to Russell's confusion between 'to say' and 'to show', that is, between significant propositions about facts and a displaying of the internal forms of language. The statements of the *Tractatus* are not propositions about the facts in the world, but are merely clarifications of the formal features of language itself.' (p. 87). Maslow is surely mistaken here. The statements of the *Tractatus* can in no way be classed with what shows or displays itself, because if this was the case they should be able to fit into the general form of a proposition. In a certain sense it is, of course, true that the statements of the *Tractatus* clarify the formal features of language for it is not until we have read the book that we know what Wittgenstein thinks about these matters, but in an important sense it is false. For, according to Wittgenstein, the formal features of language show themselves as soon as we formulate elementary propositions or picture facts to ourselves. In order that a proposition can be a picture it must possess a logical form, and as this can neither be a fact nor an object it cannot be described or named but only shown (cfr. Colombo: *Introduzione,* p. 107 and Hadot: *Réflexions sur les limites du langage,* p. 474). The formal features of language are shown when it is applied and it is this which the statements of the *Tractatus* indicate. But they themselves are neither these formal features nor descriptions of them. They are, as Wittgenstein himself says, elucidations which lead us to an understanding of what can be said and what can be shown.

Yet I do not believe that the criticism of Russell and Colombo is justified. Certainly Wittgenstein never thought of suggesting a hierarchy of languages as a 'loophole' to get out of the difficulty. As I have indicated above most of the *Tractatus* explicitly rejects the possibility of a meta-language and the theory of logical inference even seems to be a detailed attempt to show how we can do without a meta-language. Indeed, it is tempting to present the theory of inference in the book as a meta-linguistic syntax for the relations between truth-functions. But Wittgenstein carefully avoids this possibility. At the end of the book he even explicitly rejects the view that the statements of the *Tractatus* could be conceived of as a sort of meta-language. The statements in the book are nonsensical, i. e. they are not propositions but pseudo-propositions. Therefore we must really, as Hadot does, distinguish between four uses of language in connection with the *Tractatus,* namely 1. *The representing use,* which is the one we meet with in the elementary propositions, 2. *The tautological use,* which need not be explained here, 3. *The absurd use,* which is the one applied in the elucidations of the *Tractatus* and 4. *The indicative use* by which Hadot thinks of the logical form as it shows itself as a feature of descriptive propositions. The absurd use he characterizes as that 'qui engendre des pseudo-propositions: la plupart des propositions philosophiques pèchent contre les lois de la grammaire et de la syntax logique; elles comportent des signes qui n'ont pas de signification; elles n'ont donc pas de forme logique, ni de sens.' (p. 478).

As far as I can see we do most justice to Wittgenstein by conceiving of the absurd use as something answering to actions. Not only do actions alter things in one's environment but they can also be used for communicating something. I will propose two examples of this. Let us imagine that a person who is born blind is able, after an operation, to see for the first time, and now asks us what the colour blue looks like. We are excluded from answering him by means of an elementary proposition for nobody has or will ever be able to describe what blue looks like, which incidentally according to the *Tractatus* is due to the fact that a colour has no structure. Instead we may show him a blue object. Here, then, we have given him a piece of information by means of an action. Or let us say that he asks us what La Place de la Concorde looks like. Instead of applying words, we can by using the appropriate means of conveyance lead him to the place and let him see it. What he sees, then, is in a certain sense a result of the actions he has done, while guided by us, in order to arrive at the place, but when he has arrived at it these actions no longer exist. In none of these examples have we used elementary propositions or anything like them.

The statements in the *Tractatus* guide us, and are able to do this although they do not have sense. They function in this way because they are complexes of stimuli which because of our linguistic habits we perceive as communications and therefore react to in a certain way. But they are not really different from the signals we meet with in the language of animals, for instance birdsong or the red throat of the male stickleback, for like these they are not pictures or descriptions of anything but only signals, i. e. stimuli which release a certain behaviour in the organisms perceiving them. They follow each other in such a way that our reactions to them are led in a certain direction. Wittgenstein's aim is to lead us to a certain result. But the result itself (the insight of what can be said and what can only be shown) is indescribable, and no extra signal can be given in order to help us to discover what it is that has to be shown. What really happens when one opens the *Tractatus* and reads the book can perhaps be illustrated by this example. One morning a man steps out of his front door and notices an arrow painted on the pavement and pointing to the nearest corner. Being curious, he follows the arrow, but when he arrives at the corner his eye catches a new arrow pointing to the next corner. He follows this too and at the next corner again he sees yet another arrow pointing to yet another corner and so forth. Let us say that the curious man, having walked for some time, continuously following the arrows, arrives at a corner where there are no new arrows to be seen but where to his great surprise he recognizes on the pavement his gold watch which was stolen from him thirty years earlier. Presumably he will pick it up and exclaim: 'What good luck that I followed these arrows (whoever painted them) for otherwise I wouldn't have found my watch again. Now I have found it, and now it really doesn't matter whether the Highway Authorities wipe out the arrows or not. They were really only accidental means of reaching this goal (even though the person that drew them probably wanted to lead my steps to my watch).' Using this analogy I wish only to point out that even if the arrows led exactly to the gold watch, the man could not actually know whether it was what he was supposed to notice and the person that painted the arrows could not have told him this by means of arrows only. But if the person that painted the arrows knew that the man had been searching for his watch for thirty years, he would just about be certain that the other person would know what it was he was supposed to notice and recognize. This circumstance corresponds to Wittgenstein's remark in the preface to the *Tractatus:* 'Perhaps this book will be understood only by someone who has himself already had the thoughts that are expressed in it — or at least similar thoughts.' It depends on the reader what result he will arrive at. By means of signals or elucidations he can be guided to the things he is to notice. But no elucidation or elementary proposition can indicate exactly what it is the reader has to become aware of. Therefore he will not notice it unless he has had the thoughts which Wittgenstein had or at least similar thoughts (using the word 'thought' at this point in an unphilosophical sense.)

V

SOLIPSISM AND THE INEFFABLE

a. Wittgenstein's solipsism.

First I should like to define what is to be understood by solipsism. In the authoritative work by Rudolf Eisler, *Wörterbuch der philosophischen Begriffe* it is stated that 'Solipsismus .... ist die Ansicht, a) dass das eigene Ich allein das Seiende ist, dass alles Sein im eigenen Ich, im eigenen Bewusstsein beschlossen ist (extrem subjektivistischer Idealismus). Alles ist nur Inhalt des eigenen Ich, es gibt keine Objektenwelt ausser dem Ich, auch keine selbständigen, transzendenten Subjekte; insbes. sind auch die "fremden" Ichs nur als Bewusstseinsinhalt (neben dem Selbstbewusstsein) gegeben .... — b) S. kann aber auch die Ansicht heissen, dass die selbständige Realität der Objektenwelt nicht eigentlich *beweisbar* sei.' A corresponding definition can be found in J. M. Baldwin, ed.: *Dictionary of Philosophy and Psychology*. The point a) of Eisler's account is labelled solipsism, 'as metaphysics or theory of reality' here whereas point b) is called solipsism, 'as theory of knowledge'. André Lalande in his *Vocabulaire technique et critique de la philosophie* only gives the metaphysical definition. In the following I will speak of two kinds of solipsism in accordance with Eisler and Baldwin namely a) *metaphysical solipsism:* Only the I exists. No world of objects nor other I's can be found 'outside' the I. b) *epistemological solipsism:* That something other than the I exists cannot be excluded but on the other hand cannot be proved either. Obviously if the metaphysical solipsism is true the problem with which the epistemological solipsism is concerned is abolished, whereas the opposite is not the case.

The reason why I start with these definitions is that the discussion of Wittgenstein's solipsism is sometimes concerned with Wittgenstein's use of this term. Stenius, for instance, (*Wittgenstein's 'Tractatus'*, p. 221n) supported by Hintikka's article, mentioned above, criticizes Urmson for understanding by solipsism 'the doctrine that there are no other minds' instead of 'the doctrine that there is no external world', and adheres to Hintikka's view that by 'solipsism' Wittgenstein really means 'idealism' although idealism of a special kind (cfr. Hintikka: *Wittgenstein's 'Solipsism'*, p. 91).

The discussion of the solipsism of Wittgenstein is so multifarious that it will hardly be profitable to give an account of it here. I shall consider some of the viewpoints of the discussion when I have proposed my own interpretation of the solipsism of the *Tractatus*.

Before examining Wittgenstein's text I will briefly state the presuppositions Wittgenstein had when he met with the problem of solipsism, which he did not consider until the picture theory was developed.

We have learnt that language consists solely of elementary propositions and truth-functions. Furthermore we have seen that although propositions have a sense which can be known in advance of empirical investigations it is necessary to compare them with reality in order to determine whether they are true or false. Hence, Wittgenstein's philosophy contains a dualism between the facts we call thoughts or propositions on the one side and the facts described by propositions on the other side. Gian Carlo Colombo has clearly characterized this dualism as a *gnoseological dualism*. Colombo opens his passage on this dualism (*Introduzione*, pp. 95–98) by saying that he will not accuse Wittgenstein of having introduced a dualism like the ones of Descartes or Spinoza for their dualistic views are not only gnoseological but ontological as well. Wittgenstein's dualism is not ontological because both thoughts and propositions are considered facts. 'But the dualism arises as soon as we consider thought and proposition not taken for themselves but in connection with their ability to represent when the symbolism is introduced.' ('Ma il dualismo nasce quando si considerino pensiero e proposizione non in se, ma nel loro valore rappresentativo, quando cioè si introduca il simbolismo.', p. 95). For, as said, a proposition has to be compared with something other than itself if we are to determine its truth-value and according to the logical symbolism it *must have* a truth-value. A proposition is verified or falsified by means of a confrontation with reality. 'But', Colombo writes, 'how the confrontation is carried out the *Tractatus* does not tell. This silence gives rise to the suspicion that some presuppositions must be found. Schlick broke the silence when saying that the verification consits in showing whether the reality possesses the same logical form as the proposition dealing with it. In order to do this nothing further is needed. The verification of the sense consisted in making certain that a logical form of the proposition was present. The verification of the truth consists in making oneself sure of the presence of two things: the form of the proposition, and the form of the corresponding fact and furthermore, clearly, in stating their identity.' ('Ma come si compia il confronto il *Tractatus* non dice. Questo silenzio fa sospettare che vi siano dei presupposti. Schlick lo ha rotto, dicendo che la verifica consiste nel rilevare se la realta possiede la stessa forma logica della proposizione che le si referisce: per far questo non v'e bisogno di nulla di nuovo: la verifica del senso consisteva nell' accertare la presenza di una forma logica della proposizione; la verifica della verita consiste nell' accertare due presenze: la forma della proposizione e quella del fatto corrispondente, nonche, evidentemente, nel constatare la loro identita.' p. 97). Colombo refers to some articles of Schlick, *Positivismus und Realismus, The Future of Philosophy, A New Philosophy of Experience* and *Form and Content* and asserts that Schlick's formulation serves as a perfect interpretation of Wittgenstein's ideas.

Further on I will return to the question of how the confrontation is carried out. Here, it is of interest to ask what the proposition is compared to. The answer to this question I have already given in my explanation of what Wittgenstein was obliged to consider an object. As shown in chapter I an object is something phenomenalistically simple and though Wittgenstein never succeeded in finding an instance of this concept he stuck to it on the whole, and had to do so. In this connection it is of no interest whether in following Wittgenstein's ideas we end up with *minima visibile, minima temporalia* etc. The essential thing is that 'object', 'state of affairs', and 'fact' are phenomenalistic concepts. This implies that thoughts or propositions must be confronted with sensations in order that their truth-values can be determined. I prefer to use the word 'sensation' here because it seems to me a little more neutral than the words 'idea', 'impression' and 'sense-datum'. It is difficult to define 'sensation' because as we have seen Wittgenstein can give us no example of an object. But sensations naturally must be distinguished from thoughts, memory images, and emotions. A fact must be something which appears either in the visual field, the auditory field, the tactile field or in one of the other sensuous fields and psychologically it must be described as a *Gestalt* of elements. Say that 'This apple is red' describes a proposition that has a definite sense though it may be immensely complex. The fact described by this proposition is a complex of sensations and it is beyond doubt that Colombo is right in letting Schlick's words cover Wittgenstein's view. The proposition is true if it has a certain structure in common with the sensational complex. If it hasn't it is false.

This has bearings on the problem of solipsism. For clearly there is no sense in speaking of anything existing except thoughts and sensations, according to Wittgenstein. If we assumed that something behind the sensations — causing these — existed it would immediately be clear that this 'something' could not be described because propositions only refer to sensations. Nor could it be thought of. Indeed, the supposition that something more than the sensations exists could not even be formulated because an eventual formulation would have to contain at least one word which was not a name of an object. Therefore we cannot even frame a question as to whether more than the sensations exists. For, as pointed out in 6.5: 'When the answer cannot be put into words, neither can the question be put into words. / *The riddle* does not exist. / If a question can be framed at all, it is also *possible* to answer it.'

Consequently Wittgenstein's empiricism must be a sort of neutral monism resembling the views of Russell, William James (in *Does Consciousness Exist*?), and Ernst Mach (in *Analyse der Empfindungen*). But in some respects his views are different from theirs partly because of his notions of object and fact and partly because he does not suggest any theory of how the neutral elements can form part of different connections as, for instance, physical and psychical connections. For a theory of this kind could never fit in with Wittgenstein's views. It could, of course, be formulated by means of pseudo-propositions but it could never work in practice because it would necessitate signs indicating, for instance, whether an element at a certain point of time was to be considered part of a physical or of a psychical connection, and according to the picture theory such signs cannot occur in a logically perfect symbolism. In a way Wittgenstein's view seems less ontological than, for instance, Russell's, but as I shall show further on his gnoseological dualism must inevitably imply an ontological dualism.

Whether or not Wittgenstein is, according to this, a solipsist depends solely on how we define the I. If the sensations are considered part of the I, Wittgenstein is an adherent to the doctrine of both metaphysical and epistemological solipsism. If not he is not a solipsist in one sense because he believes in something more than the I. In any case, though, he is a solipsist in the sense of the word suggested by Urmson. (*Philosophical Analysis*, pp. 134 ff). For the assumption of the existence of other minds is nonsensical because such entities could never be described by any propositions. At most one could describe the behaviour of another person, but to infer from this that the other person experienced something would not only lead to a result which could not be verified, but the inference itself would be wholly illegitimate. In a way the behaviourism of Wittgenstein must be more radical than the 'logical behaviourism' proposed by Carnap in *Psychologie in physikalischer Sprache* and Hempel in *The Logical Analysis of Psychology*. For the mere thought that other persons might have an I, sensations etc. is a nonsense, because it is a question which cannot be put into words. Wittgenstein's picture theory does not allow for any inferences based on the sensations given, or any conceptual constructions suggesting entities beyond the sensations. The language and the thought are suited only to the world of sensations. What lies beyond this can neither be said nor thought of.

Wittgenstein, however, does not consider sensations a part of the I. As stated in chapter III, *b.* he distinguishes between an empirical ego and a metaphysical subject and his solipsism is, as we shall see, connected with the relation between the metaphysical subject and the world. By 'world' we must here understand the totality of facts to which the empirical ego belongs because it consists of thoughts, which *per* definition are facts. The metaphysical subject is, as pointed out, neither an object nor a fact and therefore cannot be a part of the world but in some sense or other must be 'outside' the world. Wittgenstein's conception of a person and the world can be schematized in this way:

	The world	
The metaphysical subject = the philosophical I or self.	The empirical ego = the human soul.	The 'physical' world = the world of sensations — to which my body belongs.
Indivisible.	Complex.	Complex.
The limit of the world.	Consists of thoughts the elements of which can be investigated by psychology, and perhaps of other psychical phenomena.	Consists of facts.
A person		

According to Wittgenstein I must say that I consist of an empirical ego and a metaphysical subject. Whether my body belongs to my 'self' or not is a matter of opinion of no interest to epistemology. The world comprises all facts and therefore everything with which the subject is confronted. 'I objectively confront every object but not the I' Wittgenstein writes in the *Notebooks* (p. 80) immediately after having stated that 'the I is not an object.' But although Wittgenstein makes a sharp distinction between the metaphysical subject and the world, he does not raise the problem of how he can infer the existence of a world from the existence of the I. Berkeley's problem of the existence of an external world is not touched on at any point in the *Tractatus* or the *Notebooks*. On the contrary the existence of an I and a world is postulated: 'There are two godheads: the world and my independent I.' (*Notebooks*, p. 74). This, however, is not an arbitrary postulate. It is justified by Wittgenstein's solipsism the kernel of which is that it is nonsense to speak of a world separate from a subject. '. . . . the subject is not a part of the world but a presupposition of its existence . . .' (*Note-books*, p. 79).

Nor does the gnoseological dualism in Wittgenstein's philosophy give rise to the question whether an external world exists independent of the empirical ego. The solipsism of Wittgenstein is bound up with the relation between the world and the metaphysical subject, but in any case one could ask how we can infer the existence of a world on the basis of the existence of the empirical ego. If for a moment we suspend the assumption that the empirical ego belongs to the world, we may ask in what way can more than the existence of the empirical ego and the metaphysical subject be justified. This is a problem of inferring from the one link of the gnoseological dualism to the other, i. e. from the presence of thoughts to the existence of the facts represented by the thoughts. To all appearances, Wittgenstein has not sensed a problem here. The answer to the question, according to his view, must be that we are forced to assume that something beyond language exists, because we cannot have a language unless we have a logic and we cannot have a logic unless propositions have truth-values, which they only have if they deal with something outside language. *The gnoseo-logical dualism is not based on experience. It is a necessary consequence of the possibility of logic and therefore it cannot cause any question as to the legitimacy of inferring the existence of reality on the basis of the existence of thoughts.* Apart from this argumentation, Wittgenstein could, naturally, maintain that anybody possessing normal senses must admit the existence of sensations, which he, as mentioned above, apparently does consider a part of the empirical ego.

*

The passage on solipsism in the *Tractatus* is only a page and a half long. In my investigation of it I wish to divide it into two parts; first, the section from 5.6 to 5.62 and then the section from 5.621–5.641. The reason for this division is that Wittgenstein, as far as I can see, has been led to his solipsism in two ways, corresponding to the two parts. The first part reads:

5.6 *The limits of my language* mean the limits of my world.

5.61 Logic pervades the world: the limits of the world are also its limits.
So we cannot say in logic, 'The world has this in it, and this, but not that.' For that would appear to presuppose that we were excluding certain possibil-ities, and this cannot be the case, since it would require that logic should go beyond the limits of the world; for only in that way could it view those limits from the other side as well. / We cannot think what we cannot think; so what we cannot think we cannot *say* either.

5.62 This remark provides the key to the problem, how much truth there is in solip-sism.

> For what the solipsist *means* is quite correct; only it cannot be *said*, but makes itself manifest.
> The world is *my* world: this is manifest in the fact that the limits of *the* language (the only language I am able to understand) mean the limits of *my* world.

I have made two alterations of the text of Pears & McGuinness. In the third paragraph of 5.62 the German text reads: 'Dass die Welt *meine* Welt ist, das zeigt sich darin, dass die Grenzen der Sprache (der Sprache die allein ich verstehe) die Grenzen *meiner* Welt bedeuten.' It is beyond doubt that '*der* Sprache' must be translated as '*of the language*' and not '*of language*' as suggested by Pears & McGuinness. I will clarify this distinction in the cause of the next few pages. The translation of the paranthesis has been a matter for discussion. Miss Anscombe (*An Introduction*, p. 167), Urmson (*Philosophical Analysis*, p. 135) and Colombo (in the Italian version of the *Tractatus*, p. 255) render it 'that language which alone I understand' while Hintikka who first noticed this mistake in the English version (*Wittgenstein's 'Solipsism'*, p. 88) and Stenius (*Wittgenstein's 'Tractatus'*, p. 221) maintain that the correct translation must be 'the only language I understand'. From a philological point of view Hintikka and Stenius are right and I consider it superfluous to discuss the matter further. The translation suggested by Hintikka has been followed in Wedberg's Swedish version and my own Danish version of the *Tractatus*.

What does Wittgenstein mean by the assertion in 5.6? First we must consider in what sense we can speak of 'the limits of language'. By 'language' Wittgenstein understands a system of signs which when combined in certain ways form elementary propositions, and in addition to this a set of rules (which can only be shown) for how truth-functions are constructed out of elementary propositions. In the *Tractatus* we are not told how to construct elementary propositions. They manifest themselves as thoughts. But the rules for constructing truth-functions are shown and with these the rules of inference. What is shown is condensed to the general form $[\bar{p}, \bar{\xi}, N(\bar{\xi})]$ which indicates the external form of all propositions and could really be called the mould of language. Of course this definition of language must be distinguished from the ordinary use of the word we make when we speak of English, French, Japanese, Danish etc. as languages. All these tongues are instances of one and the same language. Whether we speak Chinese or German the smallest bits of the language containing a sense are the elementary propositions and the logical syntax is the same in all tongues. Therefore it is natural for Wittgenstein when maintaining that only one language can exist to speak of it as *the* language.

Obviously the language must have limits. These, however, cannot be indicated in the same way as we indicate the frontier between, for instance, Denmark and Germany. For the conditions of indicating the borders of a country are that we are able to move on both sides of them and that the countries on either side of the border-line can be represented in language. These conditions cannot be fulfilled when the limits of the language have to be indicated. For we are neither able to think what is on one side of the limit, the non-linguistic, nor represent this part in language (because thought and language are identical). Wittgenstein emphasizes this in 5.61 and in the preface of the *Tractatus* which is reasonable as all the problems of the book originate from this fact.

We can show that the language has limits by making sign-combinations which according to the definition of the language do not belong to it. However, we cannot think such combinations nor judge them, as pointed out in chapter III. But of course they can be written in 'language' as this word is usually conceived of. We can write 'This table penholders the book' although we cannot think it. In a strict sense of 'language' when this is taken to mean 'the totality of senseful propositions' an expression of this sort does not form part of the language. In the colloquial sense, however, the expression is considered a proposition, though an odd one, and it is this colloquial use of the word 'language' Wittgenstein makes in the preface where he writes: 'Thus the aim of the book is to set a limit to thought, or rather — not to thought, but to the expression of thoughts: for in order to be able to set a limit to thought, we should have to find both sides of the limit thinkable (i. e. we should have to be able to think what cannot be thought). / It will therefore only be in language that the limit can be set, and what lies on the other side of the limit will simply be nonsense.'

Since we can speak of both an 'internal' and an 'external' form or structure of a proposition, it follows that the limits of the language can be transcended in at least two ways. Either we can form nonsensical sign-combinations such as 'This table penholders the book' or we can form compound expressions that violate the logical syntax of language. In connection with the discussion of the limits of language Wittgenstein appears to be concerned only with the latter kind of nonsense. According to Wittgenstein we simply cannot violate the logical syntax of language while communicating. It is impossible to introduce any alternative to the existing logical rules because we never could communicate the fact that we are breaking or suspending them. If we could, this would imply that we could speak of something beyond the limits of language. Wittgenstein states this clearly in the passage 3.03–3.032 in which the word 'language' apparently is applied in the strict sense:

3.03 Thought can never be of anything illogical, since, if it were, we should have to think illogically.

3.031 It used to be said that God could create anything except what would be contrary to the laws of logic. — The reason being that we could not *say* what an 'illogical' world would look like.

3.032 It is as impossible to represent in language anything that 'contradicts logic' as it is in geometry to represent by its co-ordinates a figure that contradicts the laws of space, or to give the co-ordinates of a point that does not exist.

From 3.032 it can be seen that 'language' as used here does not comprise nonsensical formations of words as it does in the preface. The double use of this word in the *Tractatus* must be noticed as Wittgenstein's views otherwise become incomprehensible.

In addition to the mentioned ways of transcending the limits of language there are two other senses in which language can be said to be limited. One is that the language is limited in that propositions can only have two truth-values, true and false, and that a proposition cannot be conceived of without its truth-poles. The other is that the totality of elementary propositions, being identical with the totality of thoughts, must be given limits by the birth and death of the individual. Both senses have affinity with the solipsism of the *Tractatus*.

I have previously shown how Wittgenstein introduced logical space as an ontological counterpart to language. From the account I have given of logical space in chapter II, *b.* it can be seen that the limits of language and the limits of the logical space must coincide. For the logical space is constructed as a tracing of the formal features of propositions. When the logical space is reproduced in this way:

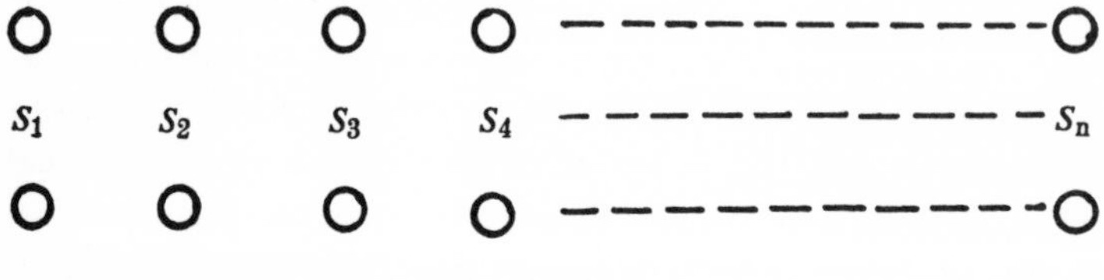

O O O O ------------O

S_1 S_2 S_3 S_4 ------------ S_n

O O O O ------------O

with the demands mentioned on p. 42 added, it is clear that any state of affairs must be an element of the series S_1, S_2, $S_3 \ldots S_n$ and that no other values of existence than the ones indicated by the upper and lower circles can be found.

In the logical space no possibility can be excluded *a priori*. The logical space indicates what is thinkable. And what is thinkable is logically possible too. To exclude a possibility in logical space as, for instance, that S_3 can ever exist, would demand a reference to something other than experience and logic. We would so to speak have to get behind experience and find a sufficient reason for the fact that S_3 could not exist. This reason could never be found *in* the world, for all states of affairs (and facts) are independent of each other. To get behind experience or outside the world, is not possible. This would mean to transcend logical space or think what cannot be thought.

The world must fall within the logical space. The world is the totality of all facts or existing states of affairs, and as the logical space indicates all possible states of affairs, any possible world can be represented by a line in the logical space as shown in chapter II, *b*.

This circumstance gives us the full understanding of 5.6 and 5.61. The limits of the language coincide with the limits of the logical space. If a combination of words is nonsensical it does not represent anything and nothing in the logical space corresponds to it. If it has sense it will be an elementary proposition (or perhaps a truth-function but this is of no interest here), and a state of affairs in the logical space will correspond to it. If we form an expression such as $p \uparrow \downarrow$, we will again meet with something nonsensical, which corresponds to nothing in the logical space, because the combination

s_K

⊗

is a forbidden combination. Everything in language which is logically legitimate can be represented in logical space.

When any possible world can be represented by a line in the logical space, obviously the limits of logical space are at the same time the limits of the world. The opposite, however, may not be the case, the limits of the world need not be the same as the limits of logical space. What in fact exists is not identical with what is logically possible. This might be the reason why Wittgenstein in 5.6 (and 5.62) writes that 'Die Grenzen meiner Sprache *bedeuten* die Grenzen meiner Welt' and not '. . . *sind* die Grenzen meiner Welt' as the limits of the language and the world do not coincide.

The next step in the understanding of this approach to solipsism is to realize why *the* language must be characterized as *my* language. For it is by virtue of the fact that the language is *my* language that the world is *my* world and that solipsism consequently becomes the only possible view. But why is the language necessarily *my* language?

Neither the *Tractatus* nor the *Notebooks* contain an explicit answer to this question. It is not, however, difficult to deduce a plausible answer from Wittgenstein's ideas. The unreflected view of language is that it consists of O-propositions and that consequently all propositions have a certain sense independent of who regards them and thinks of them. But everything is different when we are forced to say that language consists solely of W-propositions. According to the unreflected view the language is a common property, no more *mine* than *yours*. But if language consists of W-propositions only all that I can ever consider and experience as language is nothing but *my thoughts*. Even when I hear another person speaking, or read a book, the facts I perceive (the sound waves from the person, or the printing ink in the book) are pictures, according to the thought-picture theory, only because I use them as propositional signs for the thoughts which I think when hearing the person speak, or reading the book.

Already the fact that the thoughts constitute the empirical ego implies that I must speak of them as *my thoughts*. As pointed out above, the empirical ego is part of the world but at the same time it is coordinated with my I, the metaphysical subject. For although a thought already *qua* thought is a picture of a state of affairs there must be a subject connected with it which experiences that it *is* a picture of something. In some way or other, therefore, my train of thoughts is related to my I or metaphysical subject.

Language as a whole is coordinated with the metaphysical subject too. The language consists of elementary propositions but in addition possesses certain logical features which can only be shown. The fact that they are shown implies that they are shown *to* somebody or something and this something is the metaphysical subject. If there were no metaphysical subject nothing could show itself. What we call the logical structure of language only exists by virtue of an experiencing subject, and since the only language I can conceive of is the language of which the structure is displayed to me, and of which the propositions have sense for me, the language certainly is *mine*. This assertion actually is a truism. If I said that the language may have a sense to others and a structure independent of my experience, I would make the assumption which we are discussing, namely that we can assume the existence of something external, something independent of my experiences. As long as this is the question with which we are dealing, structure can only be something which shows itself to me and the language must be *my* language. It cannot exist apart from me.

The next question is how Wittgenstein infers that the world is *my* world from the fact that the language is *my* language. From what has been said above it can be seen that the limits of my language are also the limits of the logical space and therefore are the limits of every possible world. But from this it can only be inferred that 'the limits of my language are the limits of the world'. Wittgenstein, however, seems to have emphasized that by the world I only can mean 'the world as it appears in my logical space', and as the limits of the world here must lie inside the limits of my language, it is really my 'I' that determines the limits of the world.

*

We have now followed one pathway to solipsism suggested in Wittgenstein's text. The other one is presented in the passage 5.63-5.641. (At present, I shall leave 5.621 out of account but will return to it later.) The idea behind this is concentrated in a remark in the *Notebooks* which unfortunately was left out in the *Tractatus*: 'This is the way I have travelled: Idealism singles men out from the world as unique, solipsism singles me alone out, and at last I see that I too belong with the rest of the world, and so on the one side *nothing* is left over, and on the other side, as unique, *the world*. In this way idealism leads to realism if it is strictly thought out.' (*Notebooks*, p. 85). In *Tractatus* the conclusion occurs, followed by 5.64: 'Here it can be seen that solipsism, when its implications are followed out strictly, coincides with pure realism. The self of solipsism shrinks to a point without extension, and there remains the reality co-ordinated with it.'

From the quotation from the *Notebooks* it can be seen that Wittgenstein actually distinguishes between idealism and solipsism, a fact which both Hintikka and Stenius (*vide* p. 144) have overlooked. In order to understand 'the way I have travelled' which Wittgenstein speaks of we may proceed in the way he did himself when establishing the picture theory. We start by saying something that leads to some consequences which show that our starting point contained a nonsense. For instance I can proceed thus: I am in a room *R* together with a number of other persons. I maintain that as no two persons can see *R* from the same angle simultaneously we all must have different impressions of *R*. Furthermore this difference between our impressions can be reinforced on the basis of individual structural processes in our brains. Next I infer that as all of us each have our experience of *R* we mean something different by the expression 'the room *R*'. In fact I must say that when I apply this name I am referring to my experience of *R* and not to *R* itself. When one of the other persons uses the expression he is referring to his impression of *R* and so on. But the moment I realize this I understand that I cannot possibly speak of 'the room *R*' independent of my impression of *R*. I am debarred from referring in any way to that which I had, in the first place called 'the room *R*'. At this step in the argument I am forced to say that the statements that started it were pseudo-propositions because in them I referred to the room *R* independent of my impressions which — as shown in the argument — is impossible.

In this way I have been led through three stages. I started as a realist by assuming the existence of the room R independent of my experience. Then I said that each of us in the room R had an experience of R and in this way I inevitably 'singled men out from the world as unique' for the persons in R in this way were considered to be something entirely different from the other things in the room, the furniture, ashtrays etc. Now, suddenly, I had arrived at an idealistic view which amounted to each person in the room having his own experience of R and never knowing anything about R independent of this experience. First 'the room R' signified something existing independently of the mind, but now it signifies impressions. And from this stage I am led to the solipsistic view. Strictly speaking — on the gnoseological level — I know nothing but my own experiences and it is only hypothetically that I can speak of the experiences of other persons. The hypothesis that other persons experience something is a postulate beyond proof because no matter what 'evidence' I found for it, this 'evidence' could never be anything other than my own sensations or experience, and I will never be able to prove that more than my own experiences exist. This is the gnoseological solipsism at which Berkeley stopped and which is called epistemological solipsism above. It has, however, a linguistic aspect besides the gnoseological one. If I accept it, I must also accept that all the words of language are names of my sensations. I cannot even say that words used by another person are names of *his* sensations. If another person says something both he and what he says are mere phenomena in *my* world of experience. If I experience a meaning of the words he utters, this is due to the fact that I correlate them with some other sensations of mine and in this way make them a part of my private language. If I am a gnoseological solipsist I must in addition be a linguistic solipsist. I must hold the view that only one language can ever be found, *my* language, 'die Sprache die allein ich verstehe'. In this way the gnoseological solipsism is connected with the other pathway to solipsism presented in the passage 5.6–5.62.

Wittgenstein, however, does not end here. 'Solipsism singles me alone out' ('der Solipsismus scheidet mich allein aus') but this solipsism inevitably raises the question of what my 'I' is. According to the picture theory the word 'I' can only refer to an object or, if it is a shorthand for a complex expression, to a fact. But none of these possibilities is acceptable because the I cannot be a contingent fact in the world. To place the I 'outside the world' is impossible because this very expression is nonsense. But all the same the I is something, because it is stated in the *Notebooks* that it is 'a presupposition of its (the world's) existence'. In the *Tractatus* it is characterized by means of analogies partly as a point without extension (5.64) partly as a limit of the world (5.632 and 5.641). Moreover it is, as we shall see, characterized as something coinciding with the world. The realism to which Wittgenstein must return when the idealism is 'strictly thought out' is not the same as the one he started from. In 5.64 the realism reached at is called 'pure realism' which indicates that he considers this to be something different from naive realism.

Some passages in the *Notebooks* suggest that Wittgenstein, for a short period at least, has imagined and perhaps believed in a pure solipsistic view in which the world was identified with the content of his consciousness. These are on page 82 which reads 'What has history to do with me? Mine is the first and only world!', and on page 83 which reads: 'If I have been contemplating the stove, and then am told: but now all you know is the stove, my result does indeed seem trivial. For this represents the matter as if I had studied the stove as one among the many things in the world. But if I was contemplating the stove *it* was my world, and everything else colourless by contrast with it.'

*

We can now inspect more closely Wittgenstein's remarks about the second line of thought that leads him to solipsism. These are the following:

5.63 I am my world. (The microcosm.)

5.631 There is no such thing as the subject that thinks or entertains ideas.
If I wrote a book called *The World as I found it*, I should have to include a report on my body, and should have to say which parts were subordinate to my will, and which were not, etc., this being a method of isolating the subject, or rather of showing that in an important sense there is no subject; for it alone could *not* be mentioned in that book. —

5.632 The subject does not belong to the world: rather, it is a limit of the world.

5.633 Where *in* the world is a metaphysical subject to be found? You will say that this is exactly like the case of the eye and the visual field. But really you do *not* see the eye. And nothing *in the visual field* allows you to infer that it is seen by an eye.

5.6331 For the form of the visual field is surely not like this.

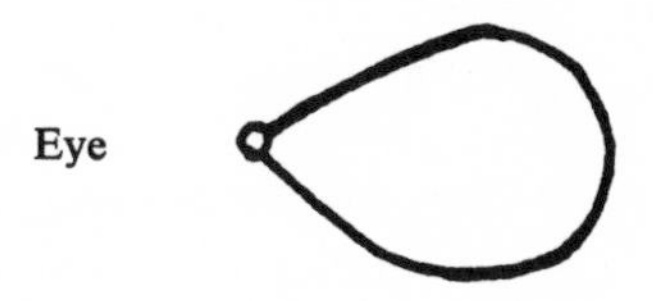

5.634 This is connected with the fact that no part of our experience is at the same time *a priori*.
Whatever we see could be other than it is.

Whatever we can describe at all could be other than it is.
There is no *a priori* order of things.

5.64 Here it can be seen that solipsism, when its implications are followed out strictly, coincides with pure realism. The self of solipsism shrinks to a point without extension, and there remains the reality co-ordinated with it.

5.641 Thus there really is a sense in which philosophy can talk about the self in a non-psychological way.
What brings the self into philosophy is the fact that 'the world is my world'.
The philosophical self is not the human being, not the human body, or the human soul, with which psychology deals, but rather the metaphysical subject, the limit of the world — not a part of it.

In the light of what I have previously said about this passage I believe it has to be understood in the following way. When I have realized that all that I can mean by the expression 'the room *R*' is *my* sensation of *R* and that I always will be in similar situations, it becomes natural to say that 'I am my world. (The microcosm)'. In the philosophical tradition in which Wittgenstein presumably grew up in Vienna, 'microcosm' signifies the individual mind's reflection of the world which is the macrocosm (cfr. Schopenhauer: *Die Welt als Wille und Vorstellung,* vol. I, § 29). Every mind is conceived of as a perceiving point which mirrors everything in its surroundings and which, because it perceives, contains elements corresponding to every perceived element of the surroundings. In the example considered, the room *R* is a part of the macrocosm, whereas my sensations of *R* form part of the microcosm which I am. By 'the world' I can only mean my microcosm for, as we have seen, I cannot experience anything but this microcosm. I never can experience the macrocosm. The world is everything which is the case. But what is the case always forms part of my microcosm. This microcosm is all I meet with from birth to death. It is all the experiences which form my life which, in turn, is the same as the totality of all facts. Therefore, clearly, the world and life are one (5.621).

5.63, however, not only indicates that by the world I must mean my microcosm but also that a certain relation can be found between the world and the I. In the paragraphs following 5.63, this is developed a little. In 5.631, which I commented on in chapter III, *b.* it is stated that I (I use the first person singular in order to give an appropriate account of the solipsism) cannot experience any subject or I in the world. It must be so because in the first place no object or fact can be entitled to be called a subject if the picture theory is valid and secondly the circumstance that the subject is a willing subject cannot reveal its connection with anything in the world because there is no necessary connection between the will and the facts of the world (*vide* chapter III, *b.*). The conclusion in 5.632 is that a subject cannot be found in the world, but the existence of a subject is not denied. It is, as pointed out above, only asserted that a subject which 'thinks or entertains ideas' (5.631) does not exist.

In 5.633 Wittgenstein attempts to indicate the relation of the subject to the world by means of an analogy: the relation of the eye to its visual field. In fact he accepts this analogy although, from a first glance at 5.633, it might look as if he rejects it. The analogy is proposed for the first time in the *Notebooks*, p. 73. After Wittgenstein has asked himself what he can possibly know about God and the purpose of life he writes among other things: 'That I am placed in it (the world) like my eye in its visual field.' This analogy has at least three aspects:

1. Just as the eye is an invisible limit of the visual field so is the subject an unobservable limit of the world.
2. From nothing in the visual field can it be inferred that it is seen by an eye. In the same way we can state that no experience reveals to us that it is experienced by a subject.
3. The visual field has no limits. We cannot, therefore, in advance tell what will fall within the limits of the field and what will not. In the same manner the world of experience is without limits so that we cannot *a priori* say what can be found in the world and what not.

1. and 2. are discussed in 5.632 and 5.633. 'The subject does not belong to the world: rather it is a limit of the world' Wittgenstein writes in 5.632, and 5.633 explains this assertion. Just as an eye cannot be found in the visual field a metaphysical subject cannot be found in the world. This is stated in the sentence: 'You will say that this is exactly like the case of the eye and the visual field.' (which is in my opinion a misleading translation of 'Du sagst, es verhält sich hier ganz wie mit Auge und Gesichtsfeld.') which seems to express a rejection of the analogy although it does not in fact do so. If it was to be considered a rejection, the next sentence would be without a motive. For the stress on the fact that 'you really do *not* see the eye' points to something which is analogous to the relation between the subject and the world and one never rejects an analogy by pointing out that at least in one respect it holds. Also the third part of 5.633 clearly shows that the analogy is accepted, and 5.6331 continues by emphasizing the third point of the analogy which Wittgenstein returns to in 6.4311.

The correct paraphrase of 5.633 must read: 'Where *in* the world is a metaphysical subject to be found? You will say that this is exactly like the case of the eye and the visual field, and you are right in saying this. But from this you must not infer that as it is possible to see an eye it may be possible to find a subject *in* the world too. For the eye, with which you perceive, you really do *not* see. And just as nothing in the visual field allows you to infer that it is seen by an eye so nothing in the total field of experience allows you to infer that it is perceived by a subject.'

The analogy incites the objection that one can easily see the perceiving eye, for instance by regarding it in a mirror. But this only shows that Wittgenstein's formulation is too rough. By a perceiving eye we must not only think of the eye-ball but of the optic nerve and braincells as well. Whether the physiological parts that enable us to see can be isolated from the organism as a whole of course is subject to doubt, but this has no importance for the validity of the analogy. What Wittgenstein should have said was that nothing in the visual field allows you to infer that it is seen by the optic cells in the brain (*via* the eye and the optic nerve). This assertion in any case is true as in looking at ourselves in a mirror we can see neither the processes in the optic nerve nor the 'picturing' in the optic cells of the brain.

With regard to point 1, Wittgenstein's analogy is instructive. In the *Notebooks* he mentions, as quoted above, that the I is placed in the world as the eye in its visual field. If we concentrate on the phenomenological experience of the visual field we realize that it is limited because we cannot see anything behind our heads. The limit between what can be seen and what cannot be seen is impossible to describe. It is common psychological knowledge that it is not even possible to describe objects situated close to this limit because they cannot be articulated clearly when placed in this remote part of the visual field. The limit itself we do not even experience although we can surely say that the visual field has a limit. When the I is characterized as a limit of the world (or as a point without extension) this presumably must be understood in the same way: All that I experience is limited because in every situation in life I meet with a perceptual whole which does not comprise everything perceivable. But I can never experience the limit between my I and my sensations.

The third point of the analogy is emphasized, then, in 5.6331. The figure presented in this paragraph must, as far as I can see, be taken to mean that the visual field has no limits as concerns the distance from the eye. If we imagine a straight line drawn from any point of the retina through the pupil no object can be placed on such a line without being perceived by the eye. The visual field does not stretch, for instance, specifically, 200 miles out into space. It does not end with a wall or a limit at a certain distance from the eye. As stated in 6.4311 'our visual field has no limits'. If it had a limit this could for example, when seen from above or from the side, have the form drawn in 5.6331. If it had a form of this kind, one could tell *a priori* in any situation what would be inside and what would be outside the visual field.

This is why Wittgenstein writes in 5.634 that what is said in 5.6331 'is connected with the fact that no part of our experience is at the same time *a priori*.' Indeed, Wittgenstein strains his analogy in point 3, and of course nothing is proved by the use of the analogy. 5.634 is no more than a postulate.

All that we learn about the difficult question regarding the relation between the I and the world can be summed up thus: The I is a limit of the world, a point without extension with which the reality is co-ordinated. The I is placed in the world like the eye in its visual field. Finally we are told in 5.63 that 'I am my world (the microcosm).' I have tried to throw light upon the first two statements but it must, indeed, be admitted that Wittgenstein could have expressed himself a little more clearly (it is of some help to know that Wittgenstein in his use of the word 'limit' is inspired by Schopenhauer (*vide* Anscombe: *An Introduction*, p. 169). The eye-visual field analogy, however, is useful in the further indication of the relation of the I to the world. For a visual field is something which only exists if the eye exists. The eye is a condition of the existence of a visual field. In the same way the subject is a necessary condition for the existence of the world. As said before this is explicitly stated in the *Notebooks*. In the *Tractatus* it is hinted on in 6.431: 'So too at death the world does not alter, but comes to an end.'

Furthermore the visual field is distinguished by being the visual field of a *certain* eye. In the same way all that I experience is not only the world but *my* world. And this world of mine is the first and only one. 'What brings the self into philosophy is the fact that 'the world is my world'' it is said in 5.641 in which it is mentioned that the I in question is not the empirical ego. The fact that the I cannot be described or experienced is no more awkward than that the eye of the vision cannot be experienced or explained if the only empirical material at hand is the visual field. Wittgenstein's solipsism really ends in a riddle. It would have been proper for him to end his passage on solipsism with the poetical remark to be found in the *Notebooks* (p. 80): 'The I, the I is what is deeply mysterious!' ('Das Ich, das Ich ist das tief Geheimnisvolle!').

*

I will now summarize what I have said about Wittgenstein's solipsism. He is led to his view along two lines. The first one begins with the fact that only one language can exist. This language is *my* language and it has limits. Because it has limits, the logical space and consequently the world have limits too. From this, however, it does not follow, as Wittgenstein thought, that the world is *my* world. This assertion is not well-founded unless we take the second line leading to solipsism into consideration. This line begins in a type of realism from which by means of Berkeleyan arguments one is led to idealism and solipsism which in this case is an epistemological solipsism, as Wittgenstein distinguishes between the subject and the world. Even the statement 'I am my world' does not wipe out this distinction. On the contrary it stresses the point that there are two 'godheads'. The subject is called a presupposition of the existence of the world but this apparently is simply to be understood in the sense in which we say that the eye is a presupposition of the existence of a visual field. The subject cannot be characterized because it lies 'outside' the world. By 'world' we do not mean something existing independently of the mind but simply the sensations I have. From a realistic point of view these sensations must be characterized as an imprint (or a mirror-image) of the world, as a microcosm. But since I only know of *this* microcosm I am excluded from describing things from the realistic point of view (In part *c.* below I shall return to this). This implies that by 'world' I can only mean 'my world' or the microcosm, and that my language can only refer to this microcosm. The microcosm, however, is not part of the I (just as the visual field is not a part of the eye). Neither is it a part of my empirical ego. It is that with which the I is confronted. The reason why Wittgenstein has to make this distinction between the I and the world of sensations is that the picture theory involves a gnoseological dualism. As mentioned above this shows itself partly in that the thoughts deal with something different from themselves, partly in that something shows itself to the metaphysical subject.

Without a subject no microcosm could exist. Therefore the end of life or the disappearance of the subject implies that the world (= my world) ceases to exist. The opposite is also the case. If no world of sensations existed there would be no eye either. For a thing to which a visual field in principle could not be co-ordinated could not be called an eye. Perhaps it is this interdependence between the eye and the world that leads Wittgenstein to write 'I am my world'. If by the I we understand not only the metaphysical subject but also the empirical ego we cannot speak of an interdependence. For it is not absurd to speak of a thinking I that has no sensations.

According to Wittgenstein's solipsism I must, if I accept it, maintain the following: What exists is '*my I*' (i. e. the metaphysical subject), *my empirical ego* and *my world* (i. e. all the experiences I have. They presuppose the existence of my I and *vice versa*.) When asked, 'Does anything exist independent of your mind?' I must answer, 'if by 'mind' you mean my empirical ego there does, but if by mind you mean the metaphysical subject, which I am, there does not. That is why I call everything *my* world.' When asked, 'Does anything exist outside 'your world', for instance the world in itself independent of all human knowledge?' I must reply, 'I am debarred from connecting any sense with expressions such as 'the world in itself', 'the world independent of my knowledge of it' etc. Therefore the question is nonsensical.' (In part *c.* of this chapter, I will return to this and try to show that Wittgenstein does, in fact, accept 'the existence' of something 'outside' the world thus contradicting his solipsistic view.) When asked, 'Do other persons or minds exist?' I must answer, 'In the meaning which the word 'person' has to me (as a name of certain complexes of sensations) persons do exist in *my world*. I cannot, however, assume that other minds or subjects exist. I may be able to connect some sense to the expression 'metaphysical subject' but according to the picture theory this expression is not a name of anything and as my language can only picture possible things in my world I cannot even in my logical space propound the possibility that other metaphysical subjects exist. Consequently it is logically impossible for them to exist.'

It must be noticed though, that Wittgenstein has probably thought of the possibility that other persons exist and in his unphilosophical moments he even seems to assume that they do (*vide* the preface and 6.43). It must not be forgotten, either, that the *Tractatus* is in fact addressed to a reader who is to attain the same knowledge as its author. Wittgenstein has undoubtedly imagined that there could be many subjects each with a private world co-ordinated with them and therefore many private languages too. But he does not deal with the problem such an assumption raises (for instance, how any communication between these different subjects could ever be established). Rather he suppresses this possibility which according to the picture theory is a nonsense. Even if I could formulate the existence of other subjects in pseudo-propositions yet the picture theory must exclude all other subjects than my own. So even if Wittgenstein has sometimes imagined that the right theory must be a sort of collective solipsism or 'perspectivism' he has been bound to reject such a theory and accept that his world was the first and the last existing world.

As mentioned above there is a problem connected with his use of the term 'pure realism'. From his point of view, however, I might say that I have come to the conclusion that only I and my world exist and that the world is something real, which although it presupposes a subject does not contain subjective features. Whereas for instance the realism of John Locke was a view in which the existence of primary qualities was accepted while the secondary were considered dependent on the nature of the subject, Wittgenstein's view does not imply any discussion whether some qualities are primary and others secondary. My world is dependent on my existence and *vice versa*. But everything in my world is equally real, nothing is more subjective than other things. Everything in the world is something which I 'objectively confront' (cfr. *Notebooks,* p. 80). Therefore the realism which I must acclaim must be safeguarded against all the objections which have been raised against traditional realism (e. g. the realism represented by Engels and Lenin). Perhaps this is why Wittgenstein wishes to call his view 'pure realism'.

*

Finally I wish to comment briefly upon the works on Wittgenstein's solipsism. I have not dealt with them above, mainly because they all present a very different interpretation from mine, but also because the commentators have only written a little about the solipsism. My view may have something in common with the one presented by Domenico Campanale (*Studi*, pp. 34–44) though I doubt if Campanale himself would agree on this. None of the commentators have mentioned why Wittgenstein speaks of the microcosm and generally they only give a superficial account of his solipsistic view.

For instance, the reason why I have not examined Miss Anscombe's interpretation in this study is that she makes no mention of 5.633, 5.6331, and 5.634, while her reading of 5.6, and 5.61, seems to me somewhat rash. (cfr. *An Introduction,* p. 167 where 5.61 is simply paraphrased). I agree with her characterization of the I as 'the centre of life, or the point from which everything is seen' (p. 168) but characterizations of this sort are just as obscure as Wittgenstein's.

Some of the commentators on the *Tractatus* believe, as mentioned above, that Wittgenstein denies the existence of a metaphysical subject because he writes that there is no such thing as the subject that thinks or entertains ideas (5.631). Weinberg explicitly characterizes the solipsism of the *Tractatus* as a solipsism without a subject (*An Examination,* pp. 67 - 68, and 201 - 02). The paradoxes implied by this view have been noticed by Barone who follows Weinberg's interpretation and critisizes Wittgenstein for having used the word 'mine' (*Il solipsismo,* p. 560). Instead Barone should have seen that Wittgenstein's use of this word actually shows that Weinberg is wrong. Furthermore Barone critisizes on the basis of this the view that some facts can represent others (*Il solipsismo,* p. 569). Colombo also follows the interpretation of Weinberg but he adds that Wittgenstein could possibly have meant that the world, the life, the I, and the language, are one and the same thing (*Introduzione,* p. 114). As we have seen, this idea cannot be accepted. We only have to remember that the empirical ego is composite whereas the subject is simple in order to realize that Colombo cannot be right. Incidentally Campanale has critisized his fellow-countrymen for not having noticed that Wittgenstein assumes that an I or ego exists (cfr. *Studi,* p. 35).

As mentioned in chapter III, *b.* both Hintikka and Stenius are also mistaken here. Hintikka describes the subject as 'a complex not unlike a totality of propositions' and tries to prove this by an analysis of the passage 5.541 - 5.5421 which, however, is too brief to offer any weight of evidence. Stenius thinks — contrary to 5.631 — that the subject understands and uses language and therefore his interpretation of 5.6 must naturally differ from the one given above, although I agree with his comments on 5.62, 5.631, 5.632, 5.633, and 5.6331 (cfr. *Wittgenstein's 'Tractatus'*, pp. 221–22). As mentioned before, both Hintikka and Stenius maintain that Wittgenstein adheres to idealism. If this is to be true we must define idealism in a very special way which does not tally with the traditional definition.

Maslow mistakes the I for the empirical ego (*A Study*, p. 150) and maintains that Wittgenstein's solipsism is formal: 'Wittgenstein's 'solipsism' is not factual but formal: it points to the impossibility of stating the limits of significant language by the propositions of such language itself.' (p. 149). I hope that it can be seen from my account that we have serious reasons to believe that Wittgenstein's solipsism is 'factual' in the sense that he is forced to maintain that his world is the first and only one because it presupposes the existence of his metaphysical subject. Maslow, however, makes some essential remarks on the ineffability of the solipsism to which I will return below (part *c.*).

b. The grounds for the metaphysical subject.

Wittgenstein's solipsism is, as I hope I have shown, attached to a certain theory about the metaphysical subject. At first glance, the solipsism seems to have nothing to do with the other views of the *Tractatus* and it seems natural to ask whether Wittgenstein could have done without the metaphysical subject and thus avoided the solipsism. A closer examination, however, reveals on the one hand a connection between the solipsism and the picture theory, as pointed out above, and on the other hand that Wittgenstein's theory of logic and meaning necessitates the assumption of a metaphysical subject.

I have touched upon this point in chapter III, *b.* I said there that the comparison between a picture (or a thought or W-proposition) and a fact presupposed the existence of a 'something' that made this comparison. This 'something' necessarily had to experience in some way or other, for to compare a thought with reality is to obtain knowledge. Furthermore this 'something' could not think or entertain ideas. For if it could think, the problem it was supposed to solve would rise again, now on a higher level. These two demands are met with in Wittgenstein's notion of the metaphysical subject. Even if he had not introduced this concept in the *Tractatus* we would arrive at it as a consequence of the thesis of extensionality and the picture theory. For if we presuppose that propositions are either true of false and in addition to this deny the possibility of intensional relations between propositions, we are compelled to accept that the truth-value of a proposition can only be fixed by a comparison of it with reality. According to the thesis of extensionality (and the picture theory) no propositions can describe the relation between a proposition and a fact. Hence there must be a kind of knowledge which cannot be said or thought and therefore cannot be related to the empirical ego.

Correspondingly we can say that Wittgenstein's theory of logical inference implies the existence of a subject which can 'see', but neither think nor entertain ideas. That pvq is true if $p \cdot q$ is true cannot be described but only seen. The same counts for the tautologies. That $pv{\sim}p$ is a tautology can be seen from the propositional sign alone but it cannot be said, for '*pv∼p is a tautology*' is a pseudo-proposition. It shows itself, and the entity to which it shows itself can see it but neither describe it nor think it. Consequently that entity must be something other than the empirical ego. For similar reasons Wittgenstein's theory of identity and relations imply the existence of a metaphysical subject.

Stenius has pointed out that we really find two picture theories in the *Tractatus*, a 'descriptional picture theory' and an 'ontological picture theory' (*Wittgenstein's 'Tractatus'*, p. 177). I should like to adopt these labels though they cannot mean exactly the same here as in Stenius' book because of the difference between our interpretations of the picture theory. By the 'descriptional picture theory' I mean here the thought-picture theory. By the 'ontological picture theory' I mean the thesis that the logical features of language mirror some features of reality and in this way represent them. This view is stated most clearly in 6.13: 'Logic is not a body of doctrine, but a mirror-image of the world. / Logic is transcendental.' 5.511 reads: 'How can the all-embracing logic, which mirrors the world, use such peculiar crotchets and contrivances? Only because they are all connected with one another in an infinitely fine network, the great mirror.' 6.124 supplements these statements: 'The propositions of logic describe the scaffolding of the world, or rather they represent it...' Furthermore we find in 6.22: 'The logic of the world, which is shown in tautologies by the propositions of logic, is shown in equations by mathematics.' In 6.342 and 6.3431 it is emphasized that although Newtonian mechanics does not directly tell us anything about the world, the *way* in which it is possible to describe the world by means of mechanics tells us something about its ontological features.

'The ontological picture theory' consists in the assertion that the propositions of logic, by which we may think of the propositional and functional logic of the *Principia Mathematica*, mirror the logic of the world, i. e. ontological features. It is, however, very difficult to understand what 'the logic of the world' or 'the logical scaffolding' is. The metaphors of Wittgenstein do not offer much help. But the idea is that just as an elementary proposition according to the descriptional picture theory mirrors, and in this way, represents, the structure of a state of affairs, the tautologies (or we might as well say the general form of a proposition) mirror a structure of the world which cannot be described but which shows itself. It is another matter whether we mean the same by 'structure' in the two picture theories. I do not want to consider this difficult problem here. The question of interest at the moment is what the two picture theories presuppose about the 'knowing' person. The answer to this question is: *The descriptional picture theory presupposes the existence of a thinking ego, the empirical ego, which pictures facts. The ontological picture theory presupposes the existence of a subject which does not think but takes in the logic of the world by an act of seeing.*

It is difficult to argue in favour of this view. The best way of showing that it must be right is to show that the alternative views are impossible to hold. If there were no metaphysical subject, logical truths could not be shown. Since Wittgenstein's 'descriptional picture theory' implies that something must be shown he must necessarily introduce a subject. It plays an essential rôle in his whole system.

In chapter IV, *b.*, I mentioned another argument in favour of the existence of a metaphysical subject. I there touched upon the question how an operation of negation is performed. What really happens when we negate *p*? Seemingly the operation could be performed mechanically. We can imagine a machine constructed in such a way that all propositions which were fed into it came out negated. If the machine received the information *p* it automatically would respond *N*(*p*). In the same manner we can perhaps imagine that a human being can negate a proposition automatically without thinking. If this were so the negation-procedure could be described behaviouristically supplemented perhaps by a physiological description of the processes in the nervous system corresponding to the actions of the person performing the negation. This, however, cannot fit into Wittgenstein's view. A proposition *p* is not negated by one simply writing *N*(*p*). By writing *N*( ) we add something on the paper to the propositional sign but the sign we add has no influence on the signs which were previously on the paper (just as the number of a proposition does not affect the proposition (cfr. p. 130). What has to be negated is *p* conceived of as a picture of a state of affairs and this it is only if '*p*' is thought. The operation of negation must be applied to a thought or a W-proposition; therefore it cannot be a mechanical operation. It must be performed by something which at the same time is 'outside' the sphere of thought and yet is connected with it in such a way that, as it were, by an act of volition, it can 'do something to' the thoughts. In addition it is, as I have pointed out above, often necessary to select some propositions out of a large class of them in order to perform the operation. Here too it is really *thoughts* that have to be selected and it therefore seems natural to imagine that something 'above' the empirical ego selects. As Wittgenstein distinguishes between the human body and the empirical ego it is in any case impossible to say that the body automatically selects the thoughts to be negated.

I realize that if we say that an operation is performed by an act of volition, it can be doubted whether an operation will in fact result just because we wish it. Here conditions are the same as when Wittgenstein discusses ethical problems. Just as my wish to save the child in the example given on p. 96 might result in something quite different from the intended actions so my wish to negate *p* might result in something entirely different from the writing of or 'thought' of *N*(*p*). It is not my task, but rather the task of the adherents to the *Tractatus,* to solve this problem.

Of course we must not forget that Wittgenstein does not even mention the metaphysical subject in connection with the operation of negation. It even looks as if he has not asked himself how this operation is performed. But here — as in all other places in this book — it is not only the views which Wittgenstein explicitly states which are of interest but also the implications they have. The main doctrines of the *Tractatus* inevitably imply the existence of a metaphysical subject and this is an interesting fact no matter whether Wittgenstein was aware of it or not. Now Wittgenstein has in fact given some grounds for speaking of a subject namely those concerning ethics and the will dealt with in chapter III, *b*. The theory of the willing subject, however, does not seem to be implied by the other views in the *Tractatus*. Rather it is only a supplement to the main theses of the book.

It has often been maintained that Wittgenstein's conception of the 'I' is equal to Kant's in *Kritik der reinen Vernunft*. The last chapter of Stenius' book on Wittgenstein has the title 'Wittgenstein as a Kantian Philosopher' and in this it is held that the metaphysical subject is transcendental (p. 221). Maslow writes: 'I feel that Wittgenstein here is very close to Kant, with the 'I' in his world playing the same role that 'Transcendental Unity of Apperception' plays in Kant's phenomenal world, namely 'that unity of consciousness which precedes all data of intuitions, and by relation to which representation of objects is alone possible' . . . . ' Colombo too points to the similarity between Wittgenstein and Kant (*Introduzione*, p. 115). Undeniably there is a great similarity to be found. It can be stated that just as the transcendental apperception in Kant's philosophy guarantees the identity of the self (*Kritik der reinen Vernunft* A, p. 107–08) and connects the various

'Vorstellungen' pertaining to the individual, so the metaphysical subject in Wittgenstein's system is the only thing which preserves the identity of the individual and functions as a co-ordination-point of everything in the world (i. e. of all thoughts and sensations). But we must not overlook the fact that Wittgenstein arrives at his subject along quite different lines from Kant and that his subject cannot think. It is questionable whether Wittgenstein is in any way inspired by Kant. I believe it to be more probable that his views concerning the metaphysical subject have been inspired by Schopenhauer. In *Die Welt als Wille und Vorstellung* Schopenhauer speaks of how '. . . jene Einheit des Bewusstseins, in welchem selbst es mit dem wollenden Ich, dessen blosse Erkenntnis-Funktion es ist, als identisch sich darstellt.' (Vol. II, p. 293). These words could just as well have been written by Wittgenstein, but in spite of this, Schopenhauer is close to Kant: 'Jener Einheitspunkt des Bewusstseins, oder das theoretische Ich, ist eben Kants synthetische Einheit der Apperception, auf welche alle Vorstellungen sich wie auf eine Perlenschnur reihen und vermöge deren das "Ich denke", als Faden der Perlenschnur, "alle unsere Vorstellungen muss begleiten können."' (pp. 293–94). And Schopenhauer's localization of the I in the brain (p. 294) must have seemed to Wittgenstein a monstrosity. But undoubtedly the problems Wittgenstein is concerned with are taken from Schopenhauer's works. Wittgenstein's view concerning the interdependency between the subject and the objects can be found in *Die Welt als Wille und Vorstellung*. And the view that everything is co-ordinated with the subject which in turn can neither be described nor explained is expressed in Schopenhauer's work: 'Die Identität nun aber des Subjekts des Wollens mit dem erkennenden Subjekt vermöge welcher das Wort "Ich" beide einschliesst und bezeichnet, ist der Weltknoten und daher unerklärlich.' (Vol. III, p. 161).

It is highly improbable that Wittgenstein conceived of the metaphysical subject as a consequence of the picture theory. The truth is, rather, that, inspired by his reading of Schopenhauer, he assumed the existence of the subject and later discovered that this subject had a *raison d'etre* in connection with the relation between reality and description (i. e. with both the descriptional and the ontological picture theory). But as mentioned above it is impossible to prove this conclusively.

c. The ineffable.

As mentioned several times by Wittgenstein himself the fundamental aim of the *Tractatus* was to show what can be said and what cannot be said but only shown; or, which is the same, what can be thought and what cannot be thought. In 4.1212 it is said that 'What *can* be shown, *cannot* be said.' In addition he seems to think that what *can* be said *cannot* be shown or that in any case it would be misleading to say that it shows itself. Moreover he seems to hold the opinion that no more than what is said and what is shown is ever present in human knowledge.

This last contention, however, is not without exception. As to objects we must say that they cannot be described but only named (3.221: 'Objects can only be *named*. Signs are their representatives. I can only speak *about* them: I cannot *put them into words*. Propositions can only say *how* things are, not *what* they are.'). It is the picture theory which implies this. For description consists in that a part of the language (a W-proposition which at the same time is a fact) reproduces the structure of a state of affairs or a fact. Since an object has no structure, because it is simple, it cannot be described. On the other hand objects do not belong to that which shows itself in language. They are not represented by a feature in language which can be shown only. The way they manifest themselves has no parallel in language. Objects show themselves when we sense them and it is questionable whether this manifestation can be classed with what 'shows itself'. In any case there is the difference that while we cannot imagine that the logical features of the world and of language which show themselves can be altered, we can easily imagine that the objects we perceive are replaced by some others. It is true that the objects form the substance of the world (2.021) but on the other hand nothing in language prescribes what objects are to be found. The only thing we know for certain, if we accept the fact of logic, is that objects *must* exist. For logic presupposes that there exist propositions with a definite sense and, as we have seen, they cannot have this unless objects exist. But our knowledge of objects seems to be something different both to what can be said and to what can only be shown.

Among the things that can only be shown we must remember the sense of a proposition. The thesis of extensionality prevents us from describing the sense of a proposition because it implies that no proposition can deal with another. But the picture theory also precludes us from doing it. We can see this in the following way. If by the sense of a proposition we understand the state of affairs described by the proposition the sense of a proposition p is p_s. If we assume that a proposition q different from p is a description of the sense of p, then q must be a picture of p_s. But in this case p and q are identical. Consequently no proposition different from p can describe the sense of p.

The internal structure of an elementary proposition which it has in common with the pictured fact cannot be described. Neither can we describe parts of the structure for if this was possible these parts would be entities with sense (because to describe them would be to form propositions about them which *per* definition would have structure in common with them) and in this case we would not be concerned with elementary propositions. The structure of an elementary proposition consequently is an indivisible whole which cannot be analysed but shows itself and, as mentioned in chapter III, *a.*, shows what it is a picture of.

Among the things which are ineffable we find furthermore, as described above, the tautologies and the relations between propositions that follow from or imply each other. In a way everything formulated by means of formal concepts too must belong to the ineffable. This implies that all the statements of the *Tractatus* must be classed with what can only be shown. I believe though that it would be right to consider them as something different from the ineffable as they surely are more or less accidental formulations. The right characterization of them is that they are pseudo-propositions or elucidations. For the person that sees everything rightly they are superfluous. One could imagine that Wittgenstein had developed his views without ever having made a statement about them. In this case he would certainly know about all which shows itself and consequently elucidations cannot be classed with the ineffable.

When Wittgenstein in 5.62 writes that 'what the solipsist *means* if quite correct, only it cannot be *said*' this is immediately evident because the statements in which the solipsism is set forth are pseudo-propositions and therefore cannot belong to what can be said. Words such as 'I', 'world', and 'language' are not names and cannot therefore be parts of propositions. There is, however, a deeper reason for maintaining that any formulation of solipsism is nonsensical.

Before I give an account of this I think it is necessary to speak a little of the consequences relevant to knowledge which must result from Wittgenstein's conceptions of logic and language.

It is natural to ask, having read the *Tractatus*, whether the theses of it hold good. Is, for instance, the distinction between what can be said and what can be shown fixed, in the sense that no future experience can violate it? Is it not possible that some sort of revelation can show the human being that something exists behind his sensations and that his view of the world is relative and gives expression to a limited knowledge.

Wittgenstein has tried to forestall such questions by introducing his general form of a proposition. The general form of proposition is not only the external form of any proposition of the past and the future, but furthermore an indication of the essence of the world. 5.471 reads: 'The general propositional form is the essence of a proposition.' and in 5.4711 it is said: 'To give the essence of a proposition means to give the essence of all description, and thus the essence of the world.' The general propositional form is the form of all expressions that describe something. The things described, the facts, will, according to 5.4711, always have a certain form that enables us to describe them by means of propositions that exemplify the general form of a proposition.

As said before, all that we can conceive of as logic is expressed in the general form. If we understand the expression $[\bar{p}, \bar{\xi}, N(\bar{\xi})]$, we must at the same time understand the whole of mathematical logic and be able to calculate all tautologies. This is maintained, partly, in 5.472: 'The description of the most general propositional form is the description of the one and only general primitive sign in logic.' The fact that all tautologies mirror something of the world's form is connected with this. 6.13 reads: 'Logic is not a body of doctrine, but a mirror-image of the world. / Logic is transcendental.' And 'The logic of the world . . . . is shown in tautologies by the propositions of logic . . . .' (6.22).

There is, accordingly, a certain fixed structure which must pertain to all possible worlds. No matter what we experience, $p v \sim p$ will always be a tautology and $p \cdot \sim p$ a contradiction. No matter what event is described, the proposition describing it will either be an elementary proposition or a truth-function constructed by means of the operation of negation. What sort of experiences we will have in the future we know nothing certain about. What is thinkable is possible too (3.02) so therefore everything which we can picture to ourselves may happen. The logical scaffolding of the world, however, we cannot imagine altered. Wittgenstein adheres to a logical absolutism which indeed is difficult to justify. That we cannot think the unthinkable is a truism. But from this we cannot infer that what we cannot think now never can be thought. Not if we argue only on the basis of Wittgenstein's premisses.

*

Besides this logical absolutism, however, there is another line of thought which plays a part in Wittgenstein's theory of the limits of knowledge. It is to Maslow's credit to have brought it to light and, in the following, I will use his label for the fundamental mistake which Wittgenstein was fighting against, namely 'The Fallacy of the Angelic Point of View', though I will speak of this fallacy in more general terms than Maslow does.

According to Maslow, this fallacy consists in the following: Philosophers who adhere to solipsistic viewpoints often forget that they are shut in in their own world of sensations and ideas. This shows itself in that when giving epression to their views they look at them from the outside, from a sort of 'angelic' point of view. This is fallacious, because according to their views it has no sense to try to characterize something from an alleged 'angelic' viewpoint. 'Perhaps this fallacy should be called 'the philosophers' fallacy'.' Maslow writes. 'It consists in the pretension of having avoided the logical restrictions of what is called in contemporary philosophical literature 'the egocentric predicament', that is, the pretension that one can say something about the world from a point of view which is outside the world in which one finds oneself.' (*A Study*, p. 148).

An example can perhaps reveal the character of this fallacy better than a definition. Let us assume that I have arrived at the view that all that I can ever experience are my own sensations, thoughts, emotions and memory images. Nothing but these can be known by me. Yet it seems reasonable that I can imagine that something exists 'behind' these things I experience. Most of the philosophers from the time of Descartes and up to Kant would say that although I adhered to solipsism I could suppose for the sake of argument that something 'behind' my experiences existed, for instance a 'Ding an sich'-world. The question whether it really exists or not would be considered by many philosophers a sensible though insoluble question. In the same way many philosophers would consider it sound that I raised the question whether other minds than my own exist, although this question could not be solved by experience either. To sum up, one could say that even if it is granted that I could only and always be aware of *my* sensations, nothing precludes that I could imagine or make a theory of the nature of the world seen from an 'angelic' point of view, even though I could never verify this theory.

This way of looking at things can be criticized on positivistic grounds as one can say that we must never assume the existence of something unless the assumption can in principle be verified or falsified by experience. Ernst Mach advanced a positivism of this sort which culminated in the verification principle of the logical positivists who maintained that a sentence was devoid of sense if it could not be tested on empirical grounds. As will be known, the connection between the older forms of positivism and the views of the sensefulness of language proposed by the logical positivists is to a certain extent established by Russell and Wittgenstein. But on account of his solipsism Wittgenstein's view of these matters contains aspects which, although not considered by the logical positivists, are valuable because they draw our attention to some features of the situation we are in when seeking for knowledge, which are relevant to epistemology, independent of the question whether Wittgenstein's picture theory and its consequences are valid or not.

The special feature of Wittgenstein's solipsism is that it is at one and the same time a phenomenalistic and a linguistic solipsism. As mentioned, Wittgenstein stresses the point that the language which he understands, which is naturally the only existing language to him, can only deal with his experiences. Not only does it contain certain logical features which mirror some general features of his world of experience (which is hardly essential in this connection) but it also contains names and these names can only be representatives of objects in his world of experience. Furthermore the language is characterized as the totality of elementary propositions, while the world is characterized as the totality of facts. Since the facts are described by means of true elementary propositions we may say that an exhaustive description of the world consists of the totality of true elementary propositions.

We must notice here that Wittgenstein's theory of meaning precludes that the world and language can be defined intensionally. When asked what is to be understood by 'the world', we must answer, according to the *Tractatus,* this fact and that fact and that one and that one etc. until we have mentioned all known existing states of affairs. When asked what is to be understood by 'the language', we must in the same manner enumerate all elementary propositions. This is all that we can say about the world and the language. If, instead of these extensional definitions, we wished to make an intensional one, for instance of the world, we would have to do this by opposing the world to something else and show that everything belonging to the world possesses a defining property which does not pertain to anything outside the world. Correspondingly an intensional definition of language must consist in an indication of a common mark which everything belonging to language possesses and which does not pertain to anything outside language.

Maybe it is easiest to understand why it must be impossible to define 'language' and 'world' intensionally, according to the *Tractatus,* if we represent the argument by means of Boole's algebra. If we have a logical universe in which all elements are classified according to a certain property p we obtain two classes, a, and *non-a:*

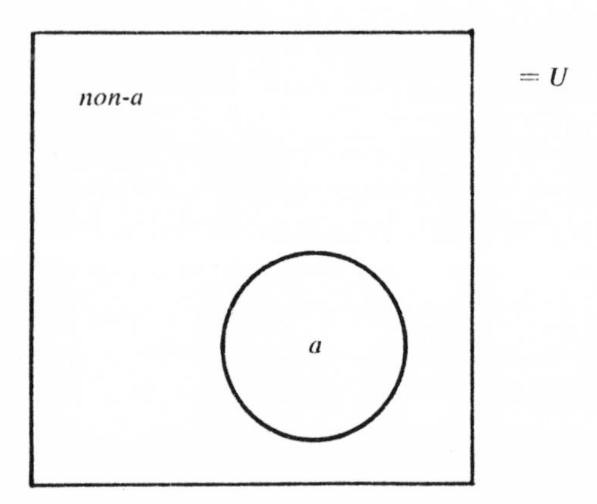

We can transfer this classification into a definition by defining a as the class of all elements possessing the property p. This definition is intensional because we are able to decide whether any arbitrarily chosen element belongs to *a*, or not, simply by testing whether it has the property *p*, or not. The presuppositions of establishing a classification and a definition of this sort are as follows:

1. The elements of *a* on one side and *non-a* on the other must differ in respect of at least one property *p*.
2. The elements of *a* and *non-a* must have at least one property in common in order that, although they belong to two different classes, they can be classed with the same logical universe.

From these two presuppositions it follows that 'existence' is not a property which can be defined intensionally. For if 'existence' is a property, then it must be possible to delimit the class of elements possessing this property in contrast to the class of elements not possessing it, which we may call the class of 'non-existence'. Furthermore it must be the case that the elements of the two classes, 'existence', and 'non-existence', respectively, must have at least one property in common. But this is impossible since it is contradictory to ascribe a property to what we call 'non-existence'.

'Existence' can be defined only extensionally, i. e. by enumerating the elements comprised by this concept. Since, *per* definition, we cannot delimit it in contrast to something else, it cannot function as a predicate-designation in propositions. For the function of a predicate-designation is to assert that the subject has a certain property which does not pertain to everything, or to class the subject with something (a class) to which it would not belong if it did not possess the property in question. Neither 'existence' nor 'exists' can have this function, however, because we can never determine what the subject should be classed with if it does not exist. Since the 'non-existing' cannot delimit the 'existing', the concept 'existence' is without limits and consequently it is nonsense to speak — by means of predicate-designations such as 'existence' or 'exists', which are not really designations at all — of classing something with the existing things.

Of course 'existence', according to the picture theory, can never occur as a predicate-designation. If it could, in the first place this would presuppose that an object named 'existence' could be found, because every element of a proposition is a name of something. If such an object could be found it would have to have itself as a property in order to exist etc. *ad infinitum*. This, however, would be impossible to picture in language. Secondly, according to 4.022, a proposition shows how things stand if it is true and it *says* that they do so stand. The picture states that the pictured state of affairs, and the objects constituting it, exists. Consequently no extra name is necessary for marking that something exists. If 'existence' or 'to exist' do not designate something, the proposition 'A exists' is, according to the picture theory, a nonsense. This, of course, can also be inferred from the fact that a proposition cannot consist of one name only because structure can only occur if at least two elements are brought together.

In returning to the example of a classification given above we can state that we cannot define U intensionally if by U we mean 'everything which exists'. U can be defined extensionally, for instance as $U = a + non\text{-}a$, but U cannot be defined intensionally unless U and Ω $(=a \cdot non\text{-}a)$ have at least one property in common. Since this is impossible, U can be defined only extensionally. This implies that nothing can be predicated about U. Or, in other words, we cannot formulate a predicative proposition containing U as a subject-designation.

*

Let us now regard Wittgenstein's conception of the language. If we consider every fact which pictures something as part of the language, then language can be defined thus:

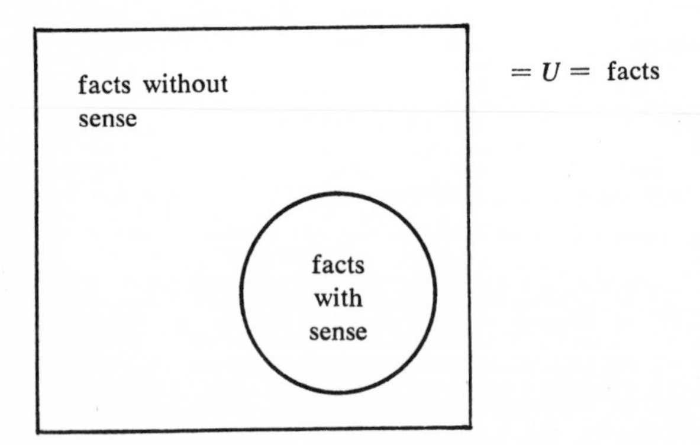

But if by 'language' we mean everything which can be thought, the situation is different. For the necessary condition for obtaining an intensional definition of 'language' is then that 'what can be thought' and 'what cannot be thought' have at least one property in common. This, however, cannot be possible. For if the act of ascribing a property to 'what cannot be thought' consists in thinking 'what cannot be thought' together with a property, we see immediately that we are involved here in the contradiction which Wittgenstein warns us against when pointing out that it is impossible to think the unthinkable. Even if this argument is not considered convincing we realize that 'what can be thought' cannot be defined intensionally unless we can a) ascribe a property p to 'what can be thought' and b) can show that 'what cannot be thought' possesses the property p too. Since 'what can be thought' is what is logically possible and 'what cannot be thought' is equivalent to what is logically impossible, it hardly can be possible to find a property common to both. No matter whether we speak of the logically possible as a formal property of language, as what is logical, or as what fits into the general propositional form, none of these predicates can be common properties for what is possible and what is not possible. Not even 'existence' could do as a common property even if it was permissible to use 'exist' as a predicate.

'What can be thought' therefore can never be delimited as an area in a logical universe. It can be defined extensionally only, i. e. 'what can be thought' can be considered a logical universe itself in which numerous distinctions can be made (we may, for instance, distinguish between thoughts in respect of the scientific topics they are about). Therefore we can never draw a limit for 'what can be thought', for this could only be done by means of a classification-procedure which makes an intensional definition possible. Hence 'language', in the sense 'what can be thought', can only be defined extensionally; we cannot set limits to it. Wittgenstein writes in the preface that we cannot 'set a limit to thought' and that 'It will therefore only be in language that the limit can be set, and what lies on the other side of the limit will simply be nonsense.' As mentioned above, by 'language', he obviously does not mean here 'the totality of W-propositions', for if so there would be no difference between language and thought in respect of the problem of setting limits. By 'language', at this point, he is, in all probability, thinking of combinations of words and propositions and clearly we can set limits in the following way:

nonsensical formations of names (and propositions)

formations of names (and propositions) with sense

$= U =$ formations of names (and propositions)

When, later in the *Tractatus,* Wittgenstein speaks of 'language' in connection with the problem of solipsism, he means by this the totality of W-propositions. I have given reasons for this assertion above and may add here that when he speaks of language as 'die Sprache, die allein ich verstehe' it is clear that nonsensical formations of names and propositions (as, for instance, 'this table penholders the book') cannot be classed with language, since they cannot even be understood.

Wittgenstein's conception of the world encounters similar difficulties. The world is the totality of facts. Facts are existing states of affairs. Consequently they can be defined in contrast to non-existing states of affairs. This definition, however, can only be made in the logical space. Here an intensional definition of both 'existing states of affairs' and 'non-existing states of affairs' can be made, where 'state of affairs' can be defined only extensionally because nothing can be opposed to this concept if the conditions 1. and 2. are to be observed. Please note that not even 'proposition', 'thought' or 'picture' can be opposed to the concept 'state of affairs' because propositions, thoughts and pictures are facts and therefore states of affairs.

When we speak of the world as what actually is manifested in our experience, i. e. as the facts, and leave out all references to the logical space, we also see that nothing can be opposed to the world. Here Wittgenstein's analogy of the eye and the visual field once again is illuminating. Just as the visual field cannot have limits, neither can my total experience. If we could see the limits of the visual field and what eventually is beyond them, we could set up something to which the visual field could be opposed. It is, however, contradictory to speak of seeing something outside the visual field. In the same way it is contradictory to speak of perceiving something beyond the total field of experience. When we speak of the visual field we cannot find anything which has one single property in common with it, and which differs from it in at least one respect. If 'existence' were a property we might define the visual field as opposed to, for instance, the auditory field, but we have to preclude this possibility. Also, we are not able to find anything having at least one property in common with the total perceptual field which at the same time differs from it in at least one respect. This is already precluded by the fact that we cannot find an extra quality pertaining to everything which we can experience besides the one that it can be experienced. Any definition of the world (= the totality of facts), therefore, can be nothing but extensional. 'The world' as well as 'the language' is a concept which cannot occur as a subject-designation in a predicative proposition.

*

The fallacy of the angelic point of view among other things consists in that we use concepts, which can only be defined extensionally, as if they were defined intensionally. In order to show this I will present an example of an epistemological mistake.

Let us regard the assertion 'life is a dream'. Although this assertion has never been maintained as a definite point of view it has functioned as a provisional legitimate assumption in many places, for instance in the philosophy of Descartes. The assertion may be founded on an argumentation such as the following one: 'I have often, when asleep, dreamt something which, while I dreamt, I thought was real. But every time this has happened I have woken and discovered that what I dreamt was not real at all. When awake I have a lot of experiences just like those when I dream, and while I have them I cannot help believing that they are more real than what I experience when dreaming at night. But taught by the experience that when I dream I am often mistaken about dream and reality, I think that what I call reality now might as well be a dream, but that this all-comprehensive dream cannot be known to be a dream until at some time I awake from it to what we might call the *real* reality, whatever that may be. The more I think it over the more convinced I am that we have no reasons whatsoever for denying that this life, the reality we look at now, is a dream.'

The fallacy in this argument is revealed as soon as we examine the conditions for using the words 'dream' and 'reality' (In Jørgensen's *Psykologi på biologisk grundlag,* chap. VI, there is an argumentation similar to the following). The starting point of the argument is that all experienced phenomena can be divided into some which are dreamt, and some which are real, since 'dream' and 'reality' at this point are defined in contrast to each other. This can be illustrated in this way:

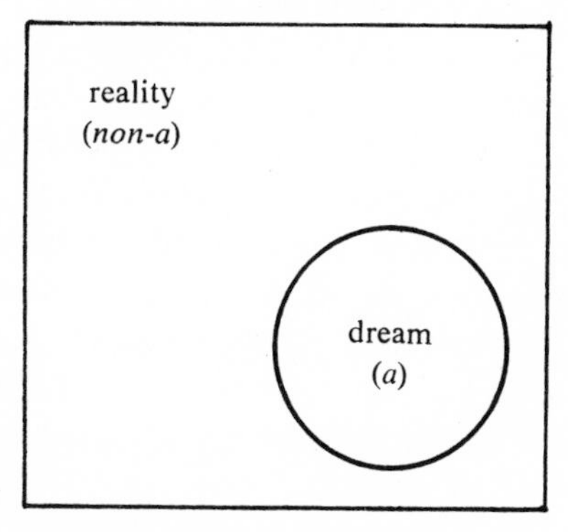

$= U =$ the totality of phenomena or experience.

Since $U = a + non\text{-}a$ the assertion that everything is a dream obtains this form:

$$(1) \quad a = a + non\text{-}a;$$

This, however, is contradictory. This contradiction can only be avoided if we maintain that by the *a* on the left side of the sign of equation we mean something different from the *a* on the right side (so by 'dream' in the assertion 'life is a dream' we do not mean the same as we normally mean). We must therefore write:

$$(2) \quad a' = a + non\text{-}a;$$

but now the question is what we really mean by *a'*.

I do not believe that it is an objection to this argument to say that dreams form part of reality and that no attention is paid to this fact in the drawing above. For if dreams are considered parts of reality, i. e. as having a property, say *b*, in common with the rest of reality we arrive at:

$$(3) \quad U = b \cdot a + b \cdot non\text{-}a;$$

If this equation is chosen as a starting point the assertion 'life is a dream' must be expressed:

$$(4) \; b \cdot a = b \cdot a + b \cdot non\text{-}a$$

But since it is legitimate to divide by *b* on both sides of the equation-sign this expresses the same as (1).

Nor do I believe that it is relevant to object that 'dream' and 'reality' are not defined sharply in the example considered. For in the example I have really considered only the structure which the argument has, no matter how 'dream' and 'reality' are defined, as long as we insist that the two concepts are opposed to each other and therefore differ in at least one aspect.

Consequently, a person who maintains that life or reality is a dream is saying something which is either a contradiction or a nonsense. It is a nonsense if we cannot get to know what *a'* signifies. When in spite of this we are tempted to say that life *might* be a dream in any case, this is because we commit the mistake of speaking as if we could view things from an angelic point of view. This fallacy is natural in the regarded example. I have often seen a person asleeping, who from his movements and talk in his sleep revealed that he was dreaming, and have had this confirmed by him after he has woken up. While he was dreaming the situation was that he believed what he experienced was true and real while I knew that it wasn't. In the same way some 'higher' being might be regarding me while I am experiencing the things I call real, and he will then know that my experiences actually are dreams only.

As mentioned above, a positivist philosopher might argue that we have to hold to what we can experience and that we must never establish hypotheses about anything beyond experience. We can, however, argue by means of indirect proof too. I now assume that a 'higher' being *can* be found outside my world of experience. Furthermore I assume that he actually registers that my experience is a dream and that I am asleep and therefore not aware of this fact. So I am not denying that beyond the phenomena I am able to perceive something might exist. My only claim is that a logical — but not necessarily an empirical — possibility must exist in order that I can take part in the knowledge possessed by the 'higher' being.

Furthermore I will presuppose that the knowledge possessed by the 'higher' being can be formulated, and as I must in advance leave open the possibility that his language is different from mine and perhaps even more perfect, I wish to distinguish between his language which I call L_1 and my own which I call L_2. I am not precluding that L_1 and L_2 might be identical. The only thing I wish to examine is whether any proposition of L_1 can be translated into a proposition belonging to L_2. For this is the necessary and sufficient condition of my taking part in the knowledge of the 'higher' being.

Now it appears, however, that if I have accepted that the conditions for applying the words 'dream' and 'reality' are as shown above, the assertion that 'life or reality is a dream' which the 'higher' being makes is incomprehensible to me. For no matter how this proposition is formulated in L_1 it can only be rendered by either of the expressions (1) or (2) in L_2. In L_2 the proposition will inevitably become a nonsense or a contradiction. As said before it will remain obscure what a' in the expression $a' = a + non\text{-}a$ signifies. Following logic, we are forced to say that $a' = U$, and even if the 'higher' being maintained that a' was really a property of U this statement of L_1 could never be translated to L_2, for in L_2 the rule that U cannot be a subject-designation in a predicative proposition is indispensable.

Since both the world and the language must be defined extensionally according to Wittgenstein, it must be impossible to say anything about these concepts. Even if a 'higher' being exists (which Wittgenstein apparently thinks, cfr. 6.432) and even if this being formulates his knowledge about the world and the language in L_1 this knowledge can never be communicated to me. For telling me something of the world and the language must be done by means of propositions in which these words are subject-designations. But as they must always, in L_2, remain extensionally defined concepts, nothing can be said of them.

Wittgenstein does not deny that the 'higher' being can have a knowledge of 'the sense of the world'. Therefore in a way he does not deny that the world can be seen from an angelic point of view either. On the other hand, however, his linguistic solipsism compels him to say that no matter what somebody can experience from an angelic viewpoint the result of it cannot be expressed in the only language which he understands. And since this language at the same time indicates the limits of the thinkable any experience from an angelic point is unthinkable. Consequently he should as well have denied the possibility of regarding the world from an angelic point of view.

Hence, Wittgenstein's assertion that it is impossible to say anything about the world (and the language) as a whole is not only founded on the fact that no elementary proposition or truth-function can describe the world as a whole but is in addition a consequence of the fact that logic determines the formal limits of language and thus lays down certain conditions for description which cannot be considered mere conventions but on the contrary appear to be indispensable conditions for any kind of description.

It is not difficult to understand that he is bound, on the basis of this knowledge, to present a totally new definition of philosophy and philosophical activity. The history of European philosophy contains so many examples of metaphysical systems starting with the fallacy of the angelic point of view that it becomes reasonable to call this fallacy 'the philosophers' fallacy' as Maslow does. Maslow, however, makes the mistake of regarding the fallacy as originated on a basis of neglecting 'the egocentric predicament'. It is obvious that if I accept 'the egocentric predicament', i. e. the view that I primarily can know of nothing but my own experiences, I am precluded from formulating anything with sense about the world seen from an angelic point of view. Maslow overlooks, however, that *it is the mere fact that the assumption of 'the egocentric predicament' dictates certain conditions for what we can and what we cannot meaningfully say that forces us to reject any possibility of the mentioned view*. And this implies that the 'fallacy' must be characterized as such not only on the basis of the adherence to the egocentric predicament but on the basis of any philosophical view implying that indispensable conditions for what we can say and think can be found. It is quite possible to maintain that other people exist and that laws of nature can be found and sufficient reasons given for them and *still* without contradiction maintain that it is impossible to look at and speak of the world from an angelic point of view. It is also possible to find views based on speaking about things from an angelic point of view which must be rejected on other grounds than the one that they are in conflict with the egocentric predicament. Plato who adhered to an absolutistic view as regards the mentioned points gives an example of the fallacy of the angelic point of view in presenting his famous cave-analogy in the seventh book of *The Republic*. As the reader will know, he characterizes the construction of the world in an analogy in which he himself plays the rôle of God (because he can regard the cave and the people in it from without just as one could think that God could regard the world from without). Apparently this analogy is a usual one of the form $\frac{a}{b} = \frac{c}{d}$, but a closer analysis shows that it is the very 'logical universe' in which he presents his cave-analogy which he intends to characterize in contrast to something else, namely the ideal world. And because of this his analogy is different from what we usually understand by an analogy since all parts of the latter are classed within the same 'sphere of existence'. In this way the cave-analogy appears to be a variant of the mistake of trying to say something about the logical universe of discourse.

Another variant of the fallacy can be found in Hume's analysis of the concepts of substance and causality in which he repeatedly argues that all experience is based on impressions and yet constantly speaks of how these impressions are produced, how some impressions come to us through the eyes, others through the ears etc. By speaking in this way he is speaking of impressions as opposed to something else which in the contexts given cannot be called 'impressions'. But this just shows that he is speaking of the world of experience as if it could be seen from a point of view according to which we can characterize impressions in contrast to something else and this contradicts his assertion that we can never have to do with anything other than impressions. Hume's philosophy is based on the mistake of believing that the concept 'impression' can be generalized so it comprises everything without losing its sense. This is impossible because the concept can only be defined in relation and contrast to other concepts which are presupposed to have as much reference to something real as 'impression' has. As long as everything can be called 'impressions', this word has no well-defined application. The inconsistency of his philosophy appears when he tries to define 'impression' because he is here compelled to look at everything from an angelic point of view and consequently apply a language which according to his fundamental theses is nonsensical.

Lektor Bertel Fønss has drawn my attention to the fact that the German philosopher J. Petzoldt has proposed viewpoints which are to a certain extent similar to the ones developed above. Petzoldt observed that many concepts in philosophical discourse are applied in a general way although they can only obtain a meaning if contrasted to the concepts they are defined by. Just as 'father' can only be defined in relation to 'son' or 'daughter', and just as 'red' can only be defined in relation to other colours, so, according to Petzoldt, 'psychical' can only have a meaning if defined in contrast to 'physical'. Therefore an assertion such as 'everything is psychical' must violate both the principle of identity and the principle of contradiction (*Einführung in die Philosophie der reinen Erfahrung*, Bd. II, p. 300–01). Also it is logically illegitimate to advance a metaphysical solipsism: 'Für den Solipsisten ist das einzig Existierende sein Ich: die Dinge und die anderen Iche sind nur seine Vorstellungen . . . Wie hat er aber . . . seinen Ichbegriff gewonnen? Doch nur im Gegensatz zu etwas, was *nicht* 'Ich' war, also im Gegensatz zum 'Du' und zu einer 'Umgebung'.' (*Einführung*, Bd. II, p. 303). The word 'mine' has a meaning only in contrast to 'yours', 'his', and 'hers'. The word 'impression' ('Vorstellung') has a meaning only in contrast to 'thing' (*Solipsismus auf praktischem Gebiet*, p. 359–62). All attempts to maintain solipsism are refuted in this way because the unambiguity of the concepts used for formulating solipsism cannot be preserved unless solipsism is invalid. To put the question 'Is everything in the world subjective' is just as futile as to ask how it can be that we experience everything the right way up when the picture on the retina is up side down. This problem is a nonsense because the visual field as a whole cannot be said to be inverted in relation to anything. In the same way it is meaningless to ask what the world as a whole is since the world cannot be contrasted with or distinguished from anything else (*Einführung*, Bd. II, p. 304–05).

Independently of Petzoldt, an argument pointing in the same direction is advanced by Dr. P. Zinkernagel in his book *Conditions for Description*, in which it is pointed out that words such as 'I' and 'subjective', or 'psychological expressions', can, on the whole, only be applied in an understandable way if we allow that words signifying things which can be said to exist independently of our perceiving them can be applied sensefully too. Since to say that a thing exists according to Zinkernagel must mean that the name of it has to be applied according to certain rules, he is, on this basis, able to criticize Berkeleyan solipsism. But Zinkernagel stresses the point, which Petzoldt did not elaborate, that the fact that some words of our language cannot be applied independently of others establishes certain conditions for description and univocal communication which we must follow when applying the mentioned concepts in order to avoid speaking nonsense. Petzoldt does not, as does Zinkernagel, draw out the consequences which these things have for the characterization of the relation between the concepts 'description' and 'reality', but on the contrary only uses them in criticism of views contrary to his own variant of empiricism.

*

As I have said before, we find in the *Tractatus* some indications that Wittgenstein does not completely deny that it may be possible to look at the world from an angelic point of view. His analogy, on which I have commented, used for showing the logical and empirical features of the physical description of the world (6.341 and 6.342) seems to show too that he considers it a possible thought that 'something' exists independently of his experiences and that it cannot be described in language. When he compares the world to black spots on a white surface he suggests in a way that it is possible to speak of the world independent of the physical description of it just as it is possible to speak of the spots on the surface without having measured and described their extent. But on the other hand the analogy shows that we *never* can speak of the world in itself as we can speak of the spots independent of our measuring them. 6.342 reads: 'The possibility of describing a picture like the one mentioned above with a net of a given form tells us *nothing* about the picture. (For that is true of all such pictures). But what *does* characterize the picture is that it can be described *completely* by a particular net with a *particular* size of mesh. / Similarly the possibility of describing the world by means of Newtonian mechanics tells us nothing about the world: but what does tell us something about it is the precise *way* in which it is possible to describe it by these means. We are also told something about the world by the fact that it can be described more simply with one system of mechanics than with another.' That there *are* certain general truths about the world shows itself only *via* certain features of *the description* of the world. The nature of these truths, however, we cannot infer.

For the sake of clarity I have maintained until now that Wittgenstein approves of something outside his world of experience, that he approves of a 'higher' being and that he thinks that even if this 'higher' being could describe the world in a language L_1 this description could not be translated into the only language he understands, L_2. However, this last assertion is not Wittgenstein's final view. What he really maintains is that L_1 can never exist. This assertion is in a way a consequence of the views described above. If no proposition of L_1 can be translated into L_2 and no word of L_1 can be defined in terms of words belonging to L_2, then we cannot find anything that entitles us to call L_1 a language. If 'language' is defined as something that can be understood or translated into something which can be understood then L_1 is not a language. The 'higher' being cannot have any language, he cannot form a proposition and cannot describe what he experiences. Wittgenstein first states that God is indifferent to *how* things are in the world. 6.432 reads: '*How* things are in the world is a matter of complete indifference for what is higher. God does not reveal himself *in* the world.' The last part of this statement is essential. For the idea is that if God really was interested in *how* things are in the world, he would have to reveal himself in the world, i. e. become a perceiving subject who experienced the world conceived of as the totality of facts. This is so because a description of *how* the world is can only consist of all true elementary propositions, i. e. the description of all facts. But these only present themselves to a perceiving subject which has the special relation to the world explained above. What God is interested in, or what the riddle of life is, is something which lies outside what I can conceive of as the world. Not even an eternal life could help me to solve the riddle of life for 'The solution of the riddle of life in space and time lies *outside* space and time.' (6.4312). Nothing can be said about that which lies 'outside' the world. For to describe is to form elementary propositions and test their truth. But such propositions can only picture facts and 'outside' the world no facts can be found according to 1 and 1.1. Therefore we cannot even ask what is 'outside' the world. 'If a question can be framed at all, it is also *possible* to answer it.' (6.5). But an answer to a question can only be either an elementary proposition or a truth-function. Consequently the only questions that can ever be raised are concerned with natural science (since the totality of true propositions according to 4.11 is the whole of natural science) and therefore they can only be about something 'in' the world.

The problem of life, then, lies 'outside' the world. Therefore it cannot be affected by the answers to all scientific questions. If all of them are answered no questions remain, not even as to the problem of life. This is expressed in 6.52: 'We feel that even when *all possible* scientific questions have been answered, the problems of life remain completely untouched. Of course there are then no questions left, and this itself is the answer.' It is moreover expressed clearly in 4.003 which ends by stating that 'the deepest problems are in fact *not* problems at all.'

Therefore no riddle exists either (cfr. 6.5). Every senseful question can in principle be answered and one can neither ask about nor have doubts about what is 'outside' the world. The scepticism Wittgenstein speaks of in 6.51 is probably therefore the view which doubts that there is something 'outside' the world, something more than the facts that shows how the world is. For scepticism is characterized as a view which doubts something which cannot even be questioned. 6.51 reads: 'Scepticism is *not* irrefutable, but obviously nonsensical, when it tries to raise doubts where no questions can be asked. / For doubt can exist only where a question exists, a question only where an answer exists, and an answer only where something *can be said*.'

That which lies outside the world Wittgenstein calls 'the mystical'. Of this nothing can be said, not even by a God who is able to view it from another point of view than I am. But *that* there *is* something, I know, for this shows itself to me partly in *that* the world exists (6.44: 'It is not *how* things are in the world that is mystical, but *that* it exists.'), partly in that I can feel the world as a limited whole (6.45: 'To view the world *sub specie aeterni* is to view it as a whole — a limited whole. / Feeling the world as a limited whole — it is this that is mystical.') This feeling probably must be explained by the fact that the world is my world and that its limits are determined by the limits of my language. For in virtue of this I come to experience the world as a limited whole the limits of which I only know from within, but because it is limited it shows that something more 'exists'. I can see that 'There are, indeed, things that cannot be put into words. They *make themselves manifest*. They are what is mystical.' (6.522). About this nothing can be said. It is this we must, according to 7, consign to silence.

It seems clear to me that this interpretation of the mystical and its relation to the world is in accordance with Wittgenstein's definition of the purpose and method of philosophy. Since all senseful questions must be classed with the natural sciences and philosophy according to 4.111 differs from the natural sciences we cannot ask a senseful question about philosophical matters. At most a philosophical book can, as the *Tractatus* does, consist of elucidations (cfr. 4.112) from which we can learn what can be said and what cannot be said but only shown. In this way we can obtain 'a logical clarification of thoughts' (4.112). To the people who still believe that it has sense to ask questions about the riddle of life, the correct philosophy is a therapy. They are shown what can be said and what cannot be said. If they still insist that more can be said than the propositions of natural science one must by means of elucidations refer to the picture theory and make it clear to them that they have failed to give a meaning to certain signs in their propositions (cfr. 6.53). In this way they will by and by learn what can be said (or thought) and what cannot be said (or thought) and when they have fully learnt where the limits of language are to be found they will grasp the meaning of life and be able to see that it cannot be expressed in language.

*

From this we can see that Wittgenstein's solipsism belongs to what can only be shown, not only because of the immediate consequences of the picture theory (that words such as 'I' and 'world' cannot be names of objects) but for another reason too. What we have learnt is, what Maslow was the first one to direct our attention to, that a correct formulation of solipsism stating that only one I exists and that the world is the world of this one I cannot be given because it presupposes that everything can be experienced from an angelic point of view. That the world is my world is true because the language is my language and the limits of language determine the limits of the world. But if we wish to speak at all of the relation between the language and the world this can be done only if it is possible to see the world and the language from outside. Whenever we state a connection between two concepts, two classes, or two fields of phenomena, we must presuppose that we can perceive or think of the two entities simultaneously. The metaphysical subject is able to look at the language and the world from outside in a certain sense (because it is able to compare elementary propositions to reality) but it can never regard its own relation to the world (just as an eye cannot compare itself to its visual field). In order to do this it would have to be outside itself and outside the world, which is impossible. It is, therefore, a necessary condition for formulating the solipsistic view to place oneself outside the world, the language, and the I. However, we have seen that any experience based on a point of view 'outside' the world cannot be expressed in language. Consequently the truth of solipsism is ineffable. Neither can the metaphysical subject formulate anything about the relation between the language and the world, in the first place because no proposition can deal with the sense of another, for which reason the relation between p and p_f is undescribable, and secondly because the metaphysical subject cannot formulate anything because it can neither speak nor think.

In this chapter I have not referred to other commentators of the *Tractatus* than Maslow because the ideas developed here are mostly related to his thoughts. In order to do justice I must therefore refer the reader to Miss Anscombe's account of the mysticism and solipsism in which among other things the distinction between the accidental belonging to the world and the non-accidental which lies 'outside' the world is emphasized (*An Introduction*, p. 170). This distinction which is presented in 6.41 serves to define the world still more from that which lies 'outside' it. However, I have not considered Miss Anscombe's account because, in my opinion, she makes the mistake of confusing that which is outside the world with Wittgenstein's thesis that the ethical in a certain sense is outside the world too. To me this seems a misleading idea. Miss Anscombe writes that Wittgenstein took over the expression 'the mystical' from Russell who meant by this an 'entirely ordinary feeling' corresponding to the one expressed in 6.52. Next she maintains that Wittgenstein's remark that 'there then is just no question left, and just this is the answer' is to be understood in connection with 6.41 in which it is said among other things that the sense of the world must lie outside the world. This may be true but she continues by explaining the passage in 6.41 that 'If there is a value that has value, it must lie outside all happening . . . For all happening . . . is accidental. What makes it non-accidental cannot be found in the world' and on the basis raises the question why Wittgenstein speaks of 'what makes it non-accidental'. To this she answers: 'To understand this, we have to understand what he says about the will. The most important remark that he makes here is: 'The facts all belong to the task set, and not to the solution' (6.4321). '*Aufgabe*', which I translate 'task set', is the German for a child's school exercise, or piece of homework. Life is like a boy doing sums. (At the end of his life he used the analogy still). Now the reason why the solution cannot bring in any facts is that it is concerned with good and evil: and the good or evil character of what is good or evil is non-accidental; it therefore cannot consist in this happening rather than that, for that is accidental.' (*An Introduction*, p. 171). I have here tried to show why it is impossible to obtain a solution to the riddle of life and have not in this place referred to what Wittgenstein writes about the good and the evil. It is true that the ethical predicates concern something not belonging to the world but this is not the mystical but the metaphysical subject which ethics is concerned with because it is a willing subject. And I do not see what statement of the *Tractatus* entitles Miss Anscombe to infer any connection between the ethical and the mystical. If we apply the analogy of the relation between the eye and the visual field we may say that Wittgenstein classes ethics with what corresponds to the eye and by the mystical he is thinking of something which corresponds to what is outside the visual field, something that determines that a visual field exists as soon as an eye exists though not determining the content of the visual field. But that which lies outside the visual field must not be mistaken for that which belongs to the eye. The fact that Wittgenstein infers from 6.41 that propositions of ethics do not exist (6.42) does not show that he identifies the ethical with the mystical but only that the subject-matter of ethics, just as the mystical, lies 'outside' the world.

I should also refer to Stenius. He ends his book with an excellent although short chapter on the ineffable. The reason why I have not found it fruitful to combine Stenius' view with mine is that we hold different views in respect of the nature of the metaphysical subject.

VI

A CRITICAL VALUATION OF THE MAIN IDEAS OF THE TRACTATUS.

a. Introduction.

In the preceding chapters I have attempted to give an explanation of a number of the main views in the *Tractatus*. This explanation is in most respects different from the views concerning the book prevailing in contemporary philosophy. It may not be an exhaustive account of the theses of the *Tractatus* (for instance I have not said much about Wittgenstein's views of mathematics and physics) but I believe that it is fairly easy to infer what we must say about these matters according to the interpretation given. For example the account which I have given of the logical parts of the book may without difficulty be adapted to Wittgenstein's few remarks on mathematics. The equations of mathematics are, like those of logic, pseudo-propositions, and proofs in mathematics as well as in logic can be presented in a *demonstratio ad oculos*-manner so no meta-language is demanded. Just like the logical truths the mathematical truths show themselves to the metaphysical subject. In the same way Wittgenstein's remarks on physics can easily be explained on account of the interpretation I have presented. To Wittgenstein, physics is an empirical science and all physical descriptions consist of elementary propositions or truth-functions of these. At the same time physics presupposes the validity of the tautologies of logic and since these belong to what can only be shown the possibility of physics must involve the existence of something in nature corresponding to the logical truths. This 'something' is 'the logic of the world' which is mirrored by the tautologies. At the same time, however, any physical description must — because it comprises presuppositions different from the tautologies — be conventional to a certain extent, since these presuppositions are neither tautologies nor empirical propositions, but are the results of arbitrary choice. We can arbitrarily decide what shall be axioms and what theorems in the physical theory (which Wittgenstein like Hertz thinks can be arranged in a deductive system) in the same way as we can decide wholly arbitrarily whether we are going to describe spots on a surface by reference to a net consisting of square, triangular or hexagonal meshes. The different descriptions we can produce in these ways are logically equally justifiable. None of them gives a better picture or impression of the essence of nature than any of the others. For according to the *Tractatus* we cannot speak of this essence. The world is a world of phenomena, and physics like all other descriptions of nature can only deal with 'observables'. Words that do not refer to 'observables' (as for instance 'force') are pseudo-names which may have a function at a certain stage in the development of science but should really be eliminated. Wittgenstein's view concerning physics must be that of a conventionalistic empiricism.

The interpretation which I have given of the *Tractatus* is based on the simple assumption that Wittgenstein's main purpose has been to draw the consequences of the thesis of extensionality (and the picture theory which is implied by it) in order to show what can be said and what cannot be said but only shown concerning human knowledge. This assumption brings out the unity of Wittgenstein's work in a clear way, as far as I can see.

The structure of this unity can be summed up in the following way. We assume that the thesis of extensionality is absolutely valid. Furthermore we assume that a logical system such as the one of the *Principia Mathematica* with all its branches can be established. (The great difference between Wittgenstein and Kant is that the latter starts from 'Das Faktum der Wissenschaft' whereas Wittgenstein starts from 'Das Faktum der Logik'). According to Wittgenstein we are then compelled to say that logic presupposes that propositions have truth-values. This in turn presupposes that they must have a sense. The question now is: How does it come about that a proposition can have a sense? This cannot be explained in any other way than through the assumption that it describes something other than itself. According to the thesis of extensionality no proposition can deal with another because the only possible connections propositions can have with each other are the ones they have in truth-functions and in a truth-function no element deals with any other. Therefore, what a proposition is about must be something non-linguistic. Moreover the circumstance that no proposition can deal with any other has the consequence that the sense of a proposition must be understood by regarding the proposition itself, because no other part of language can explain it to us. Furthermore logic prescribes that elementary propositions must exist as no truth-value otherwise could ever be determined. In addition the thesis of extensionality prescribes that internal relations between elementary propositions do not exist.

These demands are met by the picture theory according to which propositions are configurations of elements which can be seen at once to be pictures of something different from themselves. Since the elementary propositions are independent of each other so are the non-linguistic states of affairs which they describe. The circumstance that an elementary proposition must consist of indivisible elements implies that the states of affairs must consist of indivisible elements too. For a picture pictures something else by reproducing its structure while it can be seen from the picture that each element of it represents an element of reality. Furthermore we realize that the elements of a state of affairs must be indivisible for otherwise we may risk the truth of an elementary proposition implying the truth of propositions dealing with some of the parts of its subject-matter (cfr. the example of the wheel in the watch, p. 54). Consequently indivisible objects must exist linked together to states of affairs. So we see that the picture theory involves a vague, ontological view. Moreover it involves something about the mind. For the fact that propositions appear to be pictures in advance of our analysing them implies that it has no sense to speak of establishing a picturing-relation between the proposition and the described state of affairs. In a certain sense the picturing relation is given as soon as the elements of the picture are related to each other as they are. This, however, we can only understand if we conceive of propositions as thoughts which are psychical entities that by themselves point to (or mean) the things they are about. This in turn implies that there must exist a thinking ego. The fact that propositions are thoughts explains why '*A* says *p*' does not violate the thesis of extensionality. For '*A* says *p*' should be written ''*p*' says *p*' which indicates how *p* obtains its sense and therefore is a pseudo-proposition.

According to the thesis of extensionality and the picture theory any kind of meta-language is impossible. Therefore any experience of what is logically true must be impossible to formulate. Therefore logical truths must show themselves in order to be experienced. By means of an ingenious matrix-method, we can perceive that all valid inferences which cannot be formulated are established as soon as the truth-functions between which they hold are established. That this is so is due to the fact that all truth-functions can be generated by successive applications of the operation of negation. In order to perceive what is shown more than a thinking ego is necessary. Therefore we must assume the existence of a metaphysical subject besides the empirical ego. This subject cannot be a part of the world because it has a function which neither an object nor a fact could ever have. Therefore it must be simple and be opposed to the world. This definition of the metaphysical subject leads us to a solipsistic view which on account of the picture theory assumes a peculiar character. For according to the picture theory only one language can exist because by 'elementary proposition' I can only mean 'thought', and because by 'thought' I can only mean 'my thought'. In other words the language is opposed to what is nonsense. We can transcend the limits of language by constructing nonsensical combinations of signs or by breaking the rules of logic. The limits of language cannot be described in an ordinary sense. Since the language has limits so has the logical space and hereby the world is limited too because the world is a realization of a number of possibilities in the logical space. Since the language is identical to my empirical ego because every proposition is a thought which I think, the whole world is something which is coordinated with my metaphysical subject because it is this subject which compares the thoughts with reality in order to determine their truth-values. All phenomena must reveal themselves in the logical space the limits of which are identical to the limits of my language. Therefore all phenomena are coordinated with my I. By 'the world' I therefore can only mean 'my world'. Furthermore the picture theory implies that the language and the world cannot be defined intensionally. This implies that philosophical statements about these concepts must always be devoid of sense. The circumstance, however, that the world must have limits implies that it is true in a certain sense that there exists something beyond these limits. This consequence seems to contradict the solipsistic view, but on the other hand we must say that even if the world could be experienced from without as a limited whole, this experience could never be formulated. For in language we can describe only states of affairs and facts, and outside the world no facts exist because the world is defined as the totality of facts. Hence something 'mystical' exists in a certain sense although it can never be described. It is impossible to say anything about it without contradiction. Philosophers have very often forgotten that what one cannot speak of must be consigned to silence. On a whole philosophers have spent too little time on the problem of what can be said and what cannot be said. The *Tractatus* shows that by senseful propositions we must mean only elementary propositions and truth-functions of these. Once we have realized this we understand that all philosophical statements are pseudo-propositions containing words that are not names of anything (cfr. 6.53).

Briefly, this is the main line of my interpretation of the *Tractatus*. As we see, Wittgenstein proposes a total view which complies with the demands of the thesis of extensionality and in all respects renders meta-language superfluous. His starting point is a logical postulate which dictates his whole philosophy, also the empiricism which is introduced in connection with the testing of the truth of elementary propositions. In his book *Relativitet i filosofisk belysning* (pp. 95 ff) Professor Bent Schultzer suggests that the philosophy of the young Wittgenstein is absolutistic, a view which I fully approve of. However, I do not agree with Professor Schultzer's view that Wittgenstein is an adherent to an empirical absolutism. Rather he is a rationalist who 'deduces' his whole philosophy from one single assumption. Of course, though, he appears to be an empiricist if we stress the point that the truth of all elementary propositions is decided solely by empirical investigations.

In the preceding chapters I have given an account of some of the difficulties which Wittgenstein met with when developing his philosophy. In this chapter my main purpose is to point out some of the problems which are raised if we accept the views of the *Tractatus*. In section *b.*, I will consider some of the traditional objections to the *Tractatus* in light of the interpretation I have attempted to give. In section *c.*, I will consider some of the philosophical problems that are implied by my interpretation of Wittgenstein's views. First, I will sum up the difficulties attached to these views which I have already mentioned. In the following I will, for the sake of clarity, give every difficulty a number and a name. It can be said at once that Wittgenstein's views are open to criticism to such a degree that it is astonishing that his book had as great a success as it did have. Of course it contains very valuable ideas but they cannot obscure the shortcomings, and really it is surprising that nobody in the forty years that have passed since the *Tractatus* was printed has explained the aporias which one is involved in if the main ideas of the book are accepted. Indeed, Wittgenstein himself later realized that the book was insufficient in many respects. Yet he seemed to discover only a small part of its insufficiences. Recently some commentators, namely Urmson, Barone, and Colombo, have objected to the *Tractatus*. I am convinced, however, that the objections they propose in most respects can be repelled by a clever defender of Wittgenstein's ideas. The same, I believe, does not hold of the objections which I will advance here.

*

First difficulty: Is the thesis of extensionality true or valid? This is the first thing one ought to ask the adherents to the main views of the *Tractatus*. Wittgenstein gave no answer to this question. He postulated the thesis and it is impossible to find any grounds for it in his text. I cannot deal with this difficulty here as it would involve a very lengthy discussion, which would take us outside the scope of this book. But anyone who knows a little about the development of logic in this century will know too that this thesis is highly disputable.

Second difficulty: Examples of objects cannot be found. In the account given in chapter II, *c.* the possibilities of finding an interpretation of the concept of *'object'* were examined. The result was negative, and therefore it was not possible either to find an interpretation of the other concepts of the picture theory, 'state of affairs', 'name', 'elementary proposition' etc. After having published the *Tractatus,* Wittgenstein realized there was a problem hidden here. Moore writes about this: '. . . he began by pointing out that neither Russell nor he himself had produced any examples of 'atomic' propositions; and said that there was something wrong indicated by this fact, though it was difficult to say exactly what.' (*Wittgenstein's Lectures in 1930 - 33*, p. 296). *The thing to notice is not that Wittgenstein did not succeed in finding an example of an elementary proposition but that it can be shown that the picture theory in principle makes it impossible for an example ever to be found and hereby refutes itself*. We can state this on the basis of the analysis of the concept of object in chapter II. There I maintained that Wittgenstein by objects was compelled to mean phenomenological *minima*. For instance a spot in the visual field is considered an object if it appears phenomenologically to be indivisible or non-composite. A proposition such as 'The speck *A* is red' could then serve as an instance of an elementary proposition if the speck was a *minimum visibile*. It appears from *Logical Form*, however, that Wittgenstein himself began to doubt whether this conception of objects was in harmony with the thesis of extensionality. The difficulty was that if '*A* is red' is an elementary proposition its truth-value must be independent of the truth-value of any other elementary proposition. In other words, '*A* is red' must give any other elementary proposition the probability ½, and if '*A* is red' is conjugated with any other proposition the result is a truth-function which can never be a tautology or a contradiction. But now it appears that the proposition ('*A* is red') · ('*A* is blue') can never be true, so therefore it must be a contradiction. This, however, it cannot be, unless the thesis of extensionality is false. No matter what we conceived of instead of *minima visibile* the same contradiction would appear. If objects are to be distinguished in any way from each other they must be localized (supplied with space- and time-coordinates). But the moment we supply an indivisible object with space-coordinates it is impossible that other objects can have the same coordinates. An elementary proposition of the form $(x_1, y_1, z_1)P$ therefore excludes that any other object can have the set of coordinates (x_1, y_1, z_1) at the same time. Consequently we will always contradict the thesis of extensionality no matter what we choose as examples of objects.

Wittgenstein's attempt in *Logical Form* at saving the thesis of extensionality by introducing a logical principle excluding the possibility that propositions such as ('*A* is red') · ('*A* is blue') are contradictions is a bad piece of philosophy. His suggestion was, as shown in chapter II, that an expression such as ( ) *PT* only leaves room for one entity — in the same sense in which we say that there is room for only one person in a chair. In this way he tried to introduce a principle in order to preclude that the conjunction considered became a contradiction. A principle of this sort, however, must according to the *Tractatus* either be an empirical, or a logical principle. If it is empirical, we are involved in great difficulties. For in this case it is possible that some day two objects will occur in exactly the same place simultaneously which certainly would violate Leibniz's *principium identitatis indiscernibilium* which Wittgenstein apparently follows. But Wittgenstein does think, it seems, that the principle is a logical one (cfr. 6.3751). If this is the case it must show itself in the notation like all the other tautologies do. We can see that a tautology is a tautology by looking only at the propositional sign. The principle that ( ) *PT* only leaves room for one object at a time, however, cannot be formulated in such a way that its eventual truth can be gathered from the propositional sign alone or perhaps from its truth-table. Moreover, if Wittgenstein wanted to legalize this principle he would have to invent a new operation besides the operation of negation. For the truth-table of the principle (or the matrix with the top row missing, cfr. *Logical Form*, p. 170) cannot be generated by means of the operation $\bar{N}(\ )$ only. Consequently we would have in addition to give up the theory of the general form of a proposition if the analysis given in *Logical Form* was true.

Incidentally there are other traps in Wittgenstein's concept of 'object'. It may seem plausible — if we neglect the thesis of extensionality — to consider *minima visibile* objects. But how are we to determine phenomenologically *minima* in the other sensuous fields. What is, for instance, an indivisible object in the tactile field or in the auditory field? And how can we ever analyse qualities of taste and smell in order to arrive at objects? Moreover many experiences of wholes, as shown by the Gestaltpsychologists, cannot be dissected arbitrarily. For instance we may have visual experiences such as Wertheimer's φ-phenomena which cannot be dissected into *minima visibile* by means of a phenomenological analysis. Wittgenstein apparently never considered these kinds of problems.

Third difficulty: How shall we conceive of an operation of negation? I have drawn the reader's attention to this problem in chapter IV, *b.*, and pointed out that Wittgenstein in fact made three mistakes in introducing this concept. In the first place he overlooked that the negation of *p,q* is not *p|q* but *∼p,∼q*, for the negation of *p|q* is *pvq*. Secondly, he overlooked that *N*[*N*(*p*)] always must be equivalent to *p*. If the negation of *p,q* really was *p|q*, then the negation of *p|q* must be *p,q*. According to the *Tractatus*, however, it is *pvq*. Thirdly, he did not examine the procedure of selection involved in the operation of negation. Since the operation is a necessary condition for the development of the general form of a proposition these shortcomings of Wittgenstein's ideas are decisive and it is indeed strange that he did nothing in order to eliminate them.

Fourth difficulty: The relation between objects and states of affairs. As mentioned in chapter II, *b.*, there is a contradiction in maintaining that states of affairs can exist or not exist and at the same time saying that states of affairs consist of objects (2.03 and 2.031). For the objects are the substance of the world (2.021) and therefore exist, and it is unintelligible that the elements of a non-existing state of affairs should exist. This mistake in the *Tractatus* is probably a consequence of the lack of clarity as to the concepts 'state of affairs' and 'fact' in the book. Perhaps the book could be revised in this respect without the main ideas of it being affected.

Fifth difficulty: Are temporal phenomena describable according to the picture theory? This question I have dealt with in chapter II, *c*. It seems that Wittgenstein never became aware of the problem. Perhaps he would have answered that cinematic phenomena are describable by means of differential equations and that these according to the *Principia Mathematica* can be reduced to purely logical statements. But this surely is not a satisfactory answer. For if he imagined that cinematic phenomena could be described by means of mathematical equations which are reducible to a logical calculus the variables of which can have propositions as values, then all facts must be static phenomena because propositions can picture only static phenomena. If this is the case we must define 'fact' and 'state of affairs' more *sharply* than we have previously done. This we can realize in the following way. Let us imagine that a small ball is placed on the middle of a table. If I move the ball a little to the right, is it then the same fact we are presented with before and after my interference? Following his demand for 'definite sense' Wittgenstein would have to answer 'No' here. He would have to say that the moving of the ball 'produced' a new fact. We now may ask how far a ball must be moved in order that a new fact is 'produced'. According to Wittgenstein's remarks in *Logical Form* the answer must be: A distance corresponding to the horizontal extention of a *minimum visibile* (it is not contradictory to speak of the extension of a *minimum visibile* even though this is defined as not having extension. In the physical sense it might have extension in spite of its being phenomenologically indivisible). If we then imagine that the ball is exactly so small that it appears as a *minimum visibile* in the visual field and if we furthermore assume that a net of lines cross each other in the visual field as Wittgenstein suggests in *Logical Form*, then we can ascribe the coordinates (x_0, y_0) to the ball as it is lying on the middle of the table. If we move it to the right parallel to the X-axis it will traverse the points (x_1, y_0), (x_2, y_0), (x_3, y_0) . . . and so on. To this motion will correspond a series of facts which can be represented by $(x_0, y_0)\,B$, $(x_1, y_0)\,B$, $(x_2, y_0)\,B$, $(x_3, y_0)\,B$ . . . and so on. Since the coordinate-system as mentioned in chapter II, *c*., must belong to the visual field and therefore consist of *minima visibile* the ball never can be in the point $[\frac{1}{2} \cdot (x_1\text{-}x_0), y_0]$ or in any other point between x_0 and x_1, x_1 and x_2, x_2 and

x_3 . . . and so on. Even if the motion of the ball could be described as a continuous phenomenon, it is in fact a cinematographic, non-continuous phenomenon. In each point the ball must lie still for a moment (which cannot be smaller than a *minimum temporale*) and thereupon it must cease to exist in the point in question and come into being in the next one.

On the face of it it looks as if a limitation of the concept of 'fact' in this way gives us a satisfactory answer to our problem. However, it leads us to a contradiction. For we can speak only of the motion of the ball from point to point in the visual field on condition that we can speak of *the same* ball throughout the time of the motion. If we describe the motion as a series of facts this must be done by a series of elementary propositions:

At the time t_0 B is in (x_0, y_0)
– " – t_1 " – " (x_1, y_0)
– " – t_2 " – " (x_2, y_0)
– " – t_3 " – " (x_3, y_0) etc.

We can now see immediately that the definition does not preclude our formulating elementary propositions which contradict each other. Thus, the propositions 'At the time t_0 B is in (x_0, y_0)' and 'At the time t_0 B is in (x_2, y_0)' are incompatible. But this brings us into the usual conflict with the thesis of extensionality.

If we decide to say that it is not the same ball we are considering in the different points of the visual field, we meet with other difficulties. We must then maintain that what really happens when we consider the motion of the ball is that a number of *minima visibile* comes into existence and disappears successively. First one *minimum visibile* (or one ball) appears in the point $(x_0\ y_0)$. Then all of a sudden it ceases to exist and the very moment it disappears a new ball or *minimum* is created in the point (x_1, y_0). The moment this one disappears yet a new one appears but this time in the point (x_2, y_0), and so on. This view is, in the first place, incompatible with 2.027 and 2.0271 in the *Tractatus* which emphasize that objects are unalterable and subsistent. Secondly, it demands that every *minimum visibile* or ball must have its own name since a name according to the picture theory cannot signify more than one object. But this precludes us from asserting propositions of the type 'B is moving'. Thirdly, it calls for a solid ontological basis. For according to the given premisses one could imagine that objects which come into existence and cease to exist again in intervals of time smaller than a *minimum temporale* can be found just as it is conceivable that the experience of the ball at a point, for instance (x_0, y_0) lasting for some time actually is an experience of a series of balls all of them existing only for intervals of time smaller than a *minimum temporale*. We have no sufficient reasons for rejecting assumptions of these kinds (which reminds us of Russell's theory in *The Ultimate Constituents of Matter*). Therefore they cannot in principle be precluded. If the latter of them is valid, we are in a situation in which, without us knowing it, a name is a name of a series of objects, namely all the balls that appear and disappear in (x_0, y_0) during a certain interval of time. I believe that it is fairly easy to see that consequences of these kinds cannot seriously be accepted.

As mentioned Wittgenstein presumably never considered these problems. If he had done so the *Tractatus* to all appearance would have turned out quite differently from what it did.

*

To the mentioned difficulties we may add a *sixth difficulty: How do we explain the sense of other types of propositions than the descriptive ones if the picture theory is valid?* In chapter III, *c.*, I quoted Miss Anscombe's list of types of sentences which call for an explanation, and we state that Wittgenstein gives no theory for imperative and interrogative sentences. He does not even give an answer to the question whether they can have a sense or not. Inspired by Hare, Professor Stenius has tried to show that the picture theory can be worked together with the view that propositions consist of two parts, 'the *sentence-radical* (i. e. the 'phrastic' in Hare's terminology), which shows the state of affairs (real or imagined) that the sentence describes, and the *functional* component (the 'neustic' in Hare's terminology), which indicates which function the *presentation* of this state of affairs has in the language game. The state of affairs presented is the descriptive content of the sentence; the function is a semantical component which may be called its semantical mood.' (Stenius: *Wittgenstein's 'Tractatus'*, p. 161). According to this sophisticated theory the descriptive content of a picture is a picture in the sense of the *Tractatus* but 'picture' is not equal to 'sentence' because a sentence does not appear until 'the descriptive content' is united with 'the semantical mood'. This view is hardly compatible with Wittgenstein's text although Stenius apparently thinks it is. According to the thought-picture theory a W-proposition is a picture, a description, or a complete proposition, whether or not it is connected with a 'semantical mood'. The picture shows how things stand and it says *that* they do so stand (4.022). It maintains itself, as it were. Consequently an elementary proposition must always be in the indicative and the verb it contains must always be in the present tense. It cannot possibly appear combined with other 'semantical moods'. The theory Stenius advances is a great step forward in comparison with the view of the *Tractatus* but it is only possible because he gives up the thesis of extensionality and the logical atomism implied by this. For Stenius starts from the assumption that propositions need keys of interpretation in order to function as pictures and this assumption conflicts with the thesis of extensionality as pointed out in chapter III, *a*.

I leave it to others to enumerate the types of propositions which Wittgenstein did not justify with his picture theory. It is an established fact that the theory only allows for descriptive propositions in the present indicative and the problem that remains is to show that all other sentences are pseudo-propositions or nonsense. Wittgenstein did not solve this problem. He really only postulated the possibility of its solution.

b. Some known objections to the Tractatus reconsidered.

During the last ten years some criticism of the *Tractatus* has appeared. Some of the objections are of a kind that gain or lose in value according to how Wittgenstein's text is interpreted. In this section I will consider some of these objections.

In a very clear and original paper, *The Picture Theory of Meaning* Miss Edna Daitz has criticized Wittgenstein's picture theory and picture theories in general. However, much of her criticism is, as Copi has pointed out (in *Objects, Properties and Relations,* pp. 145 - 46), based on an ordinary language-conception of proposition and not on a conception such as the one of elementary propositions in the *Tractatus*. As we have seen there is a great difference between sentences of ordinary language such as 'The river is long', and elementary propositions (whatever they are), and for this reason many of Miss Daitz's objections are irrelevant to this study and are not to be considered here. In addition she has apparently not noticed that Wittgenstein maintains that formal concepts are not names. For instance her question what does 'something' signify in the sentence 'something hit me' (*The Picture Theory,* p. 188) can be answered by pointing to the fact that 'something' according to Wittgenstein is a pseudo-concept, a fact which shows that the mentioned sentence has not been thoroughly analysed.

One of the objections of Miss Daitz which has created a stir is this: If we compare a fact, such as the one that *a* has a certain relation *R* to *b*, to the description of this fact, we will observe that the fact consists of three elements, whereas the description must consist of four elements. Therefore there is not an isomorphic relation between the fact and the proposition used for describing it. The relation must always be that if the fact contains *n* elements the proposition will consist of $n + 1$ elements. 'The sentence 'Sophia hates Amos' is not identical in form with, i. e. has not the same number of elements as, the fact *Sophia hates Amos*. For the sentence is the fact *'Hates' is between 'Sophia' and 'Amos'*, i. e. it has four elements while *Sophia hates Amos* has only three. This view brings with it the consequence that all ordinary sentences have, for fact-stating purpose, one word too many!' (p. 189). The fact is *aRb*, whereas the proposition is the fact that *R* is between *a* and *b*. A certain relation must hold between the elements of the propositions and it therefore must consist of three names + one relation = four elements, whereas the fact consists of only two objects + one relation = three elements. Against this view Evans has objected (*Tractatus 3.1432*) that the fact as well as the proposition must consist of four elements, namely *a*, *b*, and *R*, and the relation holding between them. To this Copi remarks in the paper mentioned above that Evans' view involves us in an infinite regress: If the fact *aRb* consists of three elements and one relation, there must be a relation holding between the four elements we have now arrived at, and so on.

Copi also criticizes the view proposed by Miss Daitz and gives an explanation of Wittgenstein's text which is undoubtedly the right one. In 3.1432 Wittgenstein writes: 'Instead of, 'The complex sign "*aRb*" says that *a* stands to *b* in the relation *R*', we ought to put, 'That "*a*" stands to "*b*" in a certain relation says that *aRb*.'' Copi takes this to mean that the proposition describing the fact *aRb* consists of two elements only. The fact *aRb* also consists of only two elements because relations according to Wittgenstein do not exist in any ontological sense. Consequently the proposition and the fact contain the same amount of elements (*Objects, Properties and Relations*, pp. 155 - 56). This view which is developed further in Stenius' book (p. 135) seems to imply that the relation between the two elements of the proposition represents the relation between the two elements of the fact and both Copi and Stenius apparently look at the matter in this way. Copi writes that 'Any relations of objects, spatial or non-spatial, can be represented by a spatial relation of the names of those objects. That *a* has relation *R* to *b* can be represented by writing '*a*' some specified distance and direction from '*b*', and that *a* has some different relation *R*' to *b* can be presented by writing '*a*' some different distance and direction from '*b*'.' (p. 157). This view is twofold. One idea in it is that relations holding between objects can be represented by relations holding between names and this idea is in accordance with Wittgenstein's text and the thought-picture theory which I gave an account of in chapter II. The other idea, that different distances between the names in a proposition may represent different relations between objects is a more dubious view. Nothing indicates that Wittgenstein ever entertained this idea. However, the general formulation of Copi's view that propositions do not contain names of relations and need not do so is in accordance with the *Tractatus*, but it does not give a full explanation of Wittgenstein's conceptions of 'relation' and 'structure'. I will return to this in section *c.* below.

Copi leaves one of Miss Daitz's problems unanswered. She maintains that whereas a picture immediately shows what it is a picture of, this does not hold true of propositions if these have only as many elements as the facts they are pictures of. Firstly, there must be at least one word more in the proposition which tells us how it is to be understood. A picture of some cats on cushions shows what it is about but an expression such as 'cats on cushions' cannot picture anything unless we are told whether it is some, all, the neighbour's, or our own cats, that are mentioned (*The Picture Theory*, p. 196). Secondly, the proposition cannot be shown only but has to be asserted in some way or other. 'That sentences, unlike icons, do not signify *qua* entity can be brought out by comparing a sentence with an icon. Take a picture of a cushion between a cat and a mouse, and the sentence 'This adjoins that'. To speak of the sentence as the fact that 'Adjoins' is between 'this' and 'that' . . . is to regard it as three marks in ink in the way that a picture of a cushion between a cat and a mouse is three marks in ink. But a sentence does not signify because it is a pattern of marks . . .' (p. 194). This is the difficulty which Copi does not consider. As the reader will know it is solved by the thought-picture theory. As shown in chapter III, *a.*, we *can* say about a W-proposition that 'it signifies *qua* entity'. Without this addition Copi's otherwise instructive article in my opinion is not a satisfactory answer to the problems raised by Miss Daitz.

*

In his interesting introduction to the Italian version of the *Tractatus*, Colombo has called chapter VI '*Aporie Della Fondazione Wittgensteiniana*'. In this he expounds a number of difficulties which Wittgenstein's philosophy leads us to. The first aporia considered is 'Il paradossa del valore' which is really only a paradox if one starts from a certain dogmatic, philosophical basis. Colombo blames Wittgenstein for not having given sufficient reasons for why those events which actually appear in our experience are realized instead of other possible ones. It is indeed true that Wittgenstein cannot give any such reasons for, as Colombo points out, if we could discover a cause or reason *A* for why the event *a* is realized instead of another one *b*, then *A* itself must be an event *in* the world, as it otherwise could not be discovered, and therefore the problem arises again, because we have to find a reason for *A*'s occurrence. As pointed out in chapter V it would be contradictory to speak of causes or events 'outside' the world. Therefore all events must be contingent or accidental. Wittgenstein himself states this in 6.41: 'The sense of the world must lie outside the world. In the world everything is as it is, and everything happens as it does happen; *in* it no value exists — and if it did, it would have no value. / If there is any value that does have value, it must lie outside the whole sphere of what happens and is the case. For all that happens and is the case is accidental. / What makes it non-accidental cannot lie *within* the world, since if it did it would itself be accidental. / It must lie outside the world.' This is in accordance with both the picture theory and the idea of the mystical. Hence, if one wants to refute this view he must do it by proving the picture theory, and consequently the thesis of extensionality, wrong.

Another aporia, which Colombo considers, is the paradox of the meta-language, *Il paradosso del metalinguaggio,* which appears because Wittgenstein although he denies the possibility of a meta-language speaks of the relations between picture and fact, between propositions etc. in the *Tractatus.* This difficulty I have dealt with in chapter IV, *c.*, and I have there tried to defend Wittgenstein's position by pointing out that propositions can have other functions than the descriptive one. It is probable that he himself entertained this idea since he characterized the statements of the *Tractatus* as elucidations. In any case this label indicates that he did not regard them as either elementary propositions or truth-functions or as propositions endowed with sense. I do not know whether my remarks about this matter are sufficient. I will admit that there is a snag about the fact that the distinction between absurd and descriptive use of language is presented by means of the absurd use, because a statement such as 'There are two kinds of propositions, elementary propositions and elucidations' must be either an empirical or a logical truth and therefore in either case be classed with the descriptive use of language. If we are to criticize the use of pseudo-propositions in the *Tractatus* I think this is the place to start. In any case we can state a *seventh difficulty: What is the nature of Wittgenstein's presupposition that there are at least two kinds of sentences, absurd and descriptive ones?*

Colombo has based much of his criticism on 'the paradox of meta-language'. He maintains that Wittgenstein by writing the *Tractatus* has violated not only the picture theory but in addition his thesis that nothing can be said of the world as a whole and his idea that solipsism cannot be formulated. Perhaps these objections can be difficult to refute but they are not irrefutable in the way Colombo presents them. The same holds true of his idea that laws of natural science cannot be formulated according to the *Tractatus* (*Introduzione,* pp. 117 ff). The argument is that laws of nature neither can be elementary propositions nor truth-functions. Clearly they cannot be elementary propositions since they must be *general* statements. According to Colombo they cannot possibly be truth-functions because if they were they would be logical products of elementary propositions about previous experiences and consequently could not possess general validity. But Wittgenstein apparently has *not* believed that they had to have general validity. His view is that a law of nature is a propositional form based on enumerative induction. Quite another thing is that for many reasons this view is open to criticism. Wittgenstein never developed a clear philosophy of science in which the nature of classical physics and its relation to relativity theory and quantum mechanics was considered. He never tried to examine how his picture theory would fit into natural science. It is a reasonable demand that a book with so great pretensions as the *Tractatus* has should give a fairly copious account of the relation between its main ideas and the natural sciences. The problem of time in relation to the picture theory which I have touched on above is just one difficulty among many. One can blame Wittgenstein for not having dealt with problems of this kind but to a much higher degree we must blame the many philosophers who have raised the *Tractatus* to a philosophical classic without investigating the problems, which Wittgenstein neglected, before they praised the book. Besides they should have considered many other things before applauding Wittgenstein. In the following section I will point to some of these.

c. New objections.

In the preceding chapters I have not given any detailed explanation of Wittgenstein's concept 'structure' or 'logical form'. I will now make some remarks about it in order to discuss some possible objections to Wittgenstein's ideas concerning this concept. He writes very little about structure in the *Tractatus*. 2.15 reads: 'The fact that the elements of a picture are related to one another in a determinate way represents that things are related to one another in the same way. / Let us call this connexion of its elements the structure of the picture, and let us call the possibility of this structure the pictorial form of the picture.' and in 2.151 the latter concept is explained: 'Pictorial form is the possibility that things are related to one another in the same way as the elements of the picture.' It is a little disturbing that Wittgenstein speaks of both 'structure' and 'pictorial form', but the reason probably is that 'pictorial form' refers to certain a-logical features of nature which must be considered in order that the picture theory can be established. If we consider a proposition *aRb* it seems as if we can ascribe structure to it as a matter of course. But in order that this structure should enable us to describe something, it must be possible that the object *a* can have the relation *R* to the object *b*. It is, for instance, from the outset precluded that a note can be red or that a colour can have a certain weight. Therefore an expression such as 'the colour red weighs three ounces' can have no pictorial form according to 2.151. Therefore it cannot be a picture of anything. 'What any picture, of whatever form, must have in common with reality, in order to be able to depict it — correctly or incorrectly — in any way at all, is logical form, i. e. the form of reality.' (2.18). Even if we insist that it is a picture in any case it is not a 'logical picture' because the definition of this concept reads: 'A picture whose pictorial form is logical form is called a logical picture.' (2.181). According to 2.15 it looks as if only logical pictures can have a structure. The idea is briefly this. By means of names (or elements of thoughts) we can make numerous configurations. But only some of these fulfill the condition that the objects which are represented by the names can be combined in a similar way. And only these fulfilling this condition can be said to possess logical form. (This is expressed in 2.182: 'Every picture is *at the same time* a logical one . . .'). *Per* definition the concept 'structure' is used only in connection with 'logical pictures'. I have previously used the words 'configuration' and 'structure' indiscriminately. However, we now can see that a 'proposition' such as 'The colour red weighs three ounces' is a configuration of names and yet has no structure and consequently is not a picture.

Incidentally we here observe an *eighth difficulty: The picture theory presupposes that certain combinations of objects cannot occur. This presupposition has no justification.* It is not a logical truth that expressions such as 'The colour red weighs three ounces' cannot occur. For this allegation cannot be formulated as a tautology. Neither can it be proved on empirical grounds for in this case we could never introduce a precept which enables us to decide whether an arbitrarily constructed combination of names is a picture or not. Possibly Wittgenstein thought it to be an *a priori* truth when he wrote the *Tractatus*. For in this book reality is placed within the limits of the thinkable and consequently it can easily be stated that expressions such as 'The colour red weighs three ounces' never can be pictures because they are *unthinkable*. Later on, in *Logical Form*, he apparently meant that syntactical rules which prohibited sign-combinations of this sort could be found. But if these rules are to be established on empirical grounds (cfr. *Logical Form*, p. 171), we cannot construct a perfect symbolism which mirrors the general features of any possible world.

Traditionally Wittgenstein's conception of 'structure' is considered to be determined by only two things: 1. The number of elements forming the structure, and 2. The relations between these elements (*vide*, for instance, Maslow: *A Study*, pp. 89 - 90). Hence, the structure of a proposition is considered to be described exhaustively by the indication of the number of names contained in the proposition and the mutual relations between these names. But if 'structure' is defined by these two things only we meet with a problem which in short can be stated thus. Let us assume that we consider a propositional sign consisting of three elements. If this propositional sign is conceived of as a picture of a certain state of affairs the elements of it become names. For the sake of simplicity I write the propositional sign thus: N_1 N_2 N_3. If the elements are names we here can speak of the proposition as an 'immediate combination' of names. Now let us say that N_1 represents the book *B*, that N_2 represents the lamp *L* and N_3 the ashtray *A*. Let us further assume, in accordance with the view of Copi and Stenius, that the fact that N_1 is to the left of N_2 represents that *B* is to the left of *L* and the fact that N_2 is to the left of N_3 represents that *L* is to the left of *A*. Then the proposition $N_1N_2N_3$ represents the state of affairs that *B* is to the left of *A*. Let us call this state of affairs *BLA*. After we have thought this proposition for some time, we may suspend the picturing relation which we have established and start all over again. Now we let N_1 represent the chair *C*, N_2 represent the table *T* and N_3 represent the desk *D*. Again we take the fact that one name in the proposition is to the left of another to mean that the signified objects have the same relation to each other. Hence, $N_1N_2N_3$ now represents that *C* is to the left of *T* which in turn is to the left of *D*. Let us call the state of affairs pictured here *CTD*. What we have done is that we have successively applied the elements of the propositional sign as replacing-material for the elements of two different thoughts, in the first place of the thought '*BLA*', in the second of the thought '*CTD*'. If structure is determined only by the number of elements and the relations these have to each other then the thought '*BLA*' and the propositional sign $N_1N_2N_3$ must have the same structure. Similarly the thought '*CTD*' and $N_1N_2N_3$ must have structure in common, and consequently '*BLA*' and '*CTD*' have the same structure.

This conclusion, however, contradicts the picture theory. For if two thoughts have the same structure, a picturing relation can be established between them. And in this case we can for instance conceive of the thought '*CTD*' as a picture of the thought '*BLA*'. But this is not compatible with the contention that elementary propositions cannot deal with each other. If we could regard '*CTD*' as a picture of '*BLA*', then the truth of '*CTD*' would imply the existence of '*BLA*' and consequently the ego thinking the thoughts would have to think them simultaneously. Moreover we can see that if a picturing relation can be established between the two thoughts, they must both be pictures of each other. But if they are, '*CTD*' cannot be true unless '*BLA*' exists and in this case we know immediately that '*BLA*' must be true because '*CTD*' cannot be true unless it exists. Hence, the truth of '*CTD*' implies the truth of '*BLA*'. But this contradicts the thesis of extensionality.

I do not know whether Wittgenstein has considered these absurd consequences of his ideas. They might be avoided if we proceed in the following manner. We first assume that for a given language it must be true that each element of a propositional sign can function as a name of only one object. From this it follows that two objects cannot be signified by the same name and that no one object can be signified by two or more different names. As an example of the vocabulary of such language we may list:

$$\begin{array}{llllllll} L_1: & N_1, & N_2, & N_3, & N_4, & N_5, & N_6, & N_7 \\ & \downarrow & \downarrow & \downarrow & \downarrow & \downarrow & \downarrow & \downarrow \\ & O_1, & O_2, & O_3, & O_4, & O_5, & O_6, & O_7 \end{array}$$

Here we have a language, L_1, consisting of in all seven names each representing their object. By means of these names a number of propositions can be formed: N_1N_2, $N_1N_2N_3$, N_1N_3, N_2N_1, . . . etc. Now according to our assumption an arbitrary propositional sign, say $N_1N_2N_2$ cannot be used as substitution-material for more than one thought. In this way we avoid the absurd consequences mentioned above. If we decide that N_1, N_2, and N_3 can be names of other things than O_1, O_2, and O_3 respectively, this must mean that we must suspend L_1 and create a new language, L_2.

If we define the structure of a proposition not only as something determined by the number of elements and the relations between them, but in addition by the general rule which enables us to determine whether a fact in the world has a structure similar to the proposition or not, we have a concept of structure which fits with the text of the *Tractatus*. The general rule can only be established by assuming that any element of language signifies one object only. Say that we have asserted $N_1N_2N_3$ which states *BLA*. In order to maintain that $N_1N_2N_3$ is a picture of *BLA* we must observe not only that N_1 represents *B*, that N_2 represents *L*, and that N_3 represents *A* and that the relations between N_1, N_2, and N_3 are similar to the relations between *B*, *L*, and *A* but in addition we must know the general rule according to which the sphere of language (containing N_1, N_2, and N_3) and the reality are related to each other in a univocal way.

In 4.0141 Wittgenstein writes: 'There is a general rule by means of which the musician can obtain the symphony from the score, and which makes it possible to derive the symphony from the groove on the grammophone record, and using the first rule, to derive the score again. That is what constitutes the inner similarity between these things which seem to be constructed in such entirely different ways. And that rule is the law of projection which projects the symphony into the language of musical notation. It is the rule for translating this language into the language of grammophone records.' This is similar to geometrical projection. Each element of the score corresponds to only one element of the symphony (as an acoustic phenomenon) and *vice versa*. Not until this rule is laid down can we define what is meant by saying that a fact in one sphere has the same structure as a fact in the other. At the same time we can see that it is nonsense to say that two facts belonging to the same sphere have the same structure because this can only have a sense in the case where we have to do with two spheres between which a law of projection holds.

From Wittgenstein's assertion that the truth of the tautologies can be gathered from a consideration of the propositional signs only we can infer that he presupposes that a perfect symbolism has only one name for each object. If we allowed that N_1 and N_2 were both names of the same object then $(N_1N_3)v{\sim}(N_2N_3)$would be a tautology although we could not see this by considering the propositional sign only. And if we granted that N_1 signified two different objects we could not infer that $(N_1N_2)v{\sim}(N_1N_2)$ is a tautology by regarding the propositional sign only for we could never know whether the N_1 represented one thing in the brackets to the left and another thing in the brackets to the right.

We can in a way say that to give an object a name implies that all other objects too have a name and one only, in the same way as to say that a point on the line $x = y$ in a rectangular coordinate system corresponds to a point on the x-axis implies that a point on the x-axis corresponds to any other point on $x=y$ since we otherwise could not all know what was meant by the expression 'corresponds to' in the first assertion. Since names according to 3.3 only have a meaning as elements of propositions we must phrase this matter a little differently and say that to assert a proposition (or to think a thought) involves the presupposition that all objects can be named and that therefore all propositions which can be formed *can* be formed. Perhaps this is what Wittgenstein was thinking of when he wrote 3.42 in which it is said that although a proposition only determines one place in logical space 'nevertheless the whole of logical space must already be given by it.'

*

In connection with 4.0141, quoted above, the question may be raised whether a thought can picture more than one state of affairs simultaneously provided that these states of affairs have the same structure. When considering Wittgenstein's example in 4.014 it is natural to ask whether the 'musical idea' (for instance the thought of a certain chord) can be considered something which is simultaneously a picture of the written notes, the sound-waves and the groove of the gramophone record. If states of affairs were defined solely as certain configurations of elements the nature of which have no importance for the definition of them (cfr. my remark on this, page 50) we would have to answer this question in the affirmative. Perhaps we could even support it by pointing to the plural form in 3 where it is said that 'A logical picture of *facts* is a thought' (my italics). If, however, we adhere to the claim that each name can only signify one object we are compelled to say that the imagined chord either pictures the sound-waves or the written notes or the groove of the record but not two or more of these facts. Therefore the plural form in 3 is probably a slip of the pen (The right explanation perhaps is that 'der

Gedanke' might mean 'the thought' in the sense in which we speak of 'the human thought'. If so the translation by Pears & McGuinness is misleading.) But here a new difficulty appears. For if the imagined chord, the musical idea, at one moment can be a picture of the written notes and at another can be a picture of the sound-waves we are forced to say that here we actually have to do with two thoughts. The difference between them, however, is not one in respect of structure but of elements. But as soon as we say this we arrive at absurdities similar to the ones we avoided by assuming that a name was a name of one object only. How Wittgenstein would have removed these difficulties if he had sensed them I do not know. I do not intend to consider them further but will instead turn to a problem which according to Miss Anscombe (*An Introduction*, p. 67) is raised by Colombo.

This problem is simply the question: What prevents us from considering a fact a picture of a proposition? This seems just as permissible as the opposite. If p is a picture of p_f because they have the same structure, is it not reasonable then that p_f is a picture of p? It seems as if we can say with Hertz: 'Ist ein System Modell eines zweiten Systems, so ist auch umgekehrt das zweite System Modell des ersten.' (*Prinzipien der Mechanik*, p. 197). Naturally this question is relevant to Wittgenstein's philosophical ideas because if facts can be considered pictures of thoughts the distinction between the language and the world is wiped out, the gnoseological dualism is abolished and hereby the basis of the solipsism is suspended.

I have hinted at the answer to this question in my account of the thought-picture theory. There I emphasized the fact that thoughts point to something different from themselves although they are isomorphic to the pictured facts which one therefore might as well believe pointed to something different from themselves. This property of the thoughts is possessed by W-propositions as well since they *are* thoughts which consist of physical elements whereas the things we usually call thoughts consist of psychical elements only. Among all facts thoughts (and W-propositions) are singled out as a special class because they are 'directed to something' which other facts are not. Barone believes that Wittgenstein has not thought about this problem (*Il Solipsismo*, pp. 569 - 70). However, as can be seen from what I have explained in chapter III, *a.*, it is very probable that he has observed it. On the other hand it is questionable whether he realized the consequences of distinguishing between thoughts and other kinds of facts.

In the *Tractatus* no grounds are given for considering thoughts to be facts instead of starting with an ontological dualism. The most probable reason for this is — when attention is paid to the chronology of his philosophical development — that at the outset he developed an O-proposition-picture theory and did not until much later realize that it had to be replaced by a thought-picture theory. If we believe in an O-proposition-picture theory it is natural to consider pictures as facts since they occur in our experience on a line with all other facts. But even after we have accepted the thought-picture theory it is difficult to introduce an ontological dualism.

For according to the picture theory a thought must possess a structure and since structure cannot exist in itself but always must be a structure of objects we are compelled to say that thoughts are facts. Of course it would be a way out to maintain that elements of thoughts are different from objects but since objects are simple this difference would be very difficult to point out.

On the other hand the gnoseological dualism *must* imply an ontological dualism. The difference in respect of picturing between thoughts and other facts cannot be reduced to solely empirical matters. We are debarred from giving a sufficient reason for the fact that thoughts have 'a direction' whereas other facts have not and therefore we must start from the postulate that nature is made so that two fundamentally different kinds of facts can be found. It is not only the 'direction' of the thoughts that gives them a special status. Also the circumstance that thoughts in contrast to ordinary facts can be negated shows that they are very different from these. The picture theory presupposes this dualism. Whether it should be called psychophysical dualism or not is not essential. What is interesting is that the picture theory is based on an ontological assumption which can have no justification.

According to the thought-picture theory the answer to Colombo's problem is this: If by p we means 'p', then p_f cannot possibly be a picture of 'p'. For 'p' is what we (or the ego) think and in order that p_f should become a picture the elements of 'p' one by one should be replaced by the elements of p_f. But the result of this operation would be that 'p' and p_f in all essential respects would be identical. However, if by p we mean p_m then p_f can become a picture of p_m in the same way as p_m can become a picture of p_f. Let us say that p_m is $N_1N_2N_3$ and p_f is BLA. We may then think 'BLA' and use N_1, N_2, and N_3 as replacing material for the elements of this thought. Then $N_1N_2N_3$ in a certain sense (cfr. chapter III, *a*.) becomes the thought about BLA and $N_1N_2N_3$ consequently pictures BLA. We could, however, also use B, L, and A as replacing material for the thought '$N_1N_2N_3$' even if B, L, and A are things such as books, lamps and ashtrays (Wittgenstein admits this in 3.1431), and we then conceive of the propositional sign as the fact we intend to describe. The thought '$N_1N_2N_3$' can then be projected into the fact BLA which now functions as a propositional sign and at the same time is a W-proposition. But from this it appears that the two facts cannot picture each other simultaneously. And since it usually is spoken or written material which functions as propositional signs and replacing material we can in general state that it is almost always propositions (in the colloquial use of the word) that picture facts and not the other way around.

But although we can refute some natural objections to Wittgenstein's ideas simply by referring to the thought-picture theory it is clear that this theory in itself is indeed open to criticism. First of all we may ask how we can justify the postulate that thoughts point to something different from themselves. We may speak of *ninth difficulty: How can we state the reasons for the intentionality of the thoughts?* I use the term 'intentionality' here because it covers Wittgenstein's idea and at the same time stresses the similarity between him and philosophers such as Brentano, Meinong and Husserl. These philosophers have paid special attention to the fact that every psychical phenomenon is characterized by a relation to something else which we unreflectingly call the content of the phenomenon. A thought is always *about* something and that which it is about is usually called the content of the thought, although it is something different from the thought conceived of as a psychical phenomenon. According to the 'intentionalists' this fundamental characteristic of the psychical cannot be eliminated by any reduction to other phenomena and this allegation has automatically placed them as opponents of the phenomenalistic views of Mach, Avenarius and James. It is worth noticing that Wittgenstein in virtue of his thought-picture theory must be classed with the 'intentionalists', far from the views represented by Mach and Russell.

Naturally the theory of the intentionality of the thought in the *Tractatus* cannot be explained on logical grounds. We find no feature in logic which involves this idea. Not until logic is applied do we speak of picturing, but as mentioned in chapter I, *c.*, logic must not clash with its application. Since only logic contains *a priori* statements the thesis of the intentionality of the thought is not an *a priori* true assertion. Nor does it seem plausible that it should be an empirical truth. For if it is empirically true future experience might falsify it, according to the premisses of the *Tractatus*. There might occur psychical phenomena which in spite of having structure do not picture anything. Consequently it might happen that some propositions all of a sudden lose their sense. However, if the thesis of the intentionality of the thought can neither be justified logically nor empirically it cannot be justified at all according to the *Tractatus*. So here we meet with a fundamental shortcoming in Wittgenstein's philosophy.

In connection with the concept of thought other difficulties appear. I will mention them shortly. The *tenth difficulty is: Since the elements of the thoughts are objects and consequently belong to the substance of the world, is new substance, then, produced every time we have a thought?* Wittgenstein gives no answer to this question. The elements of the thoughts are objects and thoughts follow upon each other through life. Is it the same objects that occur in new configurations all the time? Did Wittgenstein believe that the total sum of the objects in the world is constant? The *Tractatus* gives us no answer to these questions but we have to have an answer to them before we can seriously accept Wittgenstein's ideas. According to 2.0271 the objects are what is unalterable and subsistent and according to 2.024 substance is what subsists independently of what is the case, i. e. what is common for all possible worlds. Thoughts must consist of objects because thoughts are pictures and pictures are facts. So what must we say about the objects of which thoughts consist? We must in accordance with this critical attitude observe another, *eleventh difficulty: What is the nature of the elements of the thoughts?* As said before (in chapter III, *a.*) Wittgenstein in a letter to Russell referred this problem to psychology. He overlooked, however, that the picture theory presupposes some formal demands to the elements of the thoughts. If we have a thought '*p*' we know that the objects in p_s represented by the elements of '*p*' must be indivisible. But this in connection with the thesis of extensionality implies that the elements of '*p*' must be indivisible too since we could otherwise form other thoughts consisting of parts of '*p*'s elements and the truth of these other thoughts would consequently not be independent of the truth-value of '*p*'. The question is whether it has any sense at all to speak of indivisible elements of thoughts. This problem Hume attacked in his *Treatise on Human Nature,* I, p. 35 where he writes: 'It is therefore certain, that the imagination reaches a *minimum* and may raise up to itself an idea, of which it cannot conceive any subdivision, and which cannot be diminished without a total annihilation. When you tell me of the thousandth and ten thousandth part of a grain of sand, I have a distinct idea of these numbers and of their different proportions; but the images which I form in my mind to represent the things themselves, are nothing different from each other, nor inferior to that image, by which I represent the grain of sand itself, which is supposed so vastly to exceed them . . . whatever we may imagine of the thing, the idea of a grain of sand is not distinguishable nor separable into twenty, much less into a thousand, ten thousand, or an infinite number of different ideas.' In the *Tractatus* it is an open question whether Wittgenstein has meant that thoughts are identical with images. But it can easily be seen that he is compelled to believe that thoughts consist of *minima.* As we have seen, the picture theory demands that our experience is built up of *minima,* for instance of *minima visibile.* Since the thought of a configuration of *minima visibile* has to be an isomorphic picture of it and since the elements of a thought have to be indivisible we must assume that psychical *minima* correspond to the *minima* in the experience. But does this imply that it is, according to Wittgenstein, impossible to think of, say, a thousandth of a *minimum visibile?* If it is we meet with serious restrictions in mathematics since for instance the infinitesimal mathematics becomes in a certain sense 'unthinkable'. If it is not we violate the thesis of extensionality since in this case we can always construct propositions about part of a *minimum* and the truth of these propositions will depend upon what originally were considered elementary propositions. No matter what we choose to say, there is at this point a problem which can never be solved by further psychological investigations.

Furthermore we can establish a *twelfth difficulty: If the elements of thoughts are indivisible how then can they be distinguished from each other?* The question of how obejects in the external world can be distinguished from each other although they are indivisible and hence do not possess any *differentiae specificae* can be answered by pointing out that we can ascribe space-coordinates to them. In any case Wittgenstein, as we have seen, has entertained this idea in *Logical Form*. Even if this view should be tenable, which I doubt, it is indeed problematic how we shall distinguish elements of thoughts from each other for these cannot possibly be ascribed space-coordinates. One may suggest that time-coordinates could be introduced since thoughts are displayed in the dimension of time but this cannot solve our problem. For a thought always consists of more than one element because it could not otherwise have structure and the elements of it must necessarily occur simultaneously in order that a certain structure can occur (conversely we can say that no element can occur in isolation. This is presupposed in the picture theory as described in chapter II, *a*.). Apparently we are here debarred from saying anything about a class of objects, namely those I call psychical elements. Also we are debarred from describing thoughts as shown above. Consequently part of the world, namely the empirical ego cannot be described at all, so a book about 'The world as I found it' (cfr. 5.631) cannot contain a description of 'the human soul' (cfr. 5.641).

In the third paragraph of 4.1121 Wittgenstein writes: 'Does not my study of sign-language correspond to the study of thought-processes, which philosophers use to consider so essential to the philosophy of logic? Only in most cases they got entangled in unessential psychological investigations, and with my method too there is an analogous risk.' We must agree with him in that this risk exists, but in addition there is a risk — which is really inevitable — that we get entangled in *essential* psychological investigations. We may, just to mention one thing, consider the following *thirteenth difficulty: How does one manage to think more than one thought at a time?* On the one hand it seems impossible that we can think 'p' and 'q' simultaneously. On the other hand it seems reasonable to say that we can think, say, $p \cdot q$. How are we to deal with this problem according to the *Tractatus?* Let us imagine that we draw on a piece of paper a spot S which lies to the right of a line L. We may then think of this state of affairs and think 'S is to the right of L'. Now let us say that the spot can be analysed into a number of *minima visibile*, m_1, m_2, m_3 . . . etc. We may then think 'm_1 is to the right of L', 'm_2 is to the right of L' and so on. Here it seems reasonable to say that if we think 'S is to the right of L' we think at the same time that all the constituents of S are to the right of L, and therefore 'm_1 is to the right of L', 'm_2 is to the right of L' etc. Consequently it looks as if in a certain sense we think many thoughts simultaneously. But is it possible that we can think at the same time 'S_l is to the left of L' and 'S_r is to the right of L'? Here, according to the *Tractatus* we ought to answer in the negative. For if this was possible, we could never put a limit to the number of thoughts which could be thought of simultaneously. If for a certain arbitrarily small moment we can think $a \cdot b$ we must be able to think $a \cdot b \cdot c \cdot d \cdot e \cdot \ldots \cdot n$ (where n is an arbitrary number) within an equally short moment. But what would it mean psychologically to think, say, 18,001.937 thoughts simultaneously? Here we seem to be led into absurdities. In my article *Tractatus 5.542* I have suggested the view that according to the *Tractatus* we can only think one thought at a time. This view is in accordance with the thought-picture theory, but it precludes that$p \cdot q$ can be conceived of as a conjunction of elementary propositions. If we think 'p' while regarding $p \cdot q$, then the conjunction actually consists of the elementary proposition p and the propositional sign q_m, and if we think 'q', the conjunction consists of the propositional sign p_m and the proposition q and should be correctly written $p_m \cdot q$. If we cannot think both 'p' and 'q' simultaneously, then what is a conjunction? It is not the simultaneous belief in or assertion of the two thoughts in question. I leave it to the reader to find an answer to this puzzling question. All I wish to point out is that Wittgenstein would inevitably have ended up in relevant, psychological problems if he had worked out the consequences of his picture theory.

There are other difficulties of a psychological character. For instance this *fourteenth difficulty: How are thoughts compared to reality?* We know that Wittgenstein imagined that the truth-value of an elementary proposition was determined by a sort of comparison of it to the fact it is about or, to express matters a little more precisely, by a comparison of the imagined state of affairs to sense-experience in order to state whether the state of affairs exists or not. But a thought cannot be compared to a sensation if by this we mean a mere taking in of impressions. In order that something sensed can be made the subject of a reflection it has to be endowed with a structure, i.e. it has to be experienced as something of a certain kind and not just as something. By using the terminology of Professor Frithiof Brandt we may distinguish between sensation and perception. Sensation is a mere taking in of impressions whereas 'in the perception of a thing a consciousness of the nature of the thing enters' (Brandt: *Psykologi*, vol. II, p. 29). If I am to compare the proposition 'The book is lying on the desk' to reality it is not sufficient that I take in the visual impressions I have when looking at the desk. I have to perceive that what I see is *a book* which is *lying on a desk*. Unless I do this no comparison can be made. The question is, however, whether it is possible at all to perceive something without at the same time having thoughts about it. If this is not the case then there is a kind of thinking which Wittgenstein has not mentioned in the *Tractatus*. In any case we must demand a psychological account of the way in which thoughts can be compared to perceptions before we can accept the picture theory.

Indeed, many other things are presupposed by the thought-picture theory and the theory of the metaphysical subject. For instance it seems to be reasonable to ask how the empirical ego is connected with the metaphysical subject. Wittgenstein would probably have answered that the empirical ego belongs to the world and therefore is not more closely related to the subject than anything else. But would this mean that we could imagine a metaphysical subject placed in a world without an empirical ego in it? This would be just as absurd as to say (cfr. the described relation between the functions of the subject and the ego in chapter V, *b*.) that we could imagine a language which had a structure but at the same time consisted only of propositions which in principle could never have a sense. The insight obtained by the subject is dependent on the thinking which is equal to the empirical ego. But how are the two 'subjects' connected? If it is nonsense to speak of a relation between them, then why is this so? Questions of this kind must be answered before we can seriously accept the picture theory and the thesis of extensionality.

Finally I wish to refer to a difficulty pointed to by Miss Daitz, a *fifteenth difficulty: How is it possible for elementary propositions to deal with something in the past?* Miss Daitz writes (*The Picture Theory*, p. 196) that ordinary pictures can never indicate what time the pictured state of affairs exists. 'We can picture a black cat but how could we picture a cat that was or will be black?' she writes. Since elementary propositions are characterized as pictures how can they deal with something in the past? Or how can we determine at all at what time the pictured fact exists? Now it must be said that Miss Daitz's conception of a picture is rather restricted (for instance she believes, while referring to the *Tractatus*, 2.171, that a spatial picture can only picture something spatial, a coloured picture only something coloured etc. which strikingly contradicts 4.014 and 4.0141) but even within the limits of her restricted conception one could attempt to give an answer to her question by proposing that all ordinary pictures could contain a calendar and a watch (forming part of the pictured fact) so that from the picture itself we could immediately gather at what time the pictured fact existed. If the black cat on the picture was sitting by the side of a calendar and a watch we could tell at what time it had been photographed, painted or drawn. We may take this suggestion to be a starting point for a more detailed answer to Miss Daitz's objection.

It is true that Wittgenstein forgot to show when writing an elementary proposition such as *aRb* how we can determine at what time the pictured fact exists. When we read *aRb* we think that *a* has the relation *R* to *b* but nothing in the thought shows at what time this holds true. If *aRb* pictures how things stand at a certain point of time, t_0, we really should write $(aRb)t_0$. But since t_o is not a name of an object this cannot be an elementary proposition. Instead we may suggest that since physical time is defined in terms of motion of bodies, t_o is a picture of a certain configuration of elements for instance those that constitute a clock. It is, however, not sufficient to refer to a clock since the series of configurations formed by the hands of the clock and the dial is periodical. We must therefore refer to physical systems in which time has a direction, i. e. in which we can define a non-psychological 'before' and 'after'. As the reader will know the notion of entropy in thermodynamics furnishes time with a direction of this kind but if all elementary propositions are to be furnished with time-indices which refer to a thermodynamical description, an elementary proposition becomes an extremely complicated affair.

Wittgenstein touches on the problem of time in *Logical Form*. From his remarks on the form of elementary propositions we can see that we really should introduce an indication of time in connection with them. We should, for instance, rather say '*P* is red at 5.30 p. m.' than '*P* is red'. If in practice we were to formulate a proposition and make sure that it is true we would have to use an stop-watch or a similar instrument and refer to it at the time at which we experience the spot *P*. But if we do so we are correlating two facts and it seems as if the proposition '*P* is red at 5.30 p. m.' is a conjunction of the two statements '*P* is red' and 'the clock shows the time 5.30 p. m.'. If it is not a conjunction, then every elementary proposition contains an indication of a point in time which is a description of a complex fact rather than a name of an object.

So we see that adherents to the picture theory meet here with a serious problem. Some might say that if we accept the thought-picture theory the problem is solved because a thought itself shows at what time the pictured fact exists but I doubt that this shows us a way out of the difficulty. In any case we can ask whether this holds true of all thoughts and how we can be sure that thoughts *always* will possess this peculiar feature.

d. Summary and conclusion.
In this chapter I have listed a number of objections to the *Tractatus* which are based partly on the interpretation I have attempted to give in chapters I-V and partly on the traditional view of the *Tractatus* where this does not contradict my own. To these objections may be added the difficulties I have pointed out while giving an account of Wittgenstein's views in the preceding chapters.

Consistent with my exposition and critique I believe that the positive and negative aspects of the *Tractatus* can be enumerated thus. By means of his truth-table method Wittgenstein has shed new light on the nature of logic by pointing to the possibility that all propositions of logic are tautologies in the sense of the *Tractatus*. Moreover he has proposed a number of valuable commentaries to Frege's and Russell's view on fundamental logical and mathematical topics. In his book he has furthermore advanced a picture theory which appears to be an interesting attempt to establish a consistent theory of meaning which does not require a meta-language. In virtue of this attempt he has started a discussion of the possibility of meta-language (although his intention was to show its impossibility) and its relation to object-language which became a central theme of the philosophical discussions in the twenties and thirties. This much can be said to be the positive contribution of the *Tractatus*. The shortcomings of the book are many because Wittgenstein never gave a complete treatment of the subjects he dealt with. Firstly, he starts from some logical premisses (the thesis of extensionality and others) which he does not bother to justify in any way. Secondly, he does not analyse the picture theory thoroughly enough to clarify whether it can be interpreted or not. Thirdly, he has not thought out at all how false propositions can be pictures. Fourthly, he has only in part developed the theory of the human mind which he realized had to be established in order that the picture theory should not violate the thesis of extensionality. Fifthly he supported the thesis of extensionality by a theory about the operation of negation which is defective in at least three respects.

Much of the *Tractatus* is therefore halffinished work. It contains some parts which have a purely philosophical interest, namely the passages on solipsism and the ineffable which, as we have seen, are in beautiful harmony with the picture theory. The theory about the ineffable particularly, seems to have a value in itself which transcends the world of thoughts in which it has appeared. The experience of the limits of language and the limits of the world is an idea which, as Wittgenstein speaks of it, is not necessarily linked with the picture theory and the other ideas of the *Tractatus*. In the account I have given of 'the fallacy of the angelic point of view' it is emphasized that it is in the first place the circumstance that certain conditions for the definition of concepts exist which preclude us from 'seeing the world from without'. In my opinion the structure of the argument can be transferred to discussions of some theories of natural science. For instance, the difference between Lorentz's and Einstein's interpretation of the Michelson-Morley experiment (and others of a similar paradoxical character) can be indicated by pointing to the fact that Lorentz by assuming that the shortening of bodies in the direction of motion was real was actually trying to establish a description based on an angelic point of view, whereas Einstein by drawing the attention to the fact that any description must be linked together with an inertial system was actually pointing to conditions for physical description which never could be dispensed with. If there were any sense in speaking of the world as seen from an angelic point of view, the question could be raised which inertial system was the objective one, for instance in matters concerning the lenght of bodies. But since the concept of length only has a meaning in connection with the possibility of performing measurements in a certain inertial system any attempt to conceive of the world as seen from an angelic point of view (i. e. to speak of absolute lengths) is an impossibility. Even if there was a God that tried to explain to us 'the absolute length' of various objects, we would never be able translate his explanation to the language we are bound to apply if we wish to describe our experiences in an unambiguous way.

The *Tractatus* is therefore, as will be understood, a very uneven achievement and, as mentioned before, it is astonishing that for so many years it could figure as a masterpiece in the philosophy of the twentieth century. Now, about forty years after its appearance, the question of its quality can no longer be of interest. It is more relevant for present day philosophers to examine whether the views which some thinkers have taken over from the *Tractatus* or based on ideas of the book imply views to which no attention is paid in the philosophy of to-day. I believe that my comments on the *Tractatus* may be of some use in this respect and I will close the book with some remarks about these matters.

In the preceding chapters I have emphasized that we can find a unity in Wittgenstein's book which does not appear from a first reading of it. I have tried to show that the thesis of extensionality determines the development of the picture theory and that this, together with the extensional view of logic, necessarily leads us to the distinction between what can be said and what can be shown and also to a solipsistic view and a theory about the ineffable and the mystical. If we adhere to an extensional view of logic — and many actually do this at present — then we must realize that it implies a theory of meaning of a certain kind. I am not maintaining that it necessarily implies a Wittgensteinian picture theory, though I believe so, but I think that I have pointed to some problems concerning the connection between the thesis of extensionality and the picture theory which are worth considering. Furthermore I hope that the account which I have given of the picture theory has pointed to some new aspects of it which will be of interest to its supporters. I believe that I have shown that we are led inevitably to a thought-picture theory if we accept that propositions are pictures and that only external relations hold between them. Furthermore I have made a point of drawing the reader's attention to some of the difficulties of this theory. For instance I am convinced that we are bound to accept the fundamental thought of the intentionality in Brentano's and Husserl's philosophy if we maintain that the picture theory is valid. On the other hand I do not wish to maintain categorically that the problems of the concept of time, the explanation of false propositions, and the exemplification of the picture theory, are insuperable. Personally I doubt that they can be solved in a satisfactory way but here I will restrict myself to saying that I hope my account of them shows that they must not be neglected but on the contrary demand a special investigation which spreads into other philosophical problems. I am convinced, though, that adherence to the picture theory involves solipsism. Perhaps I have not proved this in chapter V but it seems to me that the fact that propositions must be thoughts, if the picture theory is true, taken together with the fact that all words of language can refer only to 'observables' must lead us to solipsism. In addition I believe it is true to say that a strict formulation of the picture theory implies that no kind of meta-language can possibly be established and therefore compels us to accept Wittgenstein's views concerning philosophy and philosophical communication, as I have described them i chapter IV, *c*. I believe that I have shown this about as clearly as can be done.

If some readers regard all this as inessential work, I hope that they will consider my book at least as a contribution to the illumination of an epoch in the development of philosophy though it should not be considered a historical dissertation.

APPENDIX

Principles for the interpretation of the Tractatus.

Very often it can be of some help for the understanding of the ideas of a philosopher to examine by whom he has been influenced, with whom especially he has discussed his thoughts, which books he has read and so on. We are, however, in the case of Wittgenstein very badly equipped for this. We know that he was a pupil of Russell, that he occasionally discussed with G. E. Moore, and that in 1911 he visited Frege in Jena. And we can easily see that most of the logical and mathematical parts of the *Tractatus* are inspired by Russell and Frege and can only be understood with reference to their works. We can also see that he has read attentively *Die Welt als Wille und Vorstellung* and something of Fritz Mauthner. The passages on solipsism, will, and ethics in the *Tractatus* are conceived by Wittgenstein with Schopenhauer in mind. Also some parts can be considered as echos of Hertz. But apart from this we have large sections of the *Tractatus* which cannot be elucidated by references to other contemporary philosophers or predecessors. One would think that Wittgenstein's ontological conceptions (e. g. 'object' and 'state of affairs') revealed a connection between him and phenomenologically orientated philosophers such as Stumpf, Meinong, and Husserl. I agree, however, with Colombo (*Introduzione*, p. 24) that there are no relations between these philosophers and Wittgenstein. He is a philosophical isolationist to such an extent that we have no reasons for believing that he even knew anything of Russell's logical atomism as it developed after 1913. In any case no traces of it can be found in the *Tractatus* or the *Notebooks*. I have, therefore, wittingly, avoided all comparison between Wittgenstein's ideas and those of his contemporaries because I think that it would distort the interpretation of his philosophy to attempt to understand it in the light of Russell's, for instance.

When reading the *Tractatus* one would think that Wittgenstein had given us a good clue for distinguishing between the more and less essential parts of the book. In the footnote to the first paragraph he tells us that the decimal numbers indicate the logical (!) importance of the propositions. According to the decimal system the most important statements in the book must be the numbers 1, 2, 3, 4, 5, 6, and 7. The statements given numbers of the form *n*. 1, *n*. 2, *n*. 3 etc. are to be considered comments on statement *n*, the statements *n*. *m* 1, *n*. *m* 2 etc. are comments on the statement *n*. *m* and so on. Stenius has pointed out that Wittgenstein does not follow the system described (*vide Wittgenstein's 'Tractatus*', p. 4). He violates the system as early as 2.01, for this statement should really be a comment on 2 but this raises the question whether statements of the type *n*. 01, *n*. 02, *n*. 03 etc. are more important comments on *n* than statements of the type *n*. 1, *n*. 2, *n*. 3 etc. and it turns out that this question cannot be decided by a closer examination of Wittgenstein's text. Moreover, Wittgenstein offends his decimal system by placing some of the most important statements as comments to others which, as far as can be seen, are less important statements. As Stenius has it, the statements 1, 2, 3, 4, 5, 6, and 7 are not the most important but rather should be considered forte-passages, ending a crescendo and starting a decrescendo. From the outset we must be aware that an interpretation which strictly obeys the decimal system will lead us to serious misunderstandings of the book.

It seems reasonable to ask why Wittgenstein used numbers containing O's (in the following such numbers will be called nought-statements). Not only do we meet with numbers of the type *n*. 0*m*, but also with numbers such as 2.201, 3.001, and 5.5301. I do not think the answer is difficult to find. *Tractatus* has come into existence by a process of selection. Wittgenstein has selected a number of statements from his notebooks and arranged them in a certain way which does not correspond to their original order. Some of the statements he has revised before they were incorporated in the *Tractatus* whereas others were left unaltered. This we can see from the *Notebooks* in which a number of the statements from the *Tractatus* can be found, and in addition to these, preparations for many others of them. As he has been writing the *Tractatus* he has arrived at a situation in which he has selected some statements from the *Notebooks* which were to be placed in between statements which he had already given a number in the manuscript of the *Tractatus*. Consequently he has been compelled to introduce nought-statements. For instance, he determined that some statements were to be placed between 3 and 3.1 and therefore numbered them 3.01, 3.02, 3.03 etc. Later he has discovered yet another statement which he thought had to be placed between 3 and 3.01. This statement he then numbered 3.001 and so on. It seems that in preparing the manuscript he has also inserted statements which are not taken from the *Notebooks*. A great part of the *Tractatus*, for instance the ontological introduction, we do not find in the *Notebooks* but, of course, it cannot be precluded that Wittgenstein had another notebook from 1917 - 18 to select statements from.

The nought-statements are, to begin with, explanations of concepts introduced in the main-statements. Between 2 and 2.1 we find a number of nought-statements which explain the concepts 'fact' and 'state of affairs' in 2 and thereby unfold the whole ontological system inherent in the picture theory. Between 3 and 3.1 we find some nought-statements which deal with the concept of 'thought' in 3. Later on, though, the nought-statements are inserted more casually. One would think that all the nought-statements are inserted at a later drafting of the manuscript so that an original version, a primordial *Tractatus* could be revealed by removing them. I have examined whether anything of interest would appear by doing this and have reached a negative conclusion.

It it is true that the nought-statements are later insertions in the manuscript, other statements are also probably later insertions. It seems, for instance, that 6.1231, 6.1232, and 6.1233 are inserted after the other statements in this part of the book had been arranged. Therefore we do not have much evidence to suggest that Wittgenstein has followed the rule of the decimal system very exactly. By looking closer at a few passages of the *Tractatus*, we soon realize how little importance the decimal system has. Consider for example 4–4.1. 4 states that 'A thought is a proposition with sense'. 4.1 continues the exposition by stating that 'Propositions represent the existence and non-existence of states of affairs'. According to the decimal system 4 should be the more important of these two statements but they are in fact equally important for the understanding of the picture theory. In between these two statements a number of nought-propositions are placed. The first of them, 4.001, defines language as 'the totality of propositions'. Then comes a short explanation of the relation of language to thought (4.002). Next a little passage follows, 4.003–4.0031, which deals with the purpose of philosophy. Then comes 4.01 which is an extremely important statement: 'A proposition is a picture of reality / . . . . .' 4.011–4.016 are elaborations of this view. 4.02 which follows next is a comment to 4.016 and should therefore have been numbered 4.0161. After 4.02 comes 4.021 which in no way is a comment to 4.02 and then follows 4.022: 'A proposition shows its sense' etc. which is one of Wittgenstein's main ideas. After this we come to the passage 4.023–4.0311 which contains a number of important remarks about propositions and then comes 4.0312 which according to the decimal system should be a minor statement but which, nevertheless, expresses 'my fundamental idea' that logical constants are not representatives. Then follows again a number of important statements about 'proposition' and 'truth' before we arrive at 4.1.

As far as I can see it is very misleading to stick to the decimal system as a principle of interpretation. I have heard that von Wright has suggested that a thesis in the *Tractatus* functions as a sort of headline to the comments that immediately follow it. To a certain extent this is true, since some statements of the book are gathered in groups which are initiated by an important statement to which some comments are attached. But this rule is not followed in many places in the *Tractatus*. In some places statements are attacked to such a group without having anything to do with the content of the others. For instance, I am convinced that 5.5423 has nothing to do with the passage 5.541 - 5.5422. We have an indication of this in that the sketch of 5.5423 appears in the *Notebooks* (p. 28) at quite another time than the thesis in 5.542 and does not contain any reference to the analysis of '*A* says *p*' but this, of course, does not prove anything. However, if we take Wittgenstein's nonchalance about the decimal system into consideration, we must say that the assertion that 5.5423 belongs to the passage 5.541 - 5.5422 calls for at least as much proof as the opposite assertion. The same holds true of most of the other statements of the book.

My view is, therefore, that no fixed rule can be given for the interpretation of any single statement of the *Tractatus*. In some cases (as for instance 5.621) the statement occurs in the context in which it was first thought out in the *Notebooks,* whereas it occurs in quite a different context in the *Tractatus*. In such cases an interpretation of the statement must not render it absurd in the context in which it occurs in the *Notebooks*. In other cases the form of the statement in the *Tractatus* is different from the one in the *Notebooks*. This can give us some clues as to the interpretation but it is the whole situation which determines which form has priority. In general I believe that it is preferable to try to establish an entire view of the content of Wittgenstein's text by a rough reading of it and thereafter test the validity of it by confronting it successively with each statement in the book. After several modifications of the general view, an interpretation consistent to all the statements may or may not appear. I hope that my interpretation is of this kind.

In accordance with this view, occasionally in the explanation of a statement, I have referred to statements which according to the decimal system have nothing to do with it, while making sure that the interpretation of these other statements are in accordance with the general view which at that point of time I had suggested. After having completed my interpretation I have confronted every part of it with every statement of the *Tractatus* and made sure that nothing conflicted with it. In this procedure I have stuck to the rule that a certain statement always has to be interpreted in the same way, no matter what it is used for testing. Naturally a statement must not be read in different ways according to whether it is used for testing, say, a certain interpretation of the picture theory and thereafter a certain interpretation of the ineffable.

Of course we must take care in referring to the *Notebooks* or *Logical Form* when we give an account of ideas in the *Tractatus*. I have followed the rule that a statement from the *Notebooks* can only be taken to support an interpretation of something in the *Tractatus*, if, firstly, no statement written at a later point of time goes against it, and, secondly, it originates at a time when the idea it is used for supporting has already been advanced. For instance there is no purpose in supporting a certain interpretation of Wittgenstein's solipsism by referring to *Notes on Logic*, because the development of the solipsistic view as far as we know has initiated a long time after these were written. As to *Logical Form*, I think that this paper is closely related to the *Tractatus* and really must be considered as an attempt to solve a problem which was not solved in the *Tractatus*. However, I am not denying that there might be a greater distance in thought between the two works than I have assumed in this book.

BIBLIOGRAPHY

Allaire, E. B.: Tractatus 6.3751 (Analysis vol. 19, 1958 - 1959).

Anscombe, G. E. M.: An Introduction to Wittgenstein's Tractatus (London 1959).

Baldwin, J. M., ed.: Dictionary of Philosophy and Psychology, I-II (New York, London 1902).

Barone, F.: Il Solipsismo di Wittgenstein (Filosofia, II, pp. 543 - 570, Torino 1951).

Bergmann, G.: Stenius on the Tractatus: A Special Review (unpublished).

Berkeley, G.: An Essay Towards a new Theory of Vision (Everyman's Library, London 1950).

Berkeley, G.: A Treatise concerning the Principles of Human Knowledge (Everyman's Library, London 1950).

Bradley, F. H.: Appearance and Reality (London 1899).

Brandt, F.: Psykologi, I - II (København 1947).

Brentano, F.: Psychologie vom empirischen Standpunkt, I - II (Leipzig 1924).

Bundgaard, S.: Tallene og den abstrakte algebras grundbegreber (København 1942).

Campanale, D.: Studi su Wittgenstein (Bari 1956).

Carnap, R.: Logical Syntax of Language (London 1937).

— : Psychologie in physikalischer Sprache (Erkenntnis III, 1932/33, pp. 107–142).

Colombo, G. C. M.: Introduzione critica (in Wittgenstein, L.: Tractatus Logico-Philosophicus, Testo originale, versione italiana a fronte di G. C. M. Colombo S. J., Milano-Roma 1954).

Copi, I. M.: Objects, Properties and Relations in the Tractatus (Mind 1958, pp. 145–165).

Daitz, E.: The Picture Theory of Meaning (Mind 1953, pp. 184–201).

Eisler, R.: Wörterbuch der philosophischen Begriffe, I - III, Vierte völlig neubearbeitete Auflage (Berlin 1930).

Evans, E.: About "aRb" (Mind 1959, pp. 535–538).

— : Tractatus 3.1432 (Mind 1955).

Favrholdt, D.: Tractatus 5.542 (unpublished).

Feibleman, J. K.: Inside the Great Mirror (The Hague 1958).

Frege, G.: Compound Thoughts (Mind 1963, pp. 1–17).

— : The Thought: a Logical Inquiry (Mind 1956, pp. 289–311).

— : Translations from the Philosophical Writings of G. F. (by P. Geach and M. Black, Oxford 1960).

Hadot, P.: Réflexions sur les limites du langage a propos du "Tractatus logico-philosophicus" de Wittgenstein (Revue de Metaphysique et de Morale 1959, pp. 469–484).

Hartnack, J.: Wittgenstein og den moderne filosofi (København 1960).

Hempel, C. G.: The Logical Analysis of Psychology (in Feigl & Sellars: Readings in Philosophical Analysis, New York 1949).

Hertz, H.: Die Prinzipien der Mechanik (Leipzig 1894).

Hintikka, J.: On Wittgenstein's 'Solipsism' (Mind 1958, pp. 88–91).

Hume, D.: A Treatise of Human Nature (Everyman's Library, I - II, London 1949).

James, W.: Does Consciousness Exist? (Essays in Radical Empiricism, London 1912, pp. 1–38).

Jørgensen, J.: A Treatise of Formal Logic, vol. I - III (Copenhagen & London 1931).

Jørgensen, J.: The Development of Logical Empiricism (International Encyclopedia of Unified Science, Vol. II, 9, Chicago 1951).

Jørgensen, J.: Indledning til Logikken og Metodelæren (København 1959).

— : Psykologi på biologisk Grundlag (København 1956).

— : Towards a Theory of Inference (Theoria, vol. xxv, 3, 1959).

— : Über die Ziele und Probleme der Logistik (Erkenntnis 1932 - 33).

Lalande, A.: Vocabulaire technique et critique de la philosophie. Nouvelle edition, revue et augmentée, I - III (Paris 1928).

Lewis, C. I.: A Survey of Symbolic Logic (Berkeley 1918).

— : Implication and the Algebra of Logic (Mind 1912, pp. 522–531).

Lewis, C. I. & Langford, C. H.: Symbolic Logic (New York & London 1932).

Locke, J.: An Essay Concerning Human Understanding (ed. Frazer, I - II, Oxford 1894).

Mach, E.: Die Analyse der Empfindungen (Neunte Auflage, Jena 1922).

Malcolm, N.: Ludwig Wittgenstein, a Memoir. With a Biographical Sketch by Georg Henrik von Wright (London 1958).

Maslow, A.: A Study in Wittgenstein's Tractatus (Berkeley and Los Angeles 1961).

McColl, H.: If and Imply (Mind 1908).

Moore, G. E.: Wittgenstein's Lectures in 1930 - 33 (in G. E. Moore: Philosophical Papers, London and New York 1959, pp. 252–324).

Morris, C. W.: Six Theories of Mind (Chicago 1932).

Nagel, E. & Newman, J. R.: Gödel's Proof (New York 1958).

Nielsen, F. S.: Den logiske følgerelation (København 1962).

Petzoldt, J.: Einführung in die Philosophie der reinen Erfahrung, I - II (Leipzig 1900 - 1904).

Petzoldt, J.: Solipsismus auf praktischem Gebiet (Vierteljahrsschrift für wissenschaftliche Philosophie, Leipzig 1901, pp. 339–362).

Ramsey, F. P.: Critical Notice on Wittgenstein: Tractatus Logico-Philosophicus (Mind 1923, pp. 465–478).

Ramsey, F. P.: The Foundations of Mathematics (London 1931).

Rubin, E.: Synsoplevede Figurer (København & Kristiania 1915).

Runes, D. D., ed.: Dictionary of Philosophy (Ames, Iowa, 1956).

Russell, B.: An Inquiry into Meaning & Truth (New York 1940).

— : Introduction (in Wittgenstein: Tractatus Logico-Philosophicus, with a new Translation by D. F. Pears & B. F. McGuinness, London 1961).

Russell, B.: My Philosophical Development (London 1959).

— : Mysticism and Logic (Penguin Books, Melbourne, London and Baltimore 1953).

Russell, B.: On the Nature of Truth (Proc. of the Arist. Society, 1906 - 1907, p. 28–50).

Russell, B.: The Analysis of Mind (London & New York 1921).

— : The Philosophy of Logical Atomism I - VII (The Monist 1918 - 19).

— : The Principles of Mathematics (Second edition, London 1948).

Russell, B.: The Problems of Philosophy (London 1912).

Ryle, G.: The Concept of Mind (London 1949).

Schopenhauer, A.: Die Welt als Wille und Vorstellung (Sämmtliche Werke, I - III, ed. Grisebach, Leipzig 1892).

Schultzer, B.: Relativitet i filosofisk belysning (København 1957).

Sellars, W.: Naming and Saying (Philosophy of Science, 1962, pp. 7–26).

— : Truth and "Correspondence" (The Journal of Philosophy 1962, pp. 29–56).

Shwayder, D. S.: Critical Notice on 'Wittgenstein's 'Tractatus' '. by Erik Stenius (Mind 1963, pp. 275–288).

Stebbing, L. S.: A Modern Introduction to Logic (Fourth ed., London 1945).

Stenius, E.: Frege, Wittgenstein och bildteorin (unpublished).

— : Wittgenstein's 'Tractatus', a critical exposition of its main lines of thought (Oxford 1960).

Urmson, J. O.: Philosophical Analysis (Oxford 1958).

von Wright, G. H.: Biographical Sketch (in Malcolm: Ludwig Wittgenstein, a Memoir (London 1958)).

von Wright, G. H.: Logik, Filosofi och Språk (Stockholm 1957).

Waismann, F.: Was ist logische Analyse (The Journal of Unified Science, vol. VIII, 1939/40, pp. 265–289).

Weiler, G.: On Fritz Mauthner's Critique of Language (Mind 1958, pp. 80–87).

Weinberg, J. R.: An Examination of Logical Positivism (London & New York 1936).

Weiss, P.: Entailment and the Future of Logic (Proc. of the Seventh Congress of Phil., Oxford 1930).

Whitehead, A. N. & Russell, B.: Principia Mathematica, vol. I, First Edition (Cambridge 1910), and vol. I, Second Edition (Cambridge 1960).

Wittgenstein, L.: Notebooks 1914 - 1916 (Oxford 1961).

— : Philosophical Investigations (Oxford 1953).

— : Remarks on the Foundation of Mathematics (Oxford 1956).

— : Some Remarks on Logical Form (Proc. of the Arist. Society, Supplementary Volume IX., 1929, pp. 162–171).

Wittgenstein, L.: The Blue and Brown Books (Oxford 1960).

— : Tractatus Logico-Philosophicus (Swedish edition, translation, introduction and notes by A. Wedberg, Stockholm 1962).

Wittgenstein, L.: Tractatus Logico-Philosophicus (Danish edition, translation, introduction and notes by D. Favrholdt, København 1963).

Witt-Hansen, J.: Exposition and Critique of the Conceptions of Eddington Concerning the Philosophy of Physical Science (Copenhagen 1958).

Zinkernagel, P.: Conditions for Description (International Library of Philosophy and Scientific Method, ed. Ayer, London 1962).

INDEX OF AUTHORS